Praise for William R. Trotter's *A Frozen Hell*

"We will not often find a book written with such authority as this one by Mr. Trotter. . . . We are fortunate to have it."
—John Eisenhower, *The New York Times Book Review*

"A refreshing look into the Russo–Finnish War. . . . A balanced account that accurately describes the horrifying price both sides were forced to pay."
—*Marine Corps Gazette*

"Well-researched, eminently readable and valuable to students of military and political history."
—*The Associated Press*

"A superbly researched and engrossing account. By blending precise descriptions with evocative eyewitness accounts Trotter masterfully recreates all the heroism, tragedy and drama of a campaign whose lessons deserve far more attention."
—General John R. Galvin, former Supreme Allied Commander, Europe

"Mr. Trotter tells brilliantly a piece of history that needed telling."
—*The Washington Times*

"An immensely readable and thought-provoking book."
—*Army*

"Trotter's account is the best one yet of this unique war."
—*The Virginian-Pilot and Ledger-Star*

"It will introduce American readers with admirable clarity to battles of which most of us have known almost nothing."
—Russell Weigley, author of *Eisenhower's Generals*

"The valor of the Finns is known once more."
—*The News & Observer* (Raleigh, N.C.)

"A vivid account of desperate courage and determination."
—*Contemporary Military Reading List*, Department of the Army

"A fast-paced and even-handed introductory overview to what is at once both the most tragic and most triumphant moment of Finnish history."
—*The Courier-Journal* (Louisville, Ky.)

▲ A FROZEN HELL ▲ ▲

The Russo-Finnish Winter War of 1939–1940

WILLIAM R. TROTTER

Algonquin Books of Chapel Hill ▲ 2000 ▲ ▲

Published by
Algonquin Books of Chapel Hill
Post Office Box 2225
Chapel Hill, North Carolina 27515-2225

a division of
Workman Publishing
225 Varick Street
New York, New York 10014

LIBRARY OF CONGRESS CATALOGING-IN-PUBLICATION DATA
Trotter, William R.
   A frozen hell: the Russo-Finnish winter war of 1939–1940/
William R. Trotter.
      p.   cm.
   Includes bibliographical references and index.
   ISBN-13: 978-0-945575-22-1
   1. Russo-Finnish War, 1939–1940.   I. Title.
DL1097.T76   1991
948.9703'2—dc20   90-19968
                                                          CIP

   ISBN-13: 978-1-56512-249-9 paper

10 9

To the memory of Colonel J. N. Pease,
whose faith never wavered

▲ CONTENTS ▲ ▲

▲ ILLUSTRATIONS ▲ ▲

▲ MAPS ▲ ▲

▲ ACKNOWLEDGMENTS ▲ ▲

This book began as a research project for a seminar course in Russian history at Davidson College, in 1962–63, and continued as a thesis for a junior-year-abroad program sponsored by the Scandinavian Seminar. Ten drafts and twenty-four years later, the metamorphosis is complete, and my thanks are due to the following people who helped along the way: Mr. and Mrs. Craig Gaskell, for making it possible for me to spend a year in Finland; Dr. A. I. Lobanov-Rostovsky, warrior, scholar, and prince of the Romanov family, for his early encouragement; the late Dr. Halfdan Gregerson, of the Scandinavian Seminar; Mrs. Gunnel Wrede (affectionately known, by members of the Tuborg Gang, as "The Baroness"); my cohorts in the Tuborg Gang—Ray Myhre, Sara Evans, and Fay Tobias; Mr. Brad Absetz of Viitakivi College, Hauho, Finland, for his valuable aid as a translator and go-between; Mr. and Mrs. Jorma Reinimaa; Reserve Colonel E. Kuusaari, editor of *Kansa Taisteli*; Eino Nurmio, who was patient and unbelievably helpful during several long months of translation and who became an esteemed friend in the process; Väinö Linna, author of Finland's greatest war novel, *The Unknown Soldier*, who made me welcome in his home and gave valuable insight into the psychology of the Finnish GI; Eila Pekkanen, whose friendship remains a bright and beautiful memory even now; Erkka Maula, poet, philosopher, and sauna-freak, in honor of the hedgehog in the moonlight, the *spiritus fortis*, and the cause of "continual progress"; Dr. Louis D. Rubin, whose tough, expert editing made this book finally grow up; and the late Jean Sibelius, whose music ignited my lifelong love affair with the Finnish landscape: all else flowed from that.

▲ AUTHOR'S NOTE ▲ ▲

Place-names in Finnish are quite literal, most often constructed with a suffix that is also a noun, describing exactly what sort of terrain feature is involved. The following place-suffixes are common in this book, and a quick glance at them may help the reader visualize what some of these strange names actually stand for.

-järvi: lake
-joki: river
-lahti: bay
-niemi: cape
-ranta: beach
-saari: island
-suo: marsh
-vaara: ridge

The Finnish *ä* is pronounced like the *a* in *apple*.

The abbreviation *JR* stands for the Finnish term *jalkaväki rykmentti*, which means "infantry regiment"; 2/JR-16 is the designation for the Second Battalion, Sixteenth Regiment.

A FROZEN HELL

PART I

Onslaught and Riposte

When Stalin says "dance," a wise man dances.

—Nikita S. Khrushchev, in
Khrushchev Remembers

CHAPTER 1

The Reasons Why

At the easternmost end of the Baltic Sea, between the Gulf of Finland and the vastness of Lake Ladoga, lies the rugged, narrow Karelian Isthmus. Although the land is sternly beautiful—cut laterally by numerous clear blue lakes, tapestried with evergreen forest, and textured by outcroppings of reddish gray granite—it has little intrinsic worth. The soil grows few crops, and those grudgingly, and the scant mineral resources are hardly worth the labor of extraction. Yet there are few comparably small areas of land in all Europe that have been fought over so often and so stubbornly.

The reason is geographic. Since the beginning of European history the Karelian Isthmus has served as a land bridge between the great eastward mass of Russia and Asia and the immense Scandinavian peninsula that opens to the west. The Isthmus has been a highway for tribal migrations, a conduit for trade and cultural exchange, and a springboard for conquest. Armies have washed across it—Mongol, Teutonic, Swedish, Russian—and empires have coveted it, either as a defensive breakwater or a sally port for aggression.

An unopposed army, for example, driving eastward across the Karelian Isthmus from the point where it widens into the Finnish mainland, would be at the city limits of Leningrad in a matter of hours. That is precisely the reason why, in the waning days of 1939, the world's largest military power launched a colossal attack against one of the world's smallest nations. Soviet Russia against little Finland—history affords few examples of a conflict so overwhelmingly one-sided. And yet, for more than 100 days, Finland waged a David-and-Goliath defensive struggle of unequaled valor and determination, a backs-to-the-wall stand that stirred the hearts of freedom-loving people everywhere and that enabled Finland, though ultimately and inevitably defeated, to remain a free and sovereign nation.

Conflict between Russia and Finland became inevitable in May 1703, when Peter the Great selected a swampy, bug-infested river delta at the eastern tip of the Baltic Sea and proclaimed it the site of his new capital, St. Petersburg—his long-sought "window to the West." The fact that the land he had chosen, as well as all of Finland to the west of that point, belonged to Sweden did not deter the tsar at all. The annexation of the River Neva delta was just one more move in the power struggle being waged between the Romanov dynasty and the Swedish monarchy; the prize was domination of the Baltic and, with it, lucrative trade routes to the West.

More than 100,000 Russians died during the ten years required to drain the malarial swamps and drive the pilings on which Peter's grand city would rise. Some 236 years later, another quarter-million or so Russians, along with 25,000 Finns, would die, just because the Finnish border ran so close to that same city, now called Leningrad.

Both Russia and Sweden used Finland as a convenient battleground, much to the harm of its peaceful and bucolic inhabitants. And until Peter finally bested the Swedes, there was always a danger that Sweden might successfully attack St. Petersburg across the narrow Karelian Isthmus. "The ladies of St. Petersburg could not sleep peacefully as long as the Finnish border ran so close," Peter would later write. In order to ensure the ladies' rest, he forcibly moved the border back by conquering Viipuri, the main Swedish port on the Isthmus, along with a vast stretch of mainland Karelia.

The rest of Finland remained under Swedish suzerainty until 1809, when the entire country was ceded to Russia as a function of the general reshuffling of European boundaries that attended the Napoleonic Wars. The Swedish yoke had been both loose and benign: during much of the time that Finland was a Swedish province, its citizens enjoyed religious tolerance, freedom from censorship, and as many political rights as the citizens of most European states. All things considered, if one had to be ruled by an outside power, Sweden was not a bad choice.

After he had inherited Finland, Tsar Alexander I also left the Finns to their own devices by and large, permitting them to have autonomous schools, banks, and legal institutions. Finnish citizens who wished to advance their personal careers, or to sample a more cosmopolitan life-style than what was available locally, were able freely to enter the tsarist armed forces or climb the ladder in the vast Russian civil bureaucracy. Military service for the tsars was a favorite route for ambitious young Finns: from 1810 to the revolution of 1917, Finland supplied more than 400 generals and admirals for the Imperial forces, not the least of whom was a hero of the Russo-Japanese War of 1904–1905 named Gustav Mannerheim.

A series of repressive and heavy-handed tsars, however, ignited the nascent fires of Finnish nationalism. All traces of the former easygoing relationship between the two nations vanished when the stubborn and reactionary

Nicholas II assumed the Romanov throne in 1894. Nicholas appointed as governor-general of Finland a genuinely loathsome man named Bobrikov, who quashed any manifestation of Finnish nationalism with a ruthless hand. For the first time, Finns could be conscripted unwillingly into the tsarist army; strict censorship placed a boot on the neck of Finland's ardent class of artists and intellectuals, including the young firebrand composer Jean Sibelius, whose early tone poem *Finlandia* roused its audiences to a delirium of patriotic fervor. In 1904, to the surprise of no one, a young civil servant ran up to Bobrikov on the steps of the Senate building in Helsinki and shot him dead. Finns everywhere applauded the deed, but the immediate result was increased repression and a much greater involvement in all levels of Finnish affairs by the tsar's secret police.

The outbreak of the First World War gave the more militant Finnish nationalists a window of opportunity—now, they argued, was the time to prepare for the armed overthrow of the Russian yoke. In seeking military assistance, the Finns operated on the time-honored but dangerously simplistic theory that the enemy of one's enemy is also one's friend. They sought aid from both Germany and the Bolsheviks; both connections would haunt them for decades to come, in very different ways.

About 2,000 young Finns went to Germany for professional military training in 1915 and 1916, where they were carried on the Imperial army's order of battle as the "Twenty-seventh Prussian Jaeger Battalion." Almost every successful Finnish field commander in both the Civil War and the Winter War received his basic training in the Twenty-seventh Jaegers; veterans of that unit became, for all practical purposes, an elite professional caste.

On November 15, 1917, the Finnish Parliament openly assumed responsibility for Finnish affairs, internal and external. Lenin could spare no troops and very little attention for this sideshow of secession. Instead, he purchased Finnish neutrality vis-à-vis Russia's internal power struggle by recognizing the new Finnish government just three weeks after Finland's formal declaration of independence.

Finland did not escape the widening class struggles that threatened to tear European society apart in the closing months of World War I. Its working class had endured years of worsening conditions, wartime shortages, famines, and a declining standard of living. Constant Bolshevik agitation had aggravated the situation to the point that two rival armies had formed. Domestic Communists, discontented workers and peasants, and a small but volatile assortment of homegrown anarchists all went into the ranks of the Red Guard, which was armed, trained, and fleshed out by some 40,000 Russian soldiers stationed in Finland, many of them flaming revolutionaries.

The White Guard was the militant arm of the upper classes and the bour-
geoisie; their commander was Carl Gustav Mannerheim, a former tsarist
general recently returned to his native land.

Although the Reds held the best ground—Helsinki and the industrial
center of Tampere—the Whites had an edge in terms of military professionalism; many White units were led by former tsarist officers, and the
Jaeger Battalion alumni quickly demonstrated a tactical expertise that the
Reds could not match. Although Mannerheim opposed it—believing that
Finland was in danger of mortgaging her political future—the White government requested aid from Imperial Germany, and an expeditionary force
landed in April 1918. With this new infusion of firepower, the Whites proved
unstoppable; six weeks after the Germans landed, the Reds surrendered.

The Treaty of Tartu, signed in 1920, formalized a state of peace between
Finland and the USSR. From the Soviet government, Finland gained recog-
nition and the arctic port of Petsamo; for its part, Finland destroyed all the
fortifications on the islands in the Gulf of Finland. The questions of what to
do with the denizens of East Karelia, Finnish by heritage but Russian by law
and circumstances, remained unresolved and would exert a baleful influence
on Finnish diplomacy in years to come.

Thus ended the long and peculiar relationship between Finland and Imperial Russia. What had mostly changed by 1920, aside from the configuration of the border, was the two nations' attitudes toward each other. Trust
had been badly eroded on both sides. The Finns had learned to fear Bolshevism, and the Soviets were uncomfortable with a neighbor that had opted
for a thoroughly bourgeois system of government, had violently suppressed
its own workers, and had made room in its diplomatic bed for the German enemy.

The men who ran Finland's postwar governments did much for their country. They moved to bind the internal wounds, to lay the foundations of
economic growth, and to improve—in some respects very dramatically—
the standard of living. But in the realm of foreign relations, they tended
simply to mind their own business and assume other states would mind
theirs. Their postwar policy with regard to the Soviet Union was one of
shutting their eyes and hoping it would go away. During the early years of
Lenin's regime, when the Soviet state was fragmented by internal strife and
beset from without by interventionist armies, that approach was sufficient.
But by the end of the 1920s, with the Soviet system consolidated and Russia once more becoming a powerful factor in international affairs, the Finns
should have seen clearly that sooner or later their giant eastern neighbor
would want to have words with them about some sensitive issues.

Seeds of future war had in fact been planted at the moment of Finland's birth. Lenin's government had bitterly resented having to give up Finland so compliantly, but at the time it was done, Lenin was beset by so many other and far more dangerous and immediate threats that he simply had no alternative. The Politburo assumed that propaganda, internal domestic unrest, and a bit of routine subversion would ultimately be enough to bring Finland back into the Communist sphere.

When Joseph Stalin came to power, he did so with diplomatic perceptions that were deeply and permanently colored by his memories of the early days of the Russian civil war, when the White government of Finland had allowed both the Russian Whites and some units of the British Navy to launch attacks from the Finnish coast against Bolshevik targets in the Baltic. Stalin viewed the demilitarization of the Baltic islands—in particular the huge Aaland archipelago, a vast and beautiful necklace of hundreds of islets that lies between the land mass of Sweden and the southwest coast of Finland—with a skeptical eye; it was clear to him that any great power who wanted those islands could seize them at will, and Finland could do nothing to stop it. Control of the Aalands and of the islands in the Gulf of Finland meant control of the flow of naval traffic in the Baltic, including ship movements in and out of Leningrad and Kronstadt.

Furthermore, the discovery of large nickel deposits in the Petsamo region had altered the strategic picture considerably. Mining concessions had been given by the Finns to a British Empire consortium, and it was well known that much of Germany's iron ore came from the not-too-distant mines in northern Sweden. Thus, when Stalin came to power, there were already two Great Powers—the two, as it happened, that Stalin most feared—keenly interested in the bleak and barely habitable Arctic coast of Finland.

Completion of the Murmansk Railroad, connecting Leningrad with one of Russia's few ice-free ports, was a further source of anxiety. The land through which this vital rail line passed, in East Karelia, was often the subject of loud irredentist claims made by right-wing elements in Finnish politics. Stalin was enough of a realist to know that the Finns themselves would never dare attempt the annexation of that region by force, but it seemed at least theoretically possible that another hostile nation—Germany, for instance—might offer the Karelian provinces in exchange either for Finnish military cooperation or for simple acquiescence to the deployment of foreign soldiers on Finnish soil. Finland's protestations of neutrality, however sincerely meant, counted for little in the harsh equations of realpolitik. It was the Kremlin's belief that, in the event of another big European war, Finland would simply not be allowed to remain neutral. And the Finnish border, at its closest point, was still a mere thirty-two kilometers from the outskirts of Leningrad.

From 1918 until just before the outbreak of war in 1939, Finland's ruling politicians seem to have been remarkably obtuse when it came to understanding the Russian point of view. Not until about 1935 did the Finns realize that everything they did and said was subject to Soviet misinterpretation. It was largely in an effort to redress this attitude that the Finns launched, with great public fanfare, a policy of pan-Scandinavian neutrality. The Soviet intelligence service read the papers and heard the speeches on the radio but drew the wrong conclusions from the data they perceived.

Hitler also came out in support of Scandinavian neutrality, particularly for Finland, and postwar research has shown that he did not in fact have any territorial ambitions in that region. All he desired was for the Baltic to remain open for German shipping and for the Swedish iron ore to flow into the Ruhr factories without interruption. But as Stalin saw things, there was something decidedly suspicious about the way the Germans were making such a fuss over Finland's new regional orientation. Was Finland secretly acting as a broker between Germany and the Scandinavian states? Stalin's suspicions were aggravated by the fact that the extreme right wing in Finnish politics was soon advocating just such a duplicitous policy; theirs was all a lot of hollow imitation-fascist rhetoric, and responsible Finns dismissed it as such, but the Soviet intelligence service did not write it up that way in their reports to the Kremlin.

The Russians consistently overestimated the influence of both extremes of Finnish domestic politics. When the Great Depression finally reached Finland, its effects spawned a fascist party called the Lapuan Movement (named after a town where a mob of conservative farmers had beaten up a rally of the League of Communist Youth in late 1929), led by a rather pathetic Mussolini clone named Kosola. Most of the Lapuans' activity was mere hooliganism—taking leftists for a ride to the Russian border and bodily chucking them over the fence, smashing their mimeograph machines, and the like—but they captured sensational headlines in 1931 and 1932 with a kidnapping and an attempted *putsch*.

The kidnapping was the work of some right-wing thugs led by an ex-White general named Kurt Wallenius, and its victim was the elderly and widely loved first president of Finland, a Wilsonian law professor named K. J. Stahlberg. Threats of execution were issued when the Lapuans' demands were not met, but in the end the whole thing degenerated into a nasty little farce: Wallenius and his henchmen were too incompetent to handle the kidnapping without bungling it and too irresolute to carry out their murder threat. The Finnish public was shamed and horrified by this pointless act of lawlessness, and a general backlash against the Lapuans greatly eroded their already dwindling popular support.

A tide of rumors ushered in the year 1932, the darkest of them concerning a planned coup d'état that Wallenius was anxious to mount before the Lapuans lost all their followers. The charismatic little scoundrel had been scandalously acquitted of his role in the Stahlberg kidnapping and was now in league with a clique of fascist officers in the Civic Guard, Finland's territorial militia, totaling some 100,000 men, that traced an unbroken line of descent back to the White Guard of 1918. Finland's various Communist parties had been outlawed in late 1931, so there was no longer any highly visible leftist threat for the right wing to focus its energies on; the new Lapuan objective was nothing less than the overthrow of the duly elected constitutional government.

The uprising fared no better than had the presidential kidnapping. A core of Lapuan fanatics jumped the gun and caught Wallenius's gang of conspirators off balance. Wallenius's group hurriedly tried to mobilize its forces and succeeded in putting into motion about 6,000 armed but hopelessly confused men. An impassioned radio speech by newly elected Finnish president Svinhufvud, an authentic hero of the civil war, took the backbone out of the uprising and left the hapless Wallenius in command of no more than 300 die-hard fanatics. The rebellion expired without a shot being fired.

By the end of 1932, Finland's brief flirtation with fascism was all but over. The nation's economy had improved, and the Lapuans, largely by virtue of their brutish tactics and staggering incompetence, had managed to alienate the propertied class from which they had previously drawn both financial support and a degree of borrowed respectability. The movement fragmented into a welter of impotent crank groups, such as the minuscule Military Force party, led by a man who openly worshiped Hitler, or the dreamy-eyed Academic Karelian Society, an association of fanatical irredentists who printed maps of something called "Greater Finland," which included all of Estonia and stretched eastward as far as the Ural Mountains. One can easily imagine the impact such documents had when they fell, as several specimens did, into the hands of Stalin's intelligence operatives.

Stalin was unrealistically influenced by the headline-grabbing antics of the Lapuans, the grotesque fantasies of the Karelian irredentists, and the exaggerated reports of agents who were eager to tell the Kremlin what they thought the Kremlin wanted to hear. From remarks made during his later negotiations with the Finns, it seems clear that Stalin really did believe that the interior of Finland seethed with class antagonism and fascist plotters and

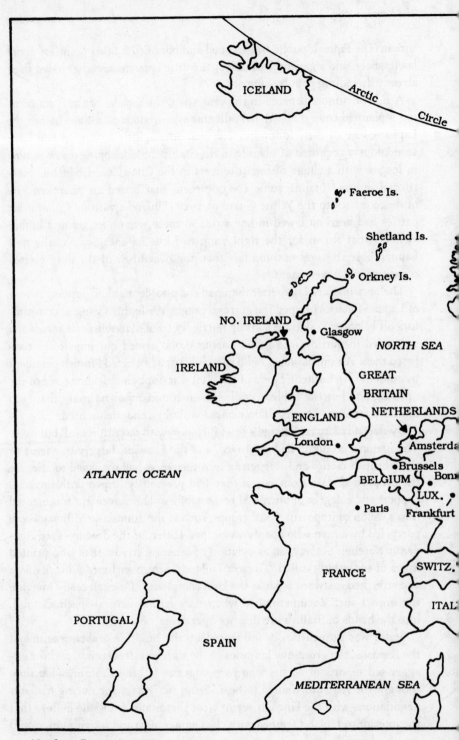

1. Northern Europe in 1939

BARENTS SEA

Petsamo

Murmansk

White Sea

Archangel

SWEDEN

FINLAND

NORWAY

Gulf of
Bothnia

Lake Ladoga

Viipuri

Helsinki

Oslo

Leningrad

Gulf of Finland

Stockholm

ESTONIA

Moscow

Riga

LATVIA

DENMARK

LITHUANIA

UNION OF SOVIET

Copenhagen

BALTIC SEA

EAST

SOCIALIST REPUBLICS

Hamburg

PRUSSIA

Berlin

Warsaw

GERMANY

POLAND

CZECHOSLOVAKIA

Munich

Vienna

Budapest

AUSTRIA

HUNGARY

ROMANIA

YUGOSLAVIA

BLACK SEA

Rome

BULGARIA

ALBANIA

TURKEY

GREECE

that all of Finnish society was undercut by smouldering grudges left over from the civil war days. Ill feeling persisted, of course—the conflict had been too bloody for all the scars to have healed in just two decades—but Moscow's estimate of its extent, importance, and potential for outside exploitation was wildly inaccurate. In fact, the old wounds were healing faster than even the Finns themselves realized; with the onset of a massive contemporary threat from the Soviet Union, those old enmities looked remote and historic.

In April 1938 came the first sign that Russia was no longer satisfied with the status quo of its relations with Finland. An MVD agent named Boris Yartsev, ostensibly a minor diplomatic official in the Helsinki embassy, approached the Finnish foreign minister, Rudolf Holsti, and suggested that it might be in Finland's best interest to agree to some secret discussions with the Soviet Union, with the aim of "improving relations" between the two countries. The reason, Yartsev claimed, was the gradual worsening of the international situation. The Soviets did not trust Nazi Germany, and if war between those two mighty powers should erupt, a glance at the map would reveal the obvious advantages Germany would gain if Hitler could use Finland as a base for operations against Russia. If such a threat were to develop, Yartsev stressed, it would not be the Red Army's intention to wait passively behind its fixed defenses but rather "to advance as far as possible to meet the enemy"—a veiled reference to the strategy of preemptive attack. If Finland were prepared to resist German pressure, then Russia would be prepared to extend all possible economic and military assistance. Russia needed some "positive guarantees" from Finland that Germany would never be allowed to use Finnish territory as a springboard to attack the USSR.

Holsti wanted to know what those "positive guarantees" might consist of, but Yartsev had reached the limits of his empowerment to speak. He could not nor would not say more. At this point Holsti brought Finnish prime minister Cajander into the discussions, and both men assured Yartsev that Finland was indeed committed to a policy of strict neutrality and would resist *any* armed incursion to the best of its ability. Yartsev indicated that Stalin was not likely to be impressed by that statement, given Finland's military weakness. But if the Finns backed up their protestations with some kind of tangible gesture, it was entirely possible that trade relations between Finland and Russia would suddenly improve. The most suitable gesture would be for Finland to cede, or lease, to the Soviet Union a number of intrinsically valueless islands in the Gulf of Finland along the seaward approaches to Leningrad.

Holsti and Cajander agreed that this move was out of the question. Even though the only people who ever went to those islets were summertime fishermen, they were still Finnish soil, and the domestic political climate would not permit them to be given to Russia.

Yartsev went back into the diplomatic chambers from whence he had emerged, and nothing further was heard about the matter until the spring of 1939. In March of that year, another Kremlin emissary broached the idea again, in somewhat more concrete terms. If Finland were willing to lease to Russia the island of Suursaari and four smaller islets in the gulf for a period of thirty years, then Russia would demonstrate good faith by offering a large slice of the disputed Karelian borderland in exchange.

Gustav Mannerheim was one of the handful of Finnish leaders privy to this second round of discussions, and he advocated giving the Russians what they wanted. The islands themselves were without value, and their loss could therefore hardly be interpreted as a blow to national prestige. It was folly, Mannerheim insisted, to adhere to such a stubborn policy vis-à-vis their giant eastern neighbor when the Finnish armed forces were not in any condition to back up that policy.

As Finland's leading soldier, Mannerheim knew what he was talking about. In the spring of 1939, the Finnish Army did not yet possess a single operational antitank gun. There were only a dozen or so modern fighter planes in the entire air force. Communications equipment was primitive; the field radios used by Finnish ground troops weighed 300 pounds, and their tubes had a tendency to explode in cold weather. Machine gun ammunition was in such short supply that gunners were restricted to a dozen rounds of live ammo per training session. The Civic Guard and reserve units drilled with wooden rifles or rusty old tsarist relics. Stocks of shells for the artillery were alarmingly low, and many of the guns themselves dated from the Russo-Japanese War of 1905. Mannerheim tried to make the politicians see the bitter truth: zeal and patriotism were fine, but those were the only commodities his army had in abundance. The army was in no condition to wage war against the biggest and most lavishly equipped army in Europe.

Mannerheim's gloomy reports were dismissed as no more than alarmist griping by an old militarist, and once again the politicians ignored this second batch of Soviet overtures. Time was growing short, however, and Russian pressure would continue to increase as the weeks went by.

That was because the Russians themselves were feeling pressured. To a Soviet strategist sitting in a map room in the Kremlin in the spring of 1939, no direction on the compass looked reassuring. And nowhere was the potential danger quite as glaring as it was in the direction of Leningrad—and Finland. Not only was Leningrad a major industrial center, it was the spiritual and cultural heart of the Communist state, the cradle of the revolution.

The city had become a powerful symbolic entity; its loss, in a war with Nazi Germany, would hurt Russia more than the loss of a million infantry. The hypothetical Russian strategist, then, would have surveyed the situation with emotions not markedly different from those that had prompted Peter the Great's concern about the sleeping ladies of Petersburg.

Stalin was no longer worried about Anglo-French cabals against him. By the spring of 1939, it had become clear that the only nation Stalin had genuine reason to fear was Nazi Germany. Already Hitler had moved into Austria, closer to the Balkans, closer to the Ukraine's wheat and the oil fields at Baku. Stalin could see as clearly as the next statesman that such bankrupt concepts as "collective security" offered no comfort, and he could certainly see that no European state, not even one as militarily contemptible as Italy, need fear the moral condemnations of the League of Nations. In view of the Western powers' long tradition of anticommunism, there seemed only the remotest chance of joining with those nations in a unified anti-German front. For Stalin and his generals, the conclusion seemed obvious: for the moment, given the realities of the day, Russia would have to go it alone. So, given the very real threat posed by Hitler, the record of close German-Finnish cooperation in 1918, and the realities of geography, the Russian viewpoint concerning Finland was not entirely unreasonable.

While events were accelerating in the northland, Hitler had been putting out secret feelers to the Kremlin. Hitler knew that Stalin needed two things: time in which to strengthen Russia's defenses, and freedom from outside intervention if Russia felt obliged, for the sake of improving its defensive posture, to gobble up some neighboring country. Alone among European leaders at that moment, Hitler was in a position to offer him both, at no additional risk to his own designs. Given Hitler's contempt for the Slavs, and his not-so-secret territorial ambitions to the east, it was obvious to both parties that this would be a marriage of convenience rather than mutual affection. Sooner or later, the deal would be revoked, probably by force, when it suited the führer to do so. Until that day came, however, the Nazi-Soviet pact was a most satisfying arrangement for both signatories.

As far as Finland was concerned, the agreement signed between the two dictatorships in August 1939 opened the way for Stalin's plans by means of an "Additional Secret Protocol," which defined the two signatories' spheres of interest in the Baltic region:

> In the event of a territorial and political rearrangement of the areas belonging to the Baltic States (Finland, Estonia, Latvia, Lithuania), the northern boundary of Lithuania shall represent the boundary of the spheres of influence of Germany and the USSR.

One week after the Nazi-Soviet pact was signed, Hitler invaded Poland. On September 17, Russia attacked Poland from the east, absorbing enough territory to give Stalin a "buffer zone" on that part of the USSR's frontier. The foreign minister of Estonia was invited to Moscow on September 22, and only one week later an agreement was signed that gave Moscow the right to station troops, aircraft, and naval units in that small Baltic nation—in effect, to annex Estonia as a satellite. The foreign ministers of Latvia and Lithuania were invited to Moscow during the first week of October, and on the fifth and eleventh of that month, they too signed "mutual assistance" treaties with the USSR that would lead to their absorption into Stalin's empire.

Another and similar summons went out on October 5, to the Finnish government in Helsinki. In form it was an invitation; in substance, it was a demand: a Finnish delegation should come to Moscow to discuss "concrete political questions." In the words of Finnish historian Max Jakobsen: "For eighteen months, Finland had conducted a muted dialogue with her great neighbor; the Russians had from time to time softly asked a favor or two, and the Finns had politely whispered their refusal. Now the tone was changed: this time, there had been steel in Molotov's voice."*

At the first high-level meeting in Moscow, on October 12, Stalin wasted no time putting his demands on the table. His main strategic problem, he said, was the vulnerability of the frontiers around Leningrad. In order to improve the city's security, he needed—indeed, he *must* have—the strongest possible assurances of continued good relations with Finland. Given the chaos that had recently engulfed Europe, he had serious fears about the possibility of an attack against that sensitive part of the Soviet Union, either from the Gulf of Finland or from the Finnish mainland.

The Soviet Union therefore demanded:

- that the frontier between Russia and Finland in the Karelian Isthmus region be moved westward to a point only 20 miles east of Viipuri, and that all existing fortifications on the Karelian Isthmus be destroyed;
- that the Finns cede to Russia the islands of Suursaari, Lavansaari, Tytarsaari, and Koivisto in the Gulf of Finland, along with most of the Rybachi Peninsula on the Arctic coast. In compensation for this, Stalin was willing to exchange 5,500 square kilometers of East Karelia, above Lake Ladoga;
- that the Finns lease to the USSR the peninsula of Hanko, and permit

*Jakobsen, Max, *The Diplomacy of the Winter War* (Cambridge, Mass.: Harvard University Press, 1961), 106.

the Russians to establish a base there, manned by 5,000 troops and some support units.

In practical terms, such concessions would mean the abandonment of Finland's main defense, the Mannerheim Line, leaving the country gravely weakened. Moreover, it was the opinion of nearly everyone in the Finnish government that these demands, as stunning as they were, were only the prelude to other, more severe demands—demands that the Finns would be powerless to reject because they would have already lost their strongest line of defense.

Foreign Minister Erkko in particular was convinced that Stalin was bluffing and that Finland needed only to stand fast and the Russians would back down. There were acrimonious discussions in Helsinki between Erkko, those who thought as he did, and Marshal Mannerheim, who kept insisting that the Russians meant what they said, would not hesitate to take what they wanted by force, and could not be stopped by Finland's armed forces.

All through the rest of October and into November, negotiations continued. The Finns were willing to compromise slightly on the Isthmus border and were willing to cede some, but not all, of the gulf islands. As for giving the Russians a base at Hanko, on the Finnish mainland, that was quite unacceptable.

Subsequent events made Stalin look so much the villain in this unfolding scenario of intimidation that it is hard to shift one's point of view to *his* side of the issue. But the effort reveals that some of his assumptions seem less paranoid than logical, and his demands, therefore, less outrageous than brutally realistic. He was, for example, absolutely accurate in his prediction that Germany would turn on the Soviet Union as soon as Hitler had achieved dominance in mainland Europe; his only mistake was in underestimating the timetable of events.

It is true that never in history had Leningrad (or St. Petersburg) been successfully attacked across the Karelian Isthmus, but the contingency existed, and the dazzling conquest of Poland had proved that if any army in the world could bring it off, it was the Wehrmacht. Stalin's proposals were a direct attempt to head off that possibility, and from his point of view the demands on Finland were both moderate and made in transparent good faith. But the Finns believed that the wily Georgian, like some shrewd Oriental merchant, had merely initiated a process of haggling by setting his price much higher than what he was really willing to settle for.

Such does not appear to have been the case. When Stalin informed the Finnish delegation that those were his minimum demands, he was quite serious, and his dismay at the Finns' hardheaded rejection was probably sincere. The stubborn and unrealistic stance adopted by the Finns appeared to Stalin as both perverse and downright suspicious. Surely the Finns must have had some kind of hidden motive for adopting such a provocative and belligerent policy; and since Finland's own armed forces were so weak, that hidden motive might well be a secret alliance with Hitler.

For their part, the Finns too believed that things could not possibly be as straightforward as they were presented to be. Stalin's proposals must have masked some darker and more sinister intention. One of Mannerheim's best staff officers, General Öhquist, was brought into the picture to study the list of Russian demands from the military point of view, and he dismissed them: "No officer with modern training could take seriously the grounds for the demands they have put to us. More likely, what they are demanding now is only the preparation for further, far-reaching demands."

His was a perceptive, if orthodox, analysis, as far as it went, but it overlooked one crucial fact: Joseph Stalin was not "an officer with modern training." Every historical indication is that the Russian negotiators were genuinely thrown off balance and deeply surprised by the Finns' intransigent response. If these original demands had been met, would Stalin then have tried to subjugate all of Finland? Would the Winter War have been fought? It is at least possible that Stalin himself did not know what his ultimate intentions toward Finland might be. The strongest argument against such a strategy of outright conquest is that it did not, in the event, happen—not after the Winter War nor even in 1944 when Stalin had every legitimate excuse to overrun the country, and could have done so with comparative ease.

Whether Stalin would truly have been satisfied with his initial "shopping list" is almost beside the point; ultimately, of course, these issues came back down to an irreducible case of right versus wrong. Finland was a sovereign nation, and it had every legal and moral right to refuse any Russian demands for territory. And the Soviet Union, for its part, had no legal or moral right to pursue its policies by means of armed aggression. Even Nikita Khrushchev admitted as much, decades later, although in the next breath he rationalized the invasion in the name of realpolitik: "There's some question whether we had any legal or moral right for our actions against Finland. Of course we didn't have any legal right. As far as morality is concerned, our desire to protect ourselves was ample justification in our own eyes." *

Russo-Finnish negotiations at the Kremlin went back and forth, round and

*Crankshaw, Edward, ed., *Khrushchev Remembers* (Boston: Little, Brown, 1970), 152.

round, and in the end got nowhere. At one of the final meetings, on November 3, Molotov dropped his mask of cool professionalism and snapped at the Finns: "Since we civilians don't seem to be making any progress, perhaps it's the soldiers' turn to speak."

On the morning of November 9, the Finnish delegates went for their final meeting with Stalin and Molotov. They communicated their government's final, inflexible rejection, restating only the relatively minor compromises that had already been put on the table and turned down by the Russians. Stalin seemed unwilling to believe his ears and continued to explore possibilities for further compromise, speaking informally and with what seemed like urgent sincerity. But after an hour of futile discussion it was obvious to everyone that the whole business had come to a dead end. Each side bade farewell to the other. Since the Finnish delegates were clearly just as upset by this outcome as the Russians, the final meeting ended with remarkably little display of animosity by anyone. The actual parting, in fact, was almost jovial. Molotov waved and said, "Au revoir!" and Stalin shook hands all around and wished the Finns "all the best." Then he went off to confer with his generals about how best to subdue this willful and obstinate little country.

It seems clear from Khrushchev's memoirs as well as other postwar Soviet documents that the Red Army planners were caught off guard by the Finns' intransigence. True, the Russians had made numerous military preparations, but those had been predicated on the contingency of a major European power moving into Finland. Little serious thought had been given to the prospect of a war against Finland alone. Now the situation had changed radically. Whatever Stalin's personal inclinations toward Finland—and at the start of negotiations, they were comparatively benign—a war of some sort now seemed inevitable.

The very sketchy evidence to emerge from post-Stalinist Russian sources suggests that Stalin was being urged to take quick action by the fire-breathing Andrei Zhdanov, political boss of Leningrad, and a clique of Leningrad District officers allied with him. This faction based its hasty and slipshod operational planning on two misconceptions: one being the belief that Finland did not have the capacity to offer more than token, face-saving resistance, and the other being the hoary Politburo delusion that the Finnish working class would rise up and paralyze its existing government, if not actually turn its guns on them, just as soon as the Red Army came across the border.

This wishful thinking was certainly reflected in official publications. A typical specimen is this excerpt from a 1938 edition of *Kranaja Gazeta*: "The Finnish Army, which for the most part is made up of peasants and workers, has no desire to pour out its blood for the benefit of landowners and the bourgeoise. . . . It is certain that if war broke out with the Soviet Union, the democratic elements of the population are ready to turn their weapons against the Fascists."* In a similar vein was a Tass report dated November 8, 1939, which stated that the families of Finland's recently mobilized reservists were so poor that many of them had neither shoes nor adequate clothing for the coming winter.

Of course Stalin, like every other isolated head of state, depended on information fed to him by a network of subordinate agencies. With the purges still fresh in every bureaucrat's mind, there was a natural tendency to tell Stalin what one supposed Stalin wished to hear. Certainly that was the case with the Russian minister in Helsinki, a servile party hack named Derevyanski, who appears to have been the source of many misconceptions about conditions inside Finland.

At the same time that Tass was reporting massive unrest among the Finnish proletariat, reports also began to appear in print citing "evidence" that "the Imperialists" were preparing to use Finland as a base for an invasion of the USSR. This was, and to a certain extent still is, the official justification given to the Soviet public for why the war was fought. It permitted the Kremlin to rationalize the apparent lunacy of a nation of 3.5 million souls attempting to invade a nation of 171 million. These claims also laid the groundwork for later explanations of the failed offensives and staggering casualties suffered by the Red Army. They could be explained away as being the result of Imperialist aid to the treacherous Finns.

The returning Finnish delegation barely had time to unpack its bags in Helsinki when word reached them that the Soviet press had unleashed a savage barrage of attacks on the Finnish government. The worst epithets were directed at Foreign Minister Erkko, who was vilified as a crowing rooster, a writhing serpent, and a phobic rat.

In its final report to the government, the Moscow delegation stated that there were three actions the Russians might take: they might do as Erkko suggested and simply abandon their claims; they might actually declare war; or they might do nothing and just wait for the international situation to move in one direction or another. "The first possibility seemed too good to be true; the second too terrible to contemplate; therefore, most people plumped for the third."†

---

*Upton, Anthony F., *Finland, 1939–1940* (Newark: University of Delaware Press, 1974), 45.
†Jakobsen, 140.

As the month of November drew to a close and no hostile Russian acts occurred, a wave of relief swept over Finland. Perhaps Erkko's gamble had paid off after all. Schoolchildren and other evacuees returned to the cities and the border districts, and the government announced that schools would reopen on December 1. The popular mood was upbeat: Finland's cause was so self-evidently just that surely the Western democracies would step in to devastate the Russians if they tried an attack.

It was touching, this inchoate faith in the national cause; it was also tragically deluded. When a delegation from the intensely patriotic National Coalition party visited Marshal Mannerheim in early November to ask for his views as Finland's leading military figure, Mannerheim gave it to them straight. Stalin was not bluffing, he said. Russia, too, felt that its cause was just. The Red Army was no pushover, in spite of all the horror stories that had leaked out about the havoc wrought by Stalin's purge of the officer corps. And as for the armed forces of Finland, the Marshal stated bluntly that their condition was critically deficient in every aspect except morale.

The politicians listened respectfully to Mannerheim, thanked him for his time, then left his office whispering among themselves that the Marshal was too old, too gloomy, too afraid of Russia, and too cautious for a proper Finn.

Mannerheim had only conveyed the essence of the uniformly grim reports that were reaching his desk. A sympathetic German military attaché warned that unless drastic moves were taken to reopen negotiations, his information indicated that soon "nothing might remain of Finland except a tale of heroism." Intelligence reports and aerial reconnaissance photos gave indications of massive troop buildups in the Leningrad area and of hundreds of tanks, guns, and planes massed openly within easy range of the frontier. Less concrete, but just as alarming, were vague reports of new railheads and unpaved roads that dead-ended in the forests just a few kilometers east of the border. The Finnish Army had just received its first shipments of Bofors antitank guns from Sweden, enough to parcel out one or two guns per regiment, no more. The situation was equally serious with regard to antiaircraft weapons. Ammunition stocks for all calibers of weapons remained critically low. Trickles of some essential items were beginning to come in, but so slowly and so haphazardly that Mannerheim finally reached a decision he had been putting off for weeks: he could no longer accept responsibility for the defense of Finland.

On November 18, and again on November 26, Mannerheim appealed to Finland's political leaders in a series of passionate and private discussions, begging them to reopen negotiations. "You must come to a diplomatic solution," he urged; "the Army is in no condition to fight!" Again the politicians listened to the Marshal respectfully, and some even agreed with him, but Erkko's ruling clique was puffed up by the belief that they had called the Soviet Bear's bluff and gotten away with it. Mannerheim had voiced similar jeremiads many times before; for the moment, Finland's ruling politicians saw no reason to budge. In disgust, Mannerheim tendered his resignation on November 27. President Kallio accepted it.

A couple of days earlier there had been a dinner meeting at the Kremlin; Khrushchev left a vivid account of it. In Stalin's apartment for the occasion were Molotov, Zhdanov, and the old-guard Finnish Communist O. W. Kuusinen, whom Stalin had already picked as his puppet ruler of a Finnish People's Republic. According to Khrushchev's account, plans for the attack on Finland had already been completed: "The consensus of the group was that the Finns should be given one last chance to accept the territorial demands which they had already rejected during the unsuccessful negotiations. If they didn't yield to our ultimatum, we would take military action. This was Stalin's idea. Naturally, I didn't oppose him."

No one in the room even voiced the possibility that the war would be anything other than a walkover. "All we had to do was raise our voices a little bit," remembered Khrushchev, "and the Finns would obey. If that didn't work, we could fire one shot and the Finns would put up their hands and surrender. Or so we thought. When I arrived at the apartment, Stalin was saying, 'Let's get started today.'"*

The war's first shots were fired on November 26. They numbered seven, and the fall of shot was pinpointed by three Finnish observation posts. These witnesses estimated that the shells detonated approximately 800 meters inside Soviet territory. That afternoon, Molotov sent Helsinki a furious note, accusing the Finns of firing an artillery barrage and claiming that the shells had killed four Russian soldiers and wounded nine others.

These were the famous "Mainila shots," named after the village nearest the explosions. The Finns did not, indeed *could* not, have fired them. Mannerheim had long since ordered all Finnish guns drawn back out of range, in order to prevent just such an incident from happening. The wording of Molotov's note indicates that he may not have known the shots were going to be fired; for an ultimatum, it contains some oddly conciliatory phrases.

For many years there was speculation that even Stalin may not have ordered the shots to be fired, and that Zhdanov did it on his own to precipi-

*Crankshaw, ed., 152.

tate a crisis and prove his zeal to his master. Again Khrushchev throws some light on the matter.

The Mainila shots, he claimed, were set up by Marshal of Artillery Kulik, a brutal and cretinous NKVD general whose military incompetence would cost the Soviet Union terribly during the first weeks of the German invasion. It is logical to assume that Zhdanov and Stalin both knew of the fabrication and condoned it. Khrushchev deals coyly with the question of who fired first at whom: "It's always like that when people start a war. They say, 'You fired the first shot,' or 'You slapped me first and I'm only hitting back.' There was once a ritual which you sometimes see in opera: someone throws down a glove to challenge someone else to a duel; if the glove is picked up, that means the challenge is accepted. Perhaps that's how it was done in the old days, but in our time it's not always so clear who starts a war." *

Helsinki replied to Molotov's note with protestations of innocence, citing Mannerheim's pullback order as proof. There was no response from Moscow. For several hours the northland held its breath. Then came the following note from the Kremlin:

As is well known, attacks by units of the Finnish armed forces against Soviet forces continue not only on the Karelian Isthmus, but also at other points along the Soviet-Finnish frontier. The Soviet Union can no longer tolerate this situation. By reason of the situation which has arisen, for which the Finnish government alone bears responsibility, the Soviet government can no longer maintain normal relations with Finland, and is obliged to recall from Finland its political and economic representatives.

A few hours later Helsinki was on fire from Soviet bombs.

*Ibid.

CHAPTER 2 ▲ ▲

The Baron

His statue looms above the avenue that bears his name, across from the Central Post Office in Helsinki, his stone gaze sweeping forever across a capital city that he conquered, ruled, yet was never really part of. That is how most people visualize him, by means of that outsized equestrian monument, and as strong-man-on-horseback statues go, it is not a bad specimen. The figure has dignity, the face wears an expression of gravity rather than bombast, and there is no phony saber for the pigeons to mock.

Carl Gustav Mannerheim towers above all other characters in the annals of the Winter War. Arguably the greatest Baltic statesman since Gustavus Adolphus, he was an elusive, complex, enigmatic, and powerful man who urgently deserves a good English-language biography. He is unlikely to get it, if only because of the linguistic difficulties of the kind of research that would be required to do justice to the subject.

Mannerheim was born in 1867, near the town of Aabo, into a prominent family of Swedish-Finnish aristocrats. His career path was a common one in those days: he chose the military, and became a member of the Finnish Corps of Cadets shortly after his fourteenth birthday. His entire subsequent career, however, can be traced directly from an incident that happened in 1886, when Mannerheim was nineteen. He went AWOL, got caught, and was expelled from the corps.

Boys will be boys, especially if their families are as well connected as the Baron's. He simply crossed the border and obtained an appointment to the tsar's Nikolaevski Cavalry School. Apparently he had already sown whatever small amount of wild oats were in his system, for his record at the cavalry school was superior, and he graduated with a lieutenant's commission in 1889.

Two years later he won a coveted posting to the elite Chevalier Guards. Among his responsibilities was the job of overseeing the dress and bearing of the interior sentries at the Winter Palace in St. Petersburg. His view of the tsarist regime was therefore obtained from a splendid elevation, permitting him almost daily contact with the royal family.

During the last Romanov coronation, in 1896, Mannerheim enjoyed a place of honor at the heart of those lavish, Mussorgskian rites: he stood at the bottom of the steps leading to the throne itself. The four-and-a-half-hour ceremony, during every minute of which he was compelled to stand motionless in full dress uniform, emblazoned itself on his mind; even half a century later he spoke of it with deep emotion, recalling the ceremony as "indescribably magnificent." * To him, the essence of the tsarist heritage was its outward grandeur; it seemed to make little if any difference to him that its embodiment was a third-rate incompetent.

When war broke out between Russia and Japan, Mannerheim chose the sterner path of professionalism. He campaigned strenuously and earned a reputation for personal bravery the hard way: his horse was shot dead from under him during a reconnaissance patrol. He was promoted to colonel as a reward for his services in this ill-starred conflict and received a mention-in-dispatches from the tsar himself.

Two years later the tsar offered Mannerheim a choice assignment: a two-year trek through Central Asia, on horseback, from Turkestan to Peking, a distance of at least 5,000 miles. Ostensibly his mission was ceremonial and scholarly, but its real object was to collect information, both topographical and political, that might be of strategic interest at some future date. Specifically, he was ordered to collect information about the attitude of local rulers toward the tsar, and to find out all he could about regional rivalries that might be usefully exploited by Russian agents.

Mannerheim traveled with a small staff and an escort of handpicked cossacks; the expedition was gone for two full years and ended up traveling nearly 9,000 miles. One reason for the extra distance was a side trip to the holy city of Lhasa, a place where few foreigners had yet ventured. Much about Mannerheim's abilities as a diplomat is revealed by the fact that he not only penetrated to the heart of Tibet but actually established a warm personal relationship with the Dalai Lama, the most sacred and least accessible ruler in Asia. In what must have been a scene straight out of a Rider Haggard novel, the reincarnation of Buddha requested, and thoroughly enjoyed receiving, lessons from the Finnish aristocrat in the art of pistol shooting. Mannerheim finished this odyssey in good health, with two massive volumes of detailed and rather pedantic observations in his saddlebags, and with a fondness for orientalia that lasted all his life.

*Mannerheim, Gustav, *Memoirs of Marshal Mannerheim* (New York: E. P. Dutton, 1945), 47.

When World War I began, Mannerheim found himself posted to the staff of the able but ill-fated General Brushilov. In 1915 he was named commander of the Twelfth Cavalry Division. In contrast to the situation in France, the eastern front had plenty of room for large, fluid engagements, and Mannerheim distinguished himself in several of them.* Eventually, he rose to the level of corps commander, but by that time the rot had set in throughout the tsarist army as a whole.

A stroke of luck removed the Baron from the front during the period immediately before and after the revolution of November 7. He had fallen from his horse, suffered a sprained ankle, and was recuperating in Odessa; otherwise, loyalist that he was, he would likely have suffered the fate of so many other aristocratic officers.

His journey back to Petrograd was distinguished by both good luck and boldness. A timid man would have traveled incognito; Mannerheim engaged a private pullman car and made the entire journey clad in the full dress uniform of an Imperial corps commander. In one of the few flashes of subjective insight to light up the otherwise arid flatness of his autobiography, the Baron described his arrival in the Petrograd railway station: "It disgusted me to see generals carrying their own kit. However, I found two soldiers who quite willingly took charge of mine."† He crossed the Finnish border just after Finland declared independence.

His return to Finland did not generate parades in the streets; after all, outside of his own class hardly anyone knew him very well. He was coming "home," but it was to a land to which he had paid little attention during the thirty-five years he had served in the Imperial army. Still, he was the most experienced warrior the Whites had, and under the circumstances, his fierce anti-Bolshevism counted for much more than his past infatuation with the tsar. Some idea of the bloody-mindedness of the campaign, and of Mannerheim's willingness to prosecute the White cause ruthlessly, can be mined from a reading of his Order of the Day for March 14, 1918: "The hour has come, the hour for which the whole nation is waiting. Your starving and martyred brothers and sisters in southern Finland fix their last hope on you. The mutilated bodies of the murdered citizens and the ruins of the burnt-

*And in the process, he nearly brought about the death of the man who first encouraged the writing of this book, back in 1962. When he was a young subaltern in the tsarist army, Prince A. I. Lobanov-Rostovsky served in Brushilov's campaign. One morning, his division was flanked and nearly trapped because the cavalry unit supposed to be screening its right wing had instead ridden off in a Custer-like plunge for glory. The commander of that cavalry division was Carl Gustav Mannerheim.
†Mannerheim, 112.

down villages call to Heaven: vengeance upon the traitors! Break down all obstacles! Advance, White army of White Finland!" *

By the time it was all over, there would be mutilated bodies and burnt-down villages enough to go around on both sides. During the period when the Reds controlled Helsinki, Tampere, and much of southern Finland, the "Red Terror" duplicated, on a smaller scale, its namesake in Russia. At least 1,500 people were murdered in the winter of 1917–18. Battle deaths in the campaigns that followed eventually totaled 6,794. But worse would come.

Mannerheim earned the nickname "The Bloody Baron," not for his role as a battlefield commander, but for his perceived role in the ghastly events that happened after the guns fell silent. At least 80,000 Red sympathizers—women and children not excepted—were herded into makeshift concentration camps. Almost 10,000 died in them during the next six months. The "White Terror" that swept Finland paid the Reds back with heavy interest; hangings and firing-squad executions totaled more than 8,000.

This episode was the most shameful in Finnish history, and even at this date, the extensive research on the period has not been able to assign a precise portion of blame to Mannerheim. Conditions throughout rural Finland were hideous during the winter of 1918: hunger was rampant (from some remote districts, there were rumors of cannibalism), and an influenza epidemic raged in the camps unchecked by any efforts on the part of the Whites who ran them.

Mannerheim-haters held the Baron responsible for every death; Mannerheim's hagiographers claimed that he did not know the extent of the butchery and that, even if he had known, communications were so poor that he had little control over what was happening in the interior of the country. It is true that communications between Helsinki and much of rural Finland were poor to nonexistent, but a commander of Mannerheim's authority can usually get his orders through if he is really determined. Whether, in the heat of revenge, those orders would have been obeyed, is questionable.

Mannerheim's avowed policy for dealing with the rebellion was pragmatic and simple: shoot the leaders and put the workers back to work as quickly as possible. Nothing in the record of his life suggests a personal streak of cruelty. His only hatred was of Bolshevism, an abstraction; wholesale vindictive retribution was a tactic that fit neither his character nor his plans for Finland.

It is hard, however, to imagine that Mannerheim was not aware of what was going on in his own backyard—indeed, only a short boat ride from his

*Rintala, Marvin, *Four Finns—Political Profiles* (Berkeley: University of California Press, 1969), 30.

office—in the confines of the old tsarist fortress of Suomenlinna, in Helsinki harbor. The largest White concentration camp was there, and modern Finnish historians estimate that at least 3,000 Red prisoners were summarily killed within its walls: shot, hanged, bayoneted, and in some cases simply beaten to death. If Mannerheim did not order these killings, he surely did little to stop them, and his silence would have been taken, by the murderers, as tacit approval of their atrocities.

Whatever the Baron's degree of culpability in the White Terror, there was no denying that he had won a smashing, and permanent, victory over the Bolsheviks. At the conclusion of his campaign, Kaiser Wilhelm awarded Mannerheim the Iron Cross—thus making him the only military commander who had fought *against* Germany to receive that coveted decoration.

Mannerheim personally favored a monarchy for Finland, but the reality was that Finland had chosen to become a parliamentary democracy. Mannerheim was not comfortable with the idea of democracies, or with their squabbling and undignified political parties. He challenged the system in the first-ever presidential elections, in July 1919, and was trounced by Professor Stahlberg. Although he lobbied for the job, Stahlberg refused to appoint Mannerheim commander of the Civic Guard, fearful of giving him access to even that limited instrument of power.

The new era in European politics was decidedly not to the Baron's taste. As Marvin Rintala, one of his best biographers, states the matter:

No longer sustained by the stagnant but outwardly serene domination of the hereditary aristocracy, the Continent was buzzing with the tumultuous contentions of inexperienced parvenu bourgeois (or ostensibly proletarian) politicians. Baron Mannerheim's orderly world— where a self-perpetuating elite governed and the commoners knew their place—had suddenly disappeared. An agitated and boisterous new regime replaced it. He never became fully reconciled to Democracy; when the new Constitution was being formulated, he urged empowering as head of state "a strong hand that will not be moved by party strife or forced to fritter away the power of government by compromise," not appreciating the fact that compromise is the essence of democratic rule.*

After losing the election to Stahlberg, Mannerheim in effect was frozen out of domestic politics. He didn't fit in with any political party, and no political party knew quite what to do with him. In fact Mannerheim despised

*Forbes, Rosita, *These Men I Knew* (New York: E. P. Dutton, 1940), 240.

political parties as a species, regarding them as undisciplined, selfish, and obstructionist. His concept of political service was almost Roman, wholly oriented toward the half-mystical idea of the individual man of honor who steps forward to serve the state. In his speeches he often referred to "the will to take risks and the readiness to bear responsibility." *

Thus, by the end of 1919, Gustav Mannerheim was no more than an unemployed soldier. He dabbled in domestic affairs in two major areas: right-wing politics and charitable public works. If the combination seems paradoxical, that is because a late-twentieth-century citizen no doubt has trouble penetrating the mind-set of a nineteenth-century monarchist. He founded the Mannerheim Child Welfare Association in 1920, and two years later became chairman of the Finnish Red Cross. In both organizations he succeeded in establishing strong, effective administrations and in tying them to international networks.

Even a sympathetic biographer, however, has trouble with Mannerheim's attachment to the Lapuans. Street brawlers were never his style; the idea of Mannerheim embracing Kurt Wallenius and his bully squads seems about as likely as the image of Field Marshal Hindenburg whooping it up with the Brown Shirts in a Munich beer hall. But Mannerheim saw the Lapuans as he wanted to see them, not as they really were. He voiced the opinion that the movement was an "expression of the Finnish people's reaction to the abuse of freedom and democracy" and justified the Lapuans' violent tactics by proclaiming that "balance reasserts itself sooner or later and the moment comes when the broad masses feel instinctively that order is preferable to unbridled liberty." † The Baron had enough sense to avoid backing a loser, however, and when the public turned on the Lapuans, he subsided into rumblings and grumblings to which few people listened seriously.

During the years between wars, Mannerheim seems to have been a solitary and rather lonely figure. He lived by himself with a small retinue of servants, in a big house in the Kaivopuisto neighborhood of Helsinki. Accounts by several people who visited him there agree that the house was furnished in an austere and overwhelmingly masculine style—hunting trophies, banners, plaques, weapons, framed certificates of honor, etc. "Even while he lived there, the house was taking on the air of the museum it was to become after his death," wrote Rosita Forbes, a journalist who interviewed him just before the outbreak of hostilities.‡ Prominently displayed on the

*Rintala, 40.
†Forbes, 243.
‡Ibid., 273.

Baron's living room wall was an autographed portrait of Nicolas II. If any visitor were to remark on the appropriateness, or lack thereof, of this exhibit, Mannerheim would answer in a flat, declarative voice: "He was my emperor."

When P. E. Svinhufvud was elected president in 1931, Gustav Mannerheim was recalled to public service and given the post of chairman of the Defense Council. He worked hard to build Finland's defenses, and he was forced to fight for every *markka* in his share of the budget, often with the notoriously tight-fisted Paasikivi. Worn out from these unsavory bureaucratic struggles, he resigned again in 1937, only to be reinstated by President-elect Kallio.

When Stalin's territorial demands became known to him in October 1939, Mannerheim consistently urged a policy of conciliation. He soon got a reputation for being the ghost at the banquet, and Prime Minister Cajander finally let it be known that he was ready to accept the Marshal's resignation. Members of the then-powerful National Coalition party openly criticized Mannerheim for being too old, too afraid of the Russians, and—the most infamous criticism of all—for being a man who could not be trusted. Kallio finally agreed that the old man would have to go, only days before hostilities broke out, but the first Russian bombs fell on Helsinki just before the Baron's resignation was formally accepted. Instead of being sacked, he was instantly appointed commander in chief. Even the old knight's worst political enemies knew he was the only possible choice to lead the nation's armed forces.

By the time Mannerheim actually became president of Finland in 1944, it was a bitter and ironic triumph, a role of almost Shakespearean despair. He was seventy-seven years old, worn out from years of wartime stress, and in fragile health; his nation was ravaged, exhausted, bankrupt, and savagely truncated. During his nineteen months in office he was often too sick to conduct daily business. Eventually, and very gently, his resignation was again requested, and the Baron stepped down, choosing, characteristically enough, to retire in Switzerland rather than in Finland.

He had done much more than simply lead his nation through two wars; he had led it *out* of war with Russia, yet managed to keep it free, identity intact. Whatever one may think of this or that element of his character and career, the independence of Finland is itself his monument; that achievement alone makes him loom as a genuine hero.

All that remained to him were five sunset years of tranquil retirement, mostly spent writing his curiously dispassionate memoirs—so matter-of-fact when dealing with the apocalyptic battles against the Red Army, yet so achingly nostalgic in their brief allusions to the world of Imperial Russia, now as remote to us, and by then, probably to him as well, as the world of lost Atlantis.

Mannerheim died on January 28, 1951; the Finnish civil war had begun on January 28, 1918. The synchronicity was a final touch of irony in a life that had been filled with ironic drama. He had been a majestic actor on the stage of Baltic history. Against his few but large-scale successes must be balanced many failures, and against those failures and successes alike must be balanced the legend that shrouds him now. It is a powerful legend, but it is based on facts. Historian Marvin Rintala, author of the best English-language study of Mannerheim and a writer who could be scathingly critical of him, was finally forced to this assessment of him: "He was a noble man, as well as a nobleman." * "Mannerheim did not grow up among the masses, but in a castle. . . . he was a cosmopolite in the age of nationalism; an aristocrat in the age of democracy; a conservative in the age of revolutions." †

There is no question that Mannerheim's politics were a dizzying anomaly, so much so that perhaps they should not be judged on ideological grounds. For all his anti-Bolshevism, for all his flirtation with the grubby machinations of the Lapuans, the man was not an ideologue. All that he did, all that he said, probably every single thing that he *thought* derived from the fact of his aristocratic birth and from the worldview he inherited from that birth in a prerevolutionary, predemocratic milieu. He was "The Baron" to his fingertips. Everyone who worked with or against him, whether they liked or hated him, agreed with or detested his politics, was struck by the man's sheer physical bearing. When Hitler met Mannerheim for the first time, in June 1942, it was the führer who bowed, while the Baron remained stiffly at attention.

He was patriotic; he cared about Finland, but nationalistic zeal was not a strong part of his makeup. On the other hand, it was this very same lack of nationalistic passion that enabled him to walk his nation across an incredibly narrow tightrope in 1944, with its integrity, honor, and identity surviving on the other side. A more fire-breathing Finnish leader, Väinö Tanner, for example, might have succumbed to fantasies of last-ditch stands in the forest. History has proven this, in fact, to be Mannerheim's greatest single accomplishment. Finns today find the idea of another war with Russia all but inconceivable (although the border defenses, to be sure, remain strong). There are few Finns still alive who can remember the barbarities of 1918, while nearly every Finn living today treasures the state of peaceful relations

*Rintala, 26.
†Ibid., 22, 36.

that exists between Finland and its giant neighbor. And one of the chief architects of that situation, Mannerheim, is still respected by the majority of Finns, even if the element of reverence has long since evaporated.

The eccentric nature of Mannerheim's patriotism is perhaps nowhere so clearly illustrated as in the matter of language. Born to Swedish-speaking nobility, and quite fluent in Russian and French (which he spoke in the elegant, high-flown manner of the Romanov Court), he could also converse passably in English, Polish, and German. Yet he did not bother to learn Finnish until his fiftieth year, regarding it as a barbarous and provincial tongue, a fact that will appear strange only to readers who have never attempted to grapple with that convoluted and unwieldy language. During the civil war he required the constant services of an interpreter just so he could pass orders to the Finnish-speaking troops under his command. One modern historian, after listening to recordings of Mannerheim's wartime speeches, stated that "to put it bluntly, Mannerheim's Finnish pronunciation is beyond belief, ranking with Winston Churchill's French. Churchill, at least, did not have to govern the French." *

With very few exceptions, his closest personal friends were not Finns but other European aristocrats. He generally disliked Germans and avoided them whenever possible. The story is told of a luncheon Mannerheim was forced, by the demands of protocol, to attend in the company of a pompous and overbearing German liaison officer. While the meal was still in progress, "this German officer produced a cigar before Mannerheim had finished eating and asked if it would bother the Marshal if he smoked it. Mannerheim fixed the Wehrmacht officer with a gaze that would penetrate armor plate and cut him dead by replying evenly: 'I don't know. No one has ever tried it.' " †

By his deep, ingrained hauteur, one is irresistibly reminded of Charles de Gaulle. Even in wartime there was something curiously "withheld" about Mannerheim, a remote quality which made it hard for subordinates to approach him with new ideas. He delegated authority grudgingly. He also seems to have been aware of this defect in his leadership style, for at most of his headquarters conferences he permitted his subordinates to speak first before he delivered his own views. His corps commanders found him a hard master. Östermann judged him cold, imperious, and unreasonable and after the war had harsh things to say about his generalship. Öhquist, who had a much higher regard for Mannerheim's tactical grasp, also states that he was a

---

*Ibid., 21.
†Goodrich, Austin, *Study in Sisu* (New York: Ballantine Books, 1960), 22.

harsh man to work for, an impossible man to please. Yet many other accounts display the Marshal as being courteous, even fatherly, with subordinates of low and middle rank; noblesse oblige, surely.

Though he was an autocrat to his bones, he had nothing in common with the dictators of his time, the Hitlers and Francos and Mussolinis, and seems to have regarded them as *little* men. For Stalin he may actually have felt a certain grudging respect, for at least the proportions of Stalin's excesses were not without precedent in Russian history. But for the bureaucratic apparatus that kept Stalin in power—the purges, the gulags, the proliferation of party hacks throughout every level of Soviet society—he could only have felt contempt.

If Mannerheim's politics seem inscrutably peculiar, it is probably because they are outside of all contemporary frames of reference. Totalitarianism itself, a postdemocratic form of reactionary spasm, was almost as alien to him as democracy. His ideals came from a lost world, a world where gentlemen in glittering uniforms conducted their business over sherry in gilded drawing rooms, and then adjourned, tiara-clad ladies at their sides, for an evening at the Imperial Ballet. Gustav Mannerheim would not have been out of place in the pages of a Tolstoy novel; but in the gray and airless chambers of modern parliamentary establishments, he was as anachronistic as an envoy from the court of Versailles.

▲ CHAPTER 3 ▲ ▲

Order of Battle

Winston Churchill was not making idle hyperbole when he spoke, in the closing months of World War II, of the Red Army's having "clawed the guts out of" the Wehrmacht. By the time Berlin fell to Marshal Zhukov's armies, the Soviet war machine had become a tidal wave of brute steel and inexhaustible human reserves. Even at the end, when they were maneuvering worn-out companies against armored divisions, the Germans outfought and outkilled their Soviet counterparts by a ratio of five to one, and still it made no difference. Any Western general who would not admit to being afraid of the Red Army by 1945, with the possibly pathological exception of George Patton, was either ignorant or a liar. Nothing that has happened since 1945 has altered that menacing image: waves of tanks, hordes of men, armadas of aircraft that darkened the sky. . . .

But in the early winter of 1939, those stereotyped images did not exist. The Red Army was an unknown quantity, not just to the West but also to its own commanders and strategists. Born in the helter-skelter campaigns of the civil war, when most of the action took place in the form of large-scale partisan operations rather than conventional warfare, the Red Army was an untried, theoretically designed instrument. True, there had been a stunningly one-sided victory won by Marshal Zhukov against the Japanese at Khalkin Gol, in August 1939, but that had not been much of a contest. The Japanese were used to fighting barefoot armies of Chinese conscripts who had no air support and no significant armor; and the Japanese tanks were even more rickety, weakly armed, and mechanically unreliable than those of the Italians. Zhukov unleashed not only large formations of the latest Christie-designed armor but tactical air power on a scale the Japanese had not dreamed could exist, and he cut up their armies like so much warm butter. Moreover, all the fighting at Khalkin Gol had taken place on the open, treeless plains of Mongolia, ideal terrain for a Soviet-style blitzkrieg.

Finland would be a different story: it was the Red Army's first campaign against a modern European foe, and it would be fought in terrain about as different from Mongolia's as the surface of another planet. At least one Red Army strategist seems to have been aware of this: the chief of staff of the Red Army, General Shaposhnikov, studied the upcoming Finnish campaign with a cool, professional eye and did not like what he saw. He submitted a report to the Main Military Council that advocated a serious buildup, extensive logistical and fire-support preparation, and a rational, methodical order of battle, deploying the Red Army's very best units, even if they had to be brought in from the Far East.

Stalin seems to have dismissed the report without much discussion, treating it in fact almost as a joke. He had been told by Zhdanov and Defense Commissar Voroshilov that the Finnish business could be taken care of by the resources on hand in the Leningrad Military District, and he believed them. After all, the Red Army had just finished inundating 200,000 square kilometers of Poland, inhabited by thirteen million people, at a cost of less than a thousand casualties. Stalin was not worried.

Zhdanov's military commander, General Meretskov, at least had some doubts; in a report submitted just before the start of hostilities, he wrote, "The terrain of coming operations is split by lakes, rivers, swamps, and is almost entirely covered by forests. . . . The proper use of our forces will be difficult. . . . It is criminal to believe that our task will be easy, or only like a march, as it has been told to me by officers in connection with my inspection."*

It does not appear, however, that Meretskov was entirely free to deploy his troops according to his own best judgment. Either that, or he just wrote the report in order to cover himself in case things went wrong. Motives, true feelings, and lines of responsibility are not very clear at this level of the Soviet command even today. The whole Finnish campaign was an embarrassment to the officer caste, and even half a century later there is little discussion of it in print on the Russian side.

Whatever his reasons, Meretskov publicly took the politically correct stance that the Finnish effort would be little more than a glorified police action, requiring two weeks at the most. By the time the fighting actually started, the only concern he expressed was for controlling his forward elements, lest some overzealous panzer commander blunder across the Swedish border.

Meretskov himself would have operational control over the Seventh,

*Chew, Allen F., *The White Death* (East Lansing: Michigan State University Press, 1971), 256.

Eighth, Ninth, and Fourteenth armies—the entire Karelian front. In 1939, he was forty-two years of age. Of peasant origins, he had joined the party early, in May 1917, straight from his job as a factory worker. He distinguished himself in battle as a Red Guard and was eventually promoted to political commissar in the Red Army. Diligent if uninspired, he kept his nose clean politically, survived the purges, and by 1938 had reached the zenith of his career when Stalin appointed him commander of the Leningrad Military District.

Some idea of the optimistic mood that prevailed, and of the power wielded by political officers over their military counterparts, can be gleaned from an anecdote published in the memoirs of N. N. Voronov, a gentleman who, by World War II, had risen to the rank of chief marshal of artillery. Voronov was in charge of logistics for the guns, a task that would prove herculean, and it was in this capacity that he paid a visit to Meretskov's headquarters during the waning days of November. Meretskov welcomed him, then kept his mouth shut; most of the talking was done by the artillery officer Kulik and a commissar named Mekhlis. These two asked Voronov what sort of ammunition stocks they could draw on during the coming campaign. "That depends," replied Voronov: "Are you planning to attack or defend . . . and by the way, how much time is allotted for the operation?"

"Between ten and twelve days," was the bland reply.

Voronov was not buying that estimate; all he had to do was look at a map of Finland. "I'll be happy if everything can be resolved in two or three months." This remark was greeted with "derisive gibes." Then–Deputy Commissar Kulik then ordered Voronov to base all his ammo-consumption and fire-support estimates on the assumption that the entire Finnish operation would last twelve days, no more.[*]

Like everybody else in the military profession, Stalin's generals had been deeply impressed by the success of the Germans' blitzkrieg tactics. Armored spearheads had sliced through the enemy's main line of resistance and spread havoc in its rear, followed by masses of infantry to exploit the breakthroughs and deal with bypassed pockets of resistance, the whole thing covered by an umbrella of tactical air support and lavishly supplied with artillery. In terms of hardware and manpower, Russia certainly had all the necessary ingredients to mount its own version of the blitzkrieg.

But German tactical doctrine had been tailored to very specific central European conditions: a familiar landscape with a network of modern roads.

---

[*]Bialer, Seweryn, ed., *Stalin and His Generals* (New York: Pegasus Books, 1969), 132.

Finland was one of the worst places on Earth to attempt the application of a technique that was designed to win battles on the open, rolling, highway-veined topography of continental Europe. Much of the blitzkrieg's effectiveness stemmed from the fact that armies fighting on mainland Europe had clearly recognizable centers of supply and communication, usually not far behind the lines, which made excellent objectives for armored spearheads. Finnish conditions offered scarcely any comparable targets. Behind the frontier forest there was only more forest. Centers of communication were deep inside the country, not just twenty miles behind the lines.

Nor did the Red generals appreciate the amount of trouble the Wehrmacht had taken to perfect tactical coordination between the component arms, to ensure a reliable and redundant network of communications, and to instill in its frontline commanders a sense of drive and individual initiative. Those very qualities, if displayed in the Red Army, were more apt to earn a man a trip to the gulag than a pat on the back. Many of the battalion and regimental commanders who would lead the Russian attacks were by this time little more than groveling flunkies whose every battlefield decision had to be seconded by a political commissar before orders could go to the troops.

The blitzkrieg, in short, had been perfected for a sleek, hard-muscled, superbly trained, and passionately motivated army, such as the German General Staff had fashioned during the decades between the wars. It was quite unsuited for a ponderous, top-heavy army of ill-trained soldiers led by timid officers, overseen by inexperienced party ideologues, and sent forth to conquer a country whose terrain consists of practically nothing but natural obstacles to military operations.

The Russian generals may have thought they were imitating the Germans, but what they actually unleashed was an offensive more in keeping with an older Russian tradition, whose crude tactics relied on masses of men and sheer weight of metal. The plan called for simply overwhelming, or overawing, the Finns with a massive ground onslaught at every place on the frontier where it seemed feasible to support an attack, coupled with air raids designed to hamper Finnish communications and spread terror among the civilian populace. That populace was supposed to be so restive already that Soviet planners expected their efforts to be augmented by a large "fifth column" deep inside the country.

What happened was something very different. Lacking the freedom to exercise initiative, Russian field commanders relied on mass frontal attacks to obliterate even minor nests of opposition, incurring thousands of needless casualties in the process. Leadership beyond the NCO level was brittle, sluggish, and marked by a rigid adherence to the same primitive tactics over and over again, no matter what the actual situation. The standard of training varied wildly from unit to unit: some regiments were crack troops, well trained and supplied, while others, often thrown in at their side, were scratch units made up of raw draftees, many of whom were so ignorant they didn't even know the name of the country they were invading.

Whole divisions entered Finland with no worthwhile intelligence estimates of their opposition, guided by hopelessly inaccurate maps, yet fully burdened with truckloads of propaganda material including reams of posters and brass bands. Into some of the densest forests in the world, they brought hundreds of flat-trajectory field guns, useless except at very close range, and relatively few howitzers—guns that could shoot *over* the trees. Each Russian column lugged into the forest a full complement of modern antitank guns, even though Soviet intelligence must have known the Finns had no operational armor. Virtually useless as field guns, dozens of these weapons were captured intact by the Finns and rapidly redeployed against their former owners.

Most glaring of all, the invading troops were unprepared for winter. It was not until after the first assaults on the Mannerheim Line had been bloodily repulsed that the Russians caught on to the idea of painting their tanks white to match the environment, or of dressing their infantry in snow capes. The invaders had almost no ski training, even though some units received truckloads of wildly unreliable ski-combat manuals just before they crossed into Finland. Apparently the men were expected to become experts in their spare time.

Yet for all its glaring faults, the Russian scheme did have a few things going for it. It was early enough in the year so that conditions, on the Karelian Isthmus at least, were favorable. The surfaces of most of the bogs and smaller lakes had frozen hard enough to present no obstacle to troop movements, but little snow had fallen. There were good roads on the Isthmus, and much of the land was only lightly wooded. But the weather conditions were fickle, and if Meretskov's troops did not clean out the Finns in two weeks' time, the full fury of the subarctic winter could be counted on to ruin all timetables. Logic dictated a swift, all-out, thunderclap assault straight across the Isthmus.

But in actuality the advance on the Isthmus was cautious and poorly led. Entire columns were halted, sometimes for hours, by the merest display of Finnish resistance from a few rearguard snipers. North of the Isthmus the Russians wasted thousands of men in operations against the midsection of Finland; these seem to have been planned in the most criminally offhanded manner and then conducted for the most part with glaring incompetence.

The key to Finland was the Isthmus and only the Isthmus; the Finns knew that, and they were surprised that the enemy did not. The reason for this may not be apparent from looking at a map. The Karelian Isthmus appears narrow and sliced up by waterways, lakes, and bogs, altogether a very limited "gateway" for a mechanized invader. In contrast, the same map shows vast, thinly populated regions north of Lake Ladoga, which seem to offer enormous amounts of elbow room and opportunity for maneuver—on paper a much more attractive theater than the cramped, channelized Isthmus. The whole country, in fact, gets quite narrow, and the concept of cutting Finland in two at the "waist" looks very inviting.

But only on paper. As confined as the Karelian Isthmus is, it still offers much better terrain for a modern army than anything north of Lake Ladoga. Up there in the narrower part of Finland the forests are more dense, more primitive than words, maps, or even pictures can convey. Roads there were little better than one-lane wagon tracks, and those were often many miles apart. There was no shelter except for a few scattered farms and logging towns, set in clearings hacked out of the trees. Lateral passage between the roads was possible only for trained men on skis; men on foot could scarcely make any progress at all in midwinter, for the snowdrifts that pile up between the trees are tall enough to bury a man in a standing position.

Once committed to these regions, the invading columns would be hopelessly road bound. No matter how strong they were, a defender made mobile by skis could dance circles around them. What the Russians should have done in these areas was to infiltrate small units of ski guerrillas, which might well have slipped undetected through the forest and worked great damage in the more populated interior. But instead of small, mobile, specialist units, the Russians committed elephantine masses of conventional infantry and armor, which had no choice except to crawl westward along whatever roads they could find. The results of this strategic blundering were some of the most one-sided defeats ever inflicted on Russian troops.

At the start of hostilities, Russian forces were positioned as follows:

1. Seventh Army: On the Karelian Isthmus, under Meretskov; comprised of between twelve and fourteen divisions, with three tank brigades and a mechanized corps attached (1,000 tanks and other vehicles); its artillery strength was much augmented, even at the start; several divisions were still in the process of forming up when hostilities began; the objective was Viipuri, the breaching of the Mannerheim Line, and, ultimately, a sweep westward to Helsinki. Later on, for purposes of better operational control, this force was divided into the Seventh and Thirteenth armies.

2. Eighth Army: North of Lake Ladoga, in Ladoga-Karelia, facing the Finnish Fourth Corps under General Hägglund; composed of six rifle divisions and two tank brigades. Its mission was to turn the northern flank of the Isthmus defenses by circling around Lake Ladoga's north shore, breaking through the relatively thin Finnish lines there, and striking south, to take the Mannerheim Line from the rear. The strength the Russians managed to deploy here was considerably more than the Finns had thought possible and was one of the nastier surprises of the war for them.

3. Ninth Army: Five rifle divisions with a motley and not well documented assortment of attached armored units. This army's mission was to thrust westward, to reach as many centers of communication as possible, and to cut Finland in half if it could. Each of these divisions, however, went in unsupported, on poor and widely separated roads, with results that ranged from disappointing to disastrous.

4. Fourteenth Army: Three mediocre divisions with attached armor, based in Murmansk, intended to capture the arctic port of Petsamo and, eventually, the Lapland capital of Rovaniemi, which was Finland's only significant center of communications in the far north.

The overall concept of the Russian plan was simple: push the Finns as hard as possible from eight different directions, by means of a coordinated westward advance. The Mannerheim Line would be hammered from the front by the Seventh Army and taken in the rear by the Eighth Army, while the Ninth Army would cut Finland in two and sever its communications with Sweden. In the far north, the Fourteenth Army would prevent any help from reaching Finland through Petsamo. It must be said that if the Russians had planned their offensive carefully, and if their troops had been better prepared for the tasks assigned to them, the plan might have worked.

The strategy Mannerheim and his staff had devised for Finland was predicated on some very harsh realities. Obviously Russia was the only likely opponent, and it was a delusion to think that Finland could successfully defend itself against the Red Army for an indefinite period of time. In the long run, Finland's only real guarantee of continued existence was the conscience of Western civilization. Finland, it was hoped, would be regarded as a vital outpost of everything the Western powers stood for, and as such the country would not be allowed to vanish from the map. Thus was born a strategy designed to enable Finland to hang on long enough for outside aid to reach it. If that hope proved chimerical, the only thing left to do was to resist so fiercely that Stalin would opt for a negotiated settlement rather than total conquest. If Stalin did seek total subjugation, the Finns would fight to the last man and bullet. Mannerheim's plans, therefore, were not based on the absurd hope of outright victory, but on "the most honorable annihilation, with the faint hope that the conscience of mankind would find an alternative solution as a reward for bravery and singleness of purpose."*

Russia's initial invasion force, already vastly superior in numbers and equipment, could of course draw on a virtually limitless reservoir of replacements, whereas Finland's army would be fully extended almost from the start. Foreign military attachés in Helsinki believed that the Finns would fight stoutly, but in the face of the on-paper odds, most of them wrote off Finnish resistance as a heroic gesture that could not possibly stave off defeat for longer than a week or two.

The average Finnish soldier looked at matters much differently. He knew, in his bones, that on a man-to-man basis he was worth several of his opponents. His ancestors, as far back as recorded Finnish history existed, had fought Russians on this same soil and usually won. The Finn knew what he was fighting for and why. His stereotyped view of the Russian soldier was not flattering: Ivan was stupid, lazy, dirty, incapable of initiative, and mentally oppressed by the same forest environment that was second nature to the Finns. To be sure, the Finnish soldier was aware of the numerical odds against him, but he rendered those odds less terrible by cracking jokes about them: "They are so many, and our country is so small, where will we find room to bury them all?"

Most Finnish units were made up of men from the same geographical regions. Some of these units found themselves in action literally on their home ground, but nearly everyone fought on terrain very similar to the land he had known since childhood. Company-, platoon-, and battalion-level officers were usually well known to their men from peacetime and were often addressed by their first names or nicknames during combat. There was probably less saluting and less parade-ground spit and polish than in any other army in Europe. Finnish troops knew they were in the army to fight, not to march in parades, and in the kind of war they were called upon to fight, that was precisely the right set of priorities.

Before 1918, of course, there was formally no such thing as "the Finnish Army"—Finnish nationals gained experience in the tsar's service and, during the years immediately preceding independence, the army of Imperial Germany. Both of those nations maintained conventional armies of the type most European nations supported in the years before World War I. The Finns

*Langdon-Davies, John, *Invasion in the Snow* (Boston: Houghton Mifflin Co., 1941), 7.

serving in them would have received training designed to prepare a soldier to function in a large, carefully structured organization, whose combat arms were backed by a full array of service and support elements. Operating procedures in such armies were formalized by many years of historical tradition; things were done, in short, "by the book."

The Finnish civil war of 1918 was fought, by both sides, largely on an ad hoc basis, using whatever forces and equipment were available from week to week. The Finnish Army that emerged from that violent field was a motley agglomeration with no real personality of its own. Its units had fought with tactics and weapons borrowed from Russia one time, from Germany the next, and with an improvisatory dash of Finnish barroom savagery thrown in for good measure. Its officers were mainly veterans of the Prussian General Staff school of warfare, trained only to lead units in a large, complex, European-style standing army, complete with a full line of specialized services and support units. Their tactical training had presumed the "givens" of such an army, envisioning each unit as a component in vast 1918-style operations, which involved tens of thousands of men, hundreds of guns firing millions of stockpiled shells, each troop movement and tactic scheduled weeks in advance, the whole effort backed up by a modern industrial economy with all its ancillary networks of transportation and communications.

None of the above applied to Finland in 1918, and not much more by 1939. No matter how the new nation developed its resources, no matter how sound its economy was, no matter how its balance of trade improved, nature had still set rigorous, Spartan limits on what was possible in Finland. Its population would never be large enough to generate the manpower needed to field a massive European-style army, nor would its economy ever be rich enough to provide for the technological and logistical luxuries enjoyed by the armies of Britain, France, or America.

These conditions, far from daunting the architects of Finnish defense strategy, had an invigorating effect on their intellects. They were forced to throw out "the book" and find solutions to problems for which their professional training had not prepared them. Their task was rendered much more difficult by the parsimonious nature of the defense budgets they had to work with. In so far as it was a conscious process, their basic concept seems to have been to concentrate on the ways in which Finland's geography and national character could be developed into military assets rather than liabilities.

Infantry training was stripped to its essentials. Officers and men worked together to develop tactical doctrine and training methods specifically adapted to Finnish terrain. The forest itself dictated a heavy emphasis on individual initiative and small-unit operations, quasi-guerrilla style. Marksmanship, mental agility, woodcraft, orienteering, camouflage, and physical conditioning were stressed, and parade-ground niceties were given short shrift. Unconventional tactics—ambushes, long-range patrols, deceptions, raids—were enshrined as doctrine and refined until they fitted into the overall national strategy.

The artillery branch concentrated its attention on mortars and howitzers, the kind of light, high-angle weapons that were best suited for the terrain. The gunners developed new techniques intended to compensate for the limitations the forest placed on range-finding and observation. Every part of Finland that might eventually become a target for Finnish gun crews was meticulously mapped and ranged, to the inch, from probable battery positions. The precision and economy of their fire-control procedures would give the ammunition-starved Finnish gunners a slight edge over their more lavishly equipped Russian counterparts when the shooting started.

Finland's population was sufficient to permit a standing army of fifteen infantry divisions, each numbering 14,000 men. Because of prewar funding problems, however, there were only ten fully equipped divisions when war broke out. An eleventh division had been formed, but it had no heavy equipment; there was enough manpower on hand for two others if equipment could be found to outfit them.

Mannerheim's mobilization scheme worked tolerably well, thanks to the advance warning the Finns had. There were some problems, however, because full-scale mobilization of entire divisions had almost never been allowed during peacetime. Officers suddenly found themselves commanding larger units than they were used to. Cadre officers who had led companies in peacetime (and who had usually known most of their men by name) were suddenly thrust into the role of battalion commander, while peacetime battalion commanders suddenly found themselves leading regiments. The duties of these new ranks had to be mastered on the job, and the remarkable success of so many Finnish captains and lieutenants in doing so is a testament to the soundness of their prewar training.

All those years of having to wring every ounce of value from every penny of the defense budget actually had some positive effects. The Finnish Army was "lean and mean," experienced at getting the maximum effectiveness from its limited resources. Man for man, on its home ground, it was one of the toughest, best-led, most adaptable armies in the world. In spite of the scarcity of modern equipment, a spirit of calm confidence prevailed throughout the ranks. The men believed in themselves and their cause, and to an unusual degree they seem to have trusted their officers not to throw their lives away.

Geography dictated the basic Finnish strategy. The frontier with Russia was a thousand kilometers long, but the biggest stretch of it, from Lake Ladoga's northern shore to the Arctic Ocean, was quite impenetrable except along a handful of unpaved roads. This fact alone helped to mitigate the Russians' numerical advantage: it meant that the Finns could concentrate their strongest forces on the Karelian Isthmus and in the area immediately north of Ladoga, to prevent the outflanking of the Mannerheim Line.

In their prewar calculations the Finns had envisioned the deployment of seven Russian divisions on the Isthmus and no more than five along the whole border north of Lake Ladoga. If that had been the case, and given the conventional three-to-one ratio needed for an attacker to overcome a well-entrenched defender, then the simple numbers did not look all that disastrous for the Finns. Their main problem would be attrition over a long period of time, but there was always the hope that outside help would arrive before matters reached a crisis.

In reality, and from the very start, the situation was much grimmer. The war in Europe made the prospects of outside aid very dim indeed, and long-term attrition made eventual defeat a certainty. Finnish strategy was also undercut by the extensive preparatory work the Russians had done on their side of the border. Mannerheim had known about some of these construction projects, but many others had been carried out without the Finns catching on. Instead of the five divisions Finnish intelligence had predicted north of Lake Ladoga, the Russians deployed twelve. If Russian competence had been equal to Russian planning, the Finns would have been in serious trouble from the start.

At the beginning of the war, Mannerheim's biggest problem was not men but matériel. Shipments of antitank and antiaircraft guns were arriving in small quantities and at a glacially slow pace. The ammunition situation was alarming. At the start of hostilities, Finnish stockpiles for some essential supplies were woefully inadequate: *

Cartridges for rifles and light automatics	60 days
Shells for light fields guns	21 days
Shells for 122 mm. howitzers	24 days
Shells for heavy and coastal artillery	19 days
Gas and oil for ground units	60 days
Aviation fuel	30 days

On paper, each Finnish division could count on the support of twenty-four field guns and a dozen howitzers. Even for an army trained to do without

*Mannerheim, 324.

artillery support, those numbers were just barely adequate. In reality, many of the weapons were long overdue for retirement—museum pieces dating from the Russo-Japanese War of 1904–1905 were counted as well as modern cannon. Each division was also supported by two dozen 81 mm. mortars. Soviet artillery was not organic to a division; it was tacked on in regiment-sized packets, usually two artillery regiments for each regiment of infantry, or about three times as many guns as the Finns could field.

Russian infantry units had about the same number of light mortars as their Finnish counterparts, but each infantry regiment could also call on support from batteries of powerful 120 mm. heavy mortars. Despite the Finns' superior fire control and accuracy, their chronic ammunition shortage seldom allowed them the luxury of counterbattery or saturation fire. The Russians could afford to fire more shells of a single caliber, on a single day, than were contained in the entire Finnish reserves.

Finnish tank forces were operationally nonexistent. Antitank training had been attempted with some clattery old Renaults dating from 1918, but most Finnish soldiers had no realistic idea of what it was like to face modern panzers. Their first confrontations with Soviet armor would be traumatic.

The army's first antitank guns, 37 mm. Bofors weapons from Sweden, were uncrated just weeks before the war broke out. Few of their crews had had time even to face a dummy tank in training before they were called on to fight large formations of the real thing. The total number of Bofors guns available was so small that they were parceled out two or three to a regiment. There had been long discussions about what sort of antitank weapons should be issued to the infantry at the platoon level. The weapons finally chosen, 20 mm. Lahti antitank rifles, did not in fact reach the troops in significant numbers until after the war was over.

Finnish small arms were at least as good as those found in the Red Army. The standard infantry rifle was one of several versions of the basic Russian Moisin/Nagant design, modified in some details by Finnish ordnance experts and of overall higher manufacturing quality than its Russian counterpart. This rifle fired a 7.62 mm. round; it was a sturdy, rugged, bolt-action piece noted for its accuracy. Although the basic Moisin action had been adopted by the Russians as far back as 1891, the design was so sound that some Soviet satellite armies could still be seen using it through the 1950s.

The Finns' basic heavy machine gun was a water-cooled version of the classic Maxim gun from the Great War era. These were cumbersome and brutally heavy weapons, but they were rugged and dependable, even under severe winter conditions. The light machine gun—equivalent in its role to the American Browning Automatic Rifle of that day—was the 7.62 mm.

Lahti/Saloranta, considered by firearms experts to be one of the first really practical "light" automatics to enter service after World War I. Indeed, photos of the weapon reveal a striking resemblance to many contemporary designs. It was a fairly heavy weapon for its day—twenty-three pounds with loaded magazine—but it could be fired from a bipod or from the shoulder, using either a twenty-round box magazine or a seventy-five-round drum. The Lahti was air cooled and recoil operated, and was one of the few automatics in service anywhere at that time that permitted its gunner to switch from single shot to full automatic. In the latter mode it had a cyclic fire rate of 500 rounds per minute. It was a powerful weapon, with a muzzle velocity of 2,625 feet per second, comparable to some of today's streamlined assault rifles.

Originally, the Lahti had been designed as an export weapon, Finland's entry into the international arms market. As far as can be determined, however, the only foreign army that purchased a significant number of them was, rather oddly, the Chinese. It was not, therefore, a weapon designed for specifically Finnish conditions. Its one weakness was a certain degree of over-manufacture in its moving parts, tolerances too fine and too numerous, so that it sometimes froze in severe cold, precisely the kind of weather it would be used in. When that happened, it was sometimes possible to reactivate a frozen Lahti by the simple expedient of urinating on it.

The most interesting weapon in the Finnish arsenal, however, was the famed "Suomi" submachine gun, or "machine pistol" (*koonipistolit* in Finnish). The Suomi was one of the least-known submachine gun designs of its day, but it was actually rather influential. So effective was it in the Winter War that the Soviets paid it the ultimate compliment of copying it for their famous PPSh "burp gun" design, which would be the mainstay of Communist Bloc armies until the advent of the AK-47.

The Suomi was a splendid weapon for the kind of small-unit, bushwhacking tactics the Finnish Army excelled in. A ski patrol deep in the forest, where encounters with the enemy were likely to be sudden, close-range affairs, didn't need an accurate long-range rifle; what was needed was a meatchopper, and the Suomi filled the bill. It had half again as much muzzle velocity as a Tommy Gun (1,300 feet/second as opposed to 920) and spewed out its 9 mm. slugs at a sizzling rate of 800–900 rounds/minute. One area where it lost out against the Thompson or the German "Schmeisser" was appearance: in terms of its lines, the Suomi was as brutal looking as an ox.

Ruggedly designed, operating on the "blowback" principle, it was short enough to dangle conveniently from a skier's shoulders and could be brought into action from that position in a split second. It also had a single-shot option for aimed fire, although it was not terribly accurate beyond 100 yards in that mode. Up close, however, it was lethal. The Russians feared and hated Suomi gunners, and with good reason—one Finnish soldier would be decorated for scoring over 200 confirmed kills with his Suomi during the *motti* battles in the central forests. The preferred method of ammo feed was a seventy-round drum; the caliber was 9 mm. Twenty- and fifty-round box magazines were also available for this weapon, but they do not seem to have been used as much in the Winter War as they would be during the later "Continuation War," when a much higher percentage of Finnish soldiers were armed with rapid-fire weapons than was the case in 1939.

Because the Suomi burned ammo at a furious rate, only a few hundred of them were issued per division at the start of the war. Under combat conditions, of course, many men managed to "acquire" Suomis to replace their bolt-action rifles. In the beginning, though, only the coolest and most intelligent troopers were issued the gun; to be designated a Suomi gunner was an honor almost the equivalent of another stripe.

Interestingly, the Russians had a chance to look at the Suomi before the war and turned it down. As Marshal of Artillery Voronov tells it:

> Way back in the beginning of the 1930s, we had acquired a model of the "Suomi" submachine gun. It was even tested by a commission of specialists on infantry weapons. The commission decided that it was a "police" weapon, unsuitable for military combat operations. The design and production of such submachine guns was considered superfluous. Acting on his own initiative, the Soviet designer V. G. Federov designed during those years a low-powered submachine gun which used Nagant revolver bullets. After being tested, this submachine gun was also rejected. Now, having encountered the widespread use of submachine guns in the Finnish Army, we bitterly regretted these miscalculations.[*]

Official Red Army doctrine in 1939, Voronov goes on to say, still emphasized massed volleys of rifle fire. It was feared that if the poorly educated recruits got hold of automatic weapons, they would waste too much ammo.

There was another weapon in the Finns' arsenal, one that occasioned any number of colorful newspaper yarns, and that was the *puukko* knife, a Lapp blade about the size and heft of a Bowie knife. Most of the tales about single-handed Finns dispatching whole squads of Russians with their *puukkos* were obviously concocted by correspondents in the bars of the Helsinki hotels.

[*]Bialer, 132.

The weapon did find employment from time to time in desperate situations, but the Finnish soldier no more went looking for hand-to-hand combat than did the average soldier in any army.

The wartime Finnish division had a paper strength of 14,400 men. The average Red Army division was officially supposed to number 17,000, but the varying additions of tank and specialist troops during the Winter War make that figure only a rough approximation.

At the beginning of the war, Mannerheim's forces were deployed as follows:

1. Army of the Karelian Isthmus: Six divisions under the command of General Hugo Viktor Östermann. On the right, the southwest Isthmus, was Second Corps, under General Öhquist, composed of the Fourth, Fifth, and Eleventh divisions, along with three groups of "covering troops" operating forward of the Mannerheim Line in early December. On the left flank, from the Vuoksi Waterway to Lake Ladoga, was Third Corps, commanded by General Heinrichs, comprised of the Ninth and Tenth divisions and one detachment of covering troops.
2. Fourth Corps: Two divisions, manning a sixty-mile line extending in a roughly concave crescent from the north shore of Lake Ladoga, commanded by General Hägglund.
3. North Finland Group: Covering the remaining 625 miles to the Arctic Ocean, this collection of Civic Guards, border guards, and activated reservist units was led by General Tuompo. Its southern unit boundary with Fourth Corps ran through the town of Ilomantsi.

Mannerheim had established his wartime headquarters in the town of Mikkeli (St. Michael). He seems to have liked the symbolism. He knew the place well, for he had mounted his final campaigns against the Reds from there in 1918. Nostalgia and symbolism aside, the village was about equidistant from the Isthmus and from Fourth Corps's zone of operations and was thus a logical choice. Mannerheim had two divisions in strategic reserve, one near Viipuri at work building fortifications, and the other based at Oulu, on the Gulf of Bothnia. Both units were woefully underequipped with mortars, machine guns, radios, even skis, and not a man could be moved without Mannerheim's personal order.

▲ CHAPTER 4 ▲ ▲

First Blows

HELSINKI

At 9:20 A.M., November 30, 1939, the first Russian plane appeared over Helsinki. It dropped thousands of leaflets urging the citizens to overthrow the Mannerheim/Cajander/Erkko government, then went on to drop five light bombs in the general vicinity of Malmi Airport.

As dawn gave way to full daylight, the morning sky was bright and clear, except to the south, where a large cloud bank had formed in the direction of Estonia. At about 10:30, the forward edge of those clouds suddenly rippled with light as a wedge of nine Russian planes (SB-2 medium bombers) left cover and leveled off for a run over the capital. The leading aircraft released their first sticks of bombs over the harbor, presumably aiming at the shipping crowded there. All of the bombs fell harmlessly into the water.

Then the formation banked toward the downtown heart of the city, apparently aiming at the architecturally renowned Helsinki railroad station. Although there was no resistance and weather conditions were ideal, the Russians didn't manage to get a single hit on the station itself. They did, however, thoroughly plaster the huge public square in front of the building, killing forty civilians.

Three planes peeled off and raked the municipal airport, setting fire to one hangar. The Helsinki Technical Institute was badly hit, and several students and faculty were killed. The Russian formation then broke into small groups, and these roamed at will above the city, scattering random bundles of small incendiary bombs, doing little serious damage but causing a chaotic rash of small fires that stretched the city's fire-fighting resources to the limit. On their way out, the planes took time to strafe a complex of working-class housing units and to drop their last few high-explosive bombs on the inner city, some of which severely damaged the front of the Soviet Legation building.

Then the bombers throttled for altitude, formed into a neat formation

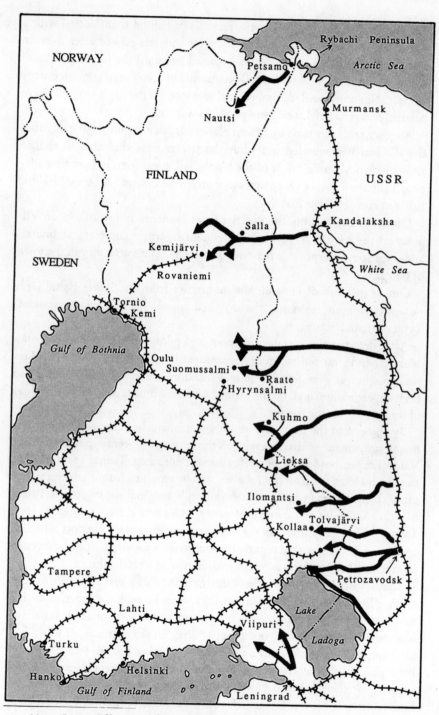

2. **Major Soviet Offensives of November 30–December 1**

again, and flew off to the east, the empty sky behind them dotted with a few puffs of smoke as Helsinki's antiaircraft batteries clawed after them in vain. None of the flak batteries had opened fire until the last moments of the raid, and not one of their shells came within 1,000 meters of an enemy aircraft. Not until the Red bombers had vanished did the city's air-raid sirens belatedly start to howl their now-pointless warning.

Another raid, this time by fifteen planes, struck at about 2:30 P.M., after the all-clear had sounded and while the streets were choked with civilian and emergency traffic. Most of the bombs fell at random, but another fifty people died and two or three times as many were injured. All told, Helsinki suffered 200 dead that first day.

On the same morning the Red Air Force launched heavy attacks on Viipuri, on the harbor at Turku, on the giant hydroelectric plant at Imatra, and—for some inexplicable reason—on a small gas mask factory in the town of Lahti.

Out in the Gulf of Finland, landing parties from the Soviet Baltic Fleet occupied without resistance the disputed islands of Sieksari, Lavansaari, Tytarsaari, and Suursaari.

After detouring past craters, corpses, and piles of flaming debris, Gustav Mannerheim's car pulled up to government headquarters. Inside the Marshal sought out President Kallio and withdrew his resignation. Kallio had been expecting him and, on the instant, activated him as commander in chief of the Finnish armed forces.

By the end of the day, the Finnish government had changed hands. The major instrument of that change was the veteran left-center political leader Väinö Tanner, head of the powerful Social Democrats. Tanner spent most of the day huddled in an air-raid shelter, and he emerged from that experience more convinced than ever that the inflexible nationalistic regime of Prime Minister Cajander and Foreign Minister Erkko would have to yield power. Tanner had already lined up the necessary parliamentary support when he approached Cajander that night, after the civilian government had moved to its wartime headquarters at Kauhajoki, northeast of Helsinki.

To soften the emotional blow, Tanner engineered a symbolic vote of confidence for Cajander in the Finnish Diet, then he took Cajander aside and told him that he had two choices: resign now with honor intact, or suffer the historical shame of being booted out of office in the morning. It was a bitter moment for Cajander: he and Erkko had worked hard to lead the nation through several relatively prosperous years, always with considerable public support for their policies. Now they were being pronounced unfit to lead Finland in time of war. Nevertheless, although there was much hard feeling in private, the public changing of the guard was accomplished with grace and dignity on the part of all concerned.

Tanner himself replaced Erkko as foreign minister. To fill Cajander's place at the prime minister's desk, Tanner picked Risto Ryti, president of the Bank of Finland. The new government's policy was clear: to reopen negotiations and end hostilities as fast as possible. To maximize Finland's bargaining power, the military strategy would be to hold on to every inch of Finnish soil and to inflict maximum casualties on the enemy—to present Stalin with such a butcher's bill that he, too, would be eager for negotiations.

While Tanner worked the diplomatic front, Ryti ran the war effort, including the campaign to obtain aid from abroad. He worked closely with Marshal Mannerheim, usually at the Marshal's headquarters rather than the civilian government's. Mannerheim refused to leave his command post when there was a battlefield crisis to deal with, which, after the first hours of the war, there usually was.

These men became, in effect, a ruling triumvirate. President Kallio and the Diet rubber-stamped their decisions, although sometimes with reluctance. On their sagacity and flexibility, and on Mannerheim's tactical grip, rested nothing less than the fate of their nation.

LADOGA-KARELIA

The entire Finnish strategy was based on a single reality and a single logical assumption. The reality was that, given the size of its army, Finland could not defend every part of its long border with the USSR. The assumption was that, given the nature of the geography, Finland would not have to.

Only on the Isthmus could a large modern army be sustained in prolonged campaigning. North of Lake Ladoga the only place Mannerheim was really concerned about was the part of Ladoga-Karelia on the north shore of the lake. There, in a fifty-to-sixty-mile-wide corridor, were two good roads that led from the border to the interior. One started at Petrozavodsk, inside Russia, and the other ran from the Murmansk railroad along the rocky coast of Lake Ladoga; the two converged near the village of Kitelä. Just a day's march beyond Kitelä was a crucial section of Finland's railroad network, along with good roads leading north and south.

This was, in fact, the "back door" to the Isthmus. The road net would support the movement of large formations, including armor, and it seemed logical for the Russians to make an attempt to break through here, wheel south, and take the Mannerheim Line from the rear.

Anticipating such a Soviet thrust, the Finns had held war games there several times during prewar maneuvers and had come up with a sound plan to deal with it. They would let the Russians come in and advance along the converging roads until they reached a strong line of prepared defenses that ran Lake Ladoga–Kitelä–Lake Syskyjärvi. Once the Russians were pinned down, with their supply lines long, thin, and vulnerable and their left flank up against Ladoga, a strong Finnish counterattack would fall on their right flank from the supposedly impassable wilderness below Loimola and Kollaa, cut off the head of their salient, and methodically destroy it.

Mannerheim and his staff had allocated what seemed like an adequate force for this task: two infantry divisions and three battalions of border troops, all of them about as well equipped as any units in the Finnish Army, organized into the Fourth Corps, under command of Major General Juho Heiskanen.

But the Russian Eighth Army, responsible for the entire Ladoga-Karelia front from Tolvajärvi to Lake Ladoga itself, had some unpleasant surprises in store for the Finns. During the fall a new railroad line had been extended from Eighth Army's main supply base at Petrozavodsk up to the border, just across from the Finnish town of Suojärvi. This strategic preparation nearly doubled the Russians' supply capability on this front. When the war broke out, they struck here not with three divisions, the maximum number Mannerheim believed they could sustain, but with five, together with a full brigade of armor. And before the war's end, they would field in this sector all or major portions of another eight divisions.

Most alarming of all was the attack of two entire divisions up at Suojärvi, a sector where Mannerheim had expected nothing stronger than reconnaissance patrols. In the opening days of the war there was virtually nothing to stop these Soviet units from outflanking the entire Fourth Corps line from the northeast, or from rolling through Tolvajärvi in a westerly thrust and running amok in the interior of Finland. It was a crisis situation from the beginning, and before it was stabilized, Mannerheim would be forced to commit one-third of his entire available reserves, seriously depleting the Finns' ability to reinforce the defenders of the Isthmus.

When Mannerheim studied his situation maps on the night of December 1, these were the threats he saw developing in Ladoga-Karelia:

1. Against the vulnerable road net at Tolvajärvi, the Russians launched their 139th Division: 20,000 men, under General Beljajev, augmented by 45 tanks and about 150 guns. In that whole critical sector, the Finns could muster at the war's beginning only 4,200 men. None of them were regular army troops, just border guards and Civic Guard reservists. Supporting this attack was the Russian Fifty-sixth

Division, which stormed across at Suojärvi then turned southwest and thrust toward Kollaa, seeking to get behind the main Finnish defensive line north of Lake Ladoga.

2. On the north shore of Ladoga itself the Russian 168th Division under General Bondarev struck at Salmi. The plan called for it to advance to a line that ran from Koirinoja to Kitelä and there join forces with the Eighteenth Division under General Kondrashev, which had attacked along the Uomaa road, parallel to and about twenty miles north of the Ladoga coastal road. The plan evolved so that the Eighteenth soon received orders to turn north toward Syskyjärvi, four miles north of the Lemetti road junction, and attack the Kollaa defense line from the rear at the same time it secured the flank of the 168th Division. Strong Finnish defensive positions kept it from ever posing a real threat to the Kollaa line, however.

THE CENTRAL FORESTS AND THE FAR NORTH

Another serious drain on Mannerheim's reserves were the powerful but isolated thrusts into the forested wilderness of central and northern Finland. North of Fourth Corps's front, the roads were so few and the terrain so utterly hostile during winter that the Finns had expected no large-scale Russian threats between Kitelä and Petsamo, their arctic toehold at the base of the Rybachi Peninsula. Instead the Russians sent eight full divisions into the forests, heavily supported by armor and artillery.

By the end of December 1, Mannerheim's maps showed the following threats developing from Petsamo south to Tolvajärvi:

1. At Petsamo the Russian 104th Division attacked by sea and by land, supported by naval gunfire and heavy coastal guns sited on the approaches to Murmansk. The Russian plan called for this division to advance down the Finns' "Arctic Highway" and capture the Lapland capital of Rovaniemi by December 12. That seemed like a reasonable proposition, since the numerical odds on this front favored the Russians by something like forty-two to one. Two regiments of the Russian 104th Division were added to this force after the initial landings and border crossings.

2. At the tiny Lapp town of Salla a two-pronged thrust was begun by the Eighty-eighth and 122d divisions. Their objective was the town of Kemijärvi, where they could pick up some good roads and from there move quickly against Rovaniemi to the southwest, linking up

there with the Petsamo invasion force. The Finns did not think the enemy's Petsamo force could negotiate the 300 miles of benighted, wind-scoured tundra between Petsamo and Rovaniemi, even if there was nobody shooting at them. Therefore the Salla thrust was considered by far the more serious threat to the Lapland capital.

3. The picturesque little village of Suomussalmi was a target simply because it blocked one side of the narrow "waist" of Finland; and it lay astride the shortest route to Oulu, Finland's most important port on the Gulf of Bothnia. Roads on the Finnish side of the border were fairly well developed in this region. The attack was opened by the 163d Division, 17,000 strong, and weighted down not only with much armor and mechanized equipment but also with such paraphernalia as brass bands, printing presses, truckloads of propaganda leaflets, and sacks of goodwill gifts, presumably for all the disaffected Finnish workers its troops would encounter in the woods. Although the Soviet political assessment was fantastic in its presumptions, it was not made up entirely out of thin air. Communist agents were known to have been active in the Suomussalmi region, and the voting patterns in national elections indicated considerable popular support for left-wing politicians and policies. Stalin obviously believed the area was ripe for "liberation," and Mannerheim, at least in the beginning, had some worries along those lines himself. In any event, if the Russians took Suomussalmi, they gained good routes to the railroad junction at Hyrynsalmi. From there, Oulu was only 150 miles away, and if Oulu fell, Finland would be cut in half.

4. The Russian Fifty-fourth Division, led by Major General Gusevski, attacked toward Kuhmo with 12,800 men, 120 pieces of artillery, and 35 tanks. Opposing their advance was a ragtag force of Finnish border guards and reservists numbering about 1,200.

5. Just south of the Kuhmo thrust, the Russian 155th Division attacked toward Lieksa, with 6,500 men, 40 guns, and a dozen tanks. Opposing it were two Finnish battalions, about 3,000 men, and 4 light, obsolete field guns.

SHIPS AGAINST FORTS

While the campaigns on land were gathering momentum, there was a flickering, shadowy naval war going on in the Gulf of Finland and adjacent waters. It was an interesting sideshow, but it did not amount to very much. There were two reasons for that. The first and most obvious is the fact that by the end of December, the Gulf of Finland had started to freeze into a vast sheet of ice. The other reason is that the navies involved did not amount to very much, either.

If there was such a thing as an "elite" force in the Red Navy of 1939, it was the Baltic Fleet—but that was not much of a distinction. The Red Navy was strictly a provincial coast defense force at that time, and technologically it was about a quarter-century behind either the Royal Navy or the German Kriegsmarine. The Baltic Fleet did occupy several of the disputed gulf islands, but these operations were unopposed. It did not have the training, the logistical structure, or the landing craft to undertake large-scale amphibious operations. Nor was it blessed with a commander in chief of strategic vision. Some idea of Stalin's competence as a naval strategist can be derived from his insistent attempts to persuade his Baltic Fleet commanders to attack Turku harbor with submarines, even though they kept pointing out to him, with words, maps, and aerial photos, that the approaches to that harbor were so shallow and strewn with reefs that no submarine could possibly survive long enough to reach a firing position.

The Finnish Navy, 13,000 men, was strictly a coast defense force. There were a dozen or so modern PT boats, some mine warfare vessels, a number of shallow-draft gunboats (some of them dating back to the tsarist era), four small submarines, and two big ships that could be described as cruisers or monitors, depending on whether one looks at their design or their function. They were named *Väinämönen* and *Ilmarinen*, after two popular heroes in the *Kalevala*, the Finnish national epic, and they had been the pride of the prewar government. They were handsome ships, and for their weight they packed considerable firepower. The one and only English-language description of these ships ever to see print states that their main batteries were 105 mm. guns, but no one ever built a cruiser-sized ship to carry such relatively puny weapons. Extant Finnish photographs clearly show a more powerful battery, and the 1940 edition of *Jane's Fighting Ships* confirms that the main guns were eight-inch, backed up by secondary guns of four-inch caliber and at least a half-dozen Bofors guns for antiaircraft protection.

It is hard to fathom why the Finnish government spent millions of marks on these ships when their deterrent value against the infinitely stronger Baltic Fleet would have been marginal at best, and when the same amount of money could have doubled the number of modern fighter planes in the air force or gone a long way toward correcting some of the field army's chronic weaknesses. These two curious vessels did brave work during the Continuation War as mobile heavy artillery, pounding Russian targets all along the Karelian Isthmus, but during the Winter War their contribution was minimal: their antiaircraft guns knocked down one or two planes over Turku harbor. Otherwise, they remained icebound for the duration of the conflict.

Most of the naval action took place in the form of classic ship-to-shore gunnery duels. The Finnish coastal artillery was something of an elite force; many of its guns were old, but they were expertly sited, powerful, and manned by keen, disciplined crews.

On December 1, the Soviet cruiser *Kirov*, escorted by two large destroyers, took on the defenses of Hanko and lost the exchange. The battle was fought under hazy conditions, so details of it are sketchy, but it is certain that one Russian destroyer, closing range recklessly, took at least one large caliber hit, sheered abruptly out of formation, and limped out to sea behind a cloud of smoke. The *Kirov* had trouble getting the range of the Hanko batteries and did them no significant damage, whereas the Finns were soon straddling it with water spouts. At least one, and possibly two, Finnish shells struck the cruiser on its stern and seriously damaged it. After retiring out of range the *Kirov* lost engine power and had to be towed back to its base at Tallin, Estonia.

Another duel, about two weeks into the war, took place in the skerries outside of Turku. Two Russian destroyers (possibly the *Gnevny* and the *Grozyaschi*) engaged batteries on Uto Island. Again, Russian fire was ineffective (and, again, one must question the competence of any naval commander who orders two destroyers to tackle a battery of ten-inch coast artillery on their own). A single Finnish shell dropped squarely amidships on one of the destroyers; both ships broke off firing after only ten minutes, made smoke, and retired. Ten minutes later the torpedo magazine of the damaged destroyer exploded, breaking the ship in two and causing it to sink in less than two minutes, with heavy loss of life.

The most dramatic of these engagements took place on December 18 and 19, just a week or so before ice brought all naval activity to a halt. The Russian battleship *Oktyabrskaya Revolutsia* sailed boldly close to the Saarenpää batteries on Koivisto Island, perhaps the most effective Finnish artillery position of the war. The bombardment was preceded by a heavy air attack, which threw up spectacular clouds of dust but did little material damage. Shortly after noon, the Russian battleship hove into range, escorted by five destroyers and a spotting plane. Two Finnish Fokkers were scrambled to nail the spotter plane, but the overzealous and highly accurate Koivisto antiaircraft gunners shot one of them down. Its pilot, Eino Luukkanen, managed to crash-land and walk away uninjured; he later became Finland's third-ranking ace. By the end of the Continuation War in 1944, he would shoot down a total of fifty-four Russian aircraft.

On this day, the Finnish guns were having trouble; one by one they fell silent after only ten minutes' fire. The battleship got closer, and its 305 mm. shells began causing casualties and damage. After furious exertions the Finnish gunners managed to get a single ten-inch rifle back in firing order, and their first few shots landed close alongside the Russian ship. The captain decided enough was enough, ordered the helm thrown over sharply, and retired out of range.

The following day, the older battleship *Marat*, heavily escorted by destroyers and light cruisers, returned to plaster the Saarenpää batteries. The Finnish commander had ordered his men to reply with only one gun at a time so that a slow but steady fire might be kept up even if weapons went out of whack again. The Russians' gunnery on this occasion was excellent—the Saarenpää site was hit by about 175 rounds, all its buildings were flattened, and the forest cover was stripped away from its battery positions.

With icy deliberation, the Finns replied with one shot at a time, seemingly to no effect. Then, just as the battleship was approaching truly lethal range, a dark column of water heaved up alongside its hull, followed by a cloud of smoke, which made precise observation difficult. Although no fires were observed, the *Marat* hurriedly retired without further combat, indicating that it had taken a hit near the waterline.

Before ice closed the seas, the Red Navy's submarines torpedoed two Finnish merchant ships and three neutrals in Finnish waterways—one Swede and two Germans—and sank an armed yacht doing escort duty. Mine fields laid by Finnish vessels, on the other hand, sank two Baltic Fleet subs.

▲ CHAPTER 5 ▲ ▲

"The People's Republic of Finland"

By far the most interesting sideshow taking place in the early hours of the Winter War was not military at all; it was an act of political vaudeville called "The Terijoki Government," or "The People's Republic of Finland."

Terijoki itself was a small village just inside Finland, the first place of any significance to be "liberated" by the Red Army, only hours after hostilities began. By 1939, the place seems to have become quietly seedy, but fifty years earlier it had been a popular seaside spa for the gentry of St. Petersburg. The Finns fought hard for Terijoki; and when they withdrew they left so many booby traps that the new government must have had a hectic time settling down to business.

To head the new puppet regime, Stalin dragged out O. W. Kuusinen and set him up as "president." Kuusinen was the most influential of all the old-guard Reds who had fled Finland in 1918. He had been the foremost Red leader during the civil war, and he grew even more doctrinaire after losing the military struggle and fleeing into exile. Kuusinen applied himself diligently to party politics in his new homeland; he did his homework, covered his flanks, came through the purges unscathed, and established for himself a reputation as a leading Marxist-Leninist theoretician. He also took care to ingratiate himself with Stalin from the earliest days of Stalin's rise to power, and his master had rewarded him by making him secretary general of the Comintern.

Now, overnight—quite literally overnight—he was installed as the head of the "Democratic Government of Finland." This ascent to high office was marked by a grandiose treaty-signing ceremony between Molotov and Kuusinen. The document began as follows:

. . . being persuaded that now, through the heroic efforts of the Red Army . . . there is to be liquidated that true focus of war-infection which the former plutocratic government of Finland had created on the borders of the Soviet Union for the benefit of the Imperialist Powers; And, since the Finnish people have created their own democratic government, which derives its support entirely from the people, the time has come to establish good relations between our countries and, with united forces, to protect the security and inviolability of our nations.*

The body of the treaty went on cheerfully to grant Stalin every concession he had ever asked of the Finns, with some additional items thrown in for good measure. In return, the whole Finnish land mass was magically rejoined with Soviet Karelia to form "The People's Republic of Finland." Broadcasts were soon made in the name of this new government, telling the captive proletariat of "plutocratic Finland" about all the wonderful reforms that would be promulgated after the Red Army had finished liberating them. Kuusinen promised that he would break up all the great landowners' estates; he also promised the workers an eight-hour day. The workers were not impressed. The eight-hour day had been legislated in Finland twenty-five years earlier, and the government's land reform program was so far advanced by 1939 that there were only a few hundred estates left in all Finland that measured more than 300 acres. Kuusinen had certainly kept up with things.

To stir up the restive masses, flights of Red bombers roamed rural Finland, dropping tens of thousands of leaflets that bore messages of this sort: "Let us not shoot each other, comrades; let us turn our guns on the common enemy: the White Guard government of Tanner and Mannerheim!!"

Kuusinen was the only person in this new regime that most Finns had ever heard of, and even he was not Stalin's first choice. That had been a gentleman named Arvo Tuominen, who was more respected inside Finland than the blustery Kuusinen. Tuominen was away in Stockholm on party business when he received a telegram from Moscow inviting him back to head up the new government. The message plunged Tuominen into an agony of indecision, robbing him of several nights' sleep. He later described the experience in a letter to a friend:

> All during that struggle, Evil whispered in my ear: just think what a position you'd get! Just think what a marvelous opportunity it would be to settle old scores! . . . but to each tempting question, my mind gave a clear answer: it would be wrong, it would be criminal . . . and behind this, it was not a picture of the free rule of the people, a glorious

*Tanner, Väinö, *The Winter War* (Stanford, Calif.: Stanford University Press, 1957), 101.

and happy life, which appeared to me as a result of this . . . war, but
the memory of hundreds of good friends who, as gaunt human ruins,
imprisoned and in slave labor, had dug canals through Russia's endless
wilderness.*

Tuominen did not wish to be an informer or a traitor; he was still, at heart,
a good Communist. He did not reveal the Soviet invasion plans he was now
privy to, but he did contact underground cells in Finland and order each man
among them to act as his conscience bade him act, thus formally absolving
them of any responsibility to Moscow. Then he burned his files and went
into hiding for the duration of the conflict.

Kuusinen seems seriously to have believed that the class struggle of 1918
would spontaneously reignite at the sound of his rallying cry. It did not.
For most working-class Finns, national pride had long since replaced Marxist
allegiance, and a massive foreign invasion unified the nation as nothing else
possibly could have, rendering all past squabbles irrelevant. No one could
think of oneself any more as just a Communist or just a Social Democrat;
now one was simply a Finn. As one working-class novelist put it: "A few
weeks ago, I would have put the word Fatherland in quotation marks, but
not any more."†

The whole Kuusinen charade was not without its comic-opera aspects. The
crowning touch was the creation of something called the "Finnish National
Army," ostensibly made up of pro-Communist Finns who had volunteered to
fight alongside their Red Army comrades for the homeland's liberation. The
whole atmosphere surrounding the Kuusinen business makes it impossible
to judge whether anyone anywhere took it seriously. Nor can anyone say for
sure whether its troops ever saw combat. It was paraded for the cameras on
one or two occasions, and eyewitnesses state that there were no more than a
thousand men on display.

Even the Russian press never claimed that the Finnish National Army
numbered more than 6,000. Certainly the vast majority of its members were
East Karelians and exiled Red Guard veterans (who must have been a bit long
in the tooth for combat by this time). Sad to say, its ranks also included some
genuine turncoats. The exact number is impossible to determine, but there
could not have been many. The biggest Russian POW camp in the war had
a population of 600 Finns; during an intense recruiting drive for the Kuusinen army, in December, a total of sixteen men are known to have signed

*Goodrich, 52.
†Jutikkala, Eino, A History of Finland (New York: Praeger, 1962), 233.

up. That small percentage probably reflects the minuscule participation of Finnish defectors in this shadowy army.

If the rest of the Kuusinen episode were not so colored by surreality, one would think the tales had to be apocryphal, but Finnish sources gleefully recount that the first few members of the Finnish National Army to go on display in Terijoki itself, guarding Kuusinen's headquarters, were dressed in Charles XIIth uniforms looted from a local museum.

Even to the more radical factions of the Finnish proletariat, the Kuusinen government looked exactly like what it was: a pathetic farce and a propaganda ploy of insulting crudeness. But having erected this puppet regime, the Soviets were reluctant to admit their folly by abandoning it upon the first snorts of derision from world opinion. And Stalin's ultimate purpose for creating the Kuusinen government was not humorous in the least. When the world press condemned Russia for naked aggression against a smaller neighbor, the Kremlin could blandly reply that the Red Army was merely going to the requested aid of the "legitimate" Finnish government. Or, as *Pravda* crowed in its front-page paean to the Kuusinen inauguration: "only the Soviet Union, which rejects in principle the violent seizure of territory and the enslavement of nations, would agree to place its armed might at disposal, not for the purpose of attacking Finland or enslaving her people, but for securing Finland's independence."

The very existence of the Kuusinen regime posed a difficult obstacle in the way of any attempt to reopen negotiations; it prolonged the war, that much is certain, and probably, if indirectly, caused the deaths of thousands of men on both sides.

Tanner's new government felt the impact almost immediately. He succeeded in placing the matter of Russia's invasion before the League of Nations. In the debates that followed, the member states reacted in a curious way: the virulence of their condemnations rose in direct proportion to their physical distance from the Soviet Union. Argentina, for example, denounced Stalin in savage, Churchillian rhetoric. The Scandinavian nations, however, issued muted and diplomatic statements of principle. In rebuttal, the Soviet Union's representative rose to object to the harsh language directed at his country. Why, Russia was not "at war" with Finland! How absurd! On the contrary, its relations with the legitimate Kuusinen government were, verifiably, the last word in cordiality and mutual trust!

In disgust, the democratic members of the League did the only thing in their power left to do; flexing what little muscle remained in that moribund congress, the League of Nations expelled the Soviet Union. It was not the sort of rebuke that Stalin was likely to lose sleep over.

CHAPTER 6

The Mannerheim Line

In the forest battles north of Lake Ladoga, the Finns beat the Russians by adopting a style of warfare different only in detail from the tactics that caused Braddock's defeat in colonial America two centuries earlier. The invader was outmaneuvered and outfought by men defending their homeland, fighting in the style that was best suited to their native terrain—guerrilla tactics on a massive scale—and compensating for their numerical and technological inferiority with speed, daring, and economy of force. The image of the outnumbered but intrepid ski warrior that emerged from those victories became, in the minds of newspaper readers the world over, the most vivid and inspiring symbol of Finnish resistance. There wasn't room in most people's minds for any other.

But in some ways, the struggle for the Karelian Isthmus proved the Finns' mettle even more than their sensational triumphs in the northern wilderness. The Isthmus gave little chance to exercise those guerrilla tactics; the restricted nature of the terrain created a classic and thoroughly conventional military situation: a heavily fortified line, its flanks protected by large bodies of water (at least until that water turned to ice), manned by stubborn defenders, being assaulted by a powerful and numerically superior attacker. The Finns would win or lose on the basis of their conventional, professional, military skills, the fiber of their discipline, the worthiness of their commanders—and above all else, on the depth and stubbornness of their *sisu*. That bristling little word was once the most famous Finnish idiom ever to become part of the outside world's vocabulary. It can be translated as "guts" or "spunk" or "grit" or "balls," or as a combination of all those words together. The word in Finnish has nuances that resist easy translation.

Largely to excuse the enormous losses they incurred during their frontal assaults against it, the Russians went to much trouble during the latter weeks of the war, and in all their published accounts of it since, to inflate the Mannerheim Line's reputation to fantastic proportions. The usual claim was that it was "as strong as" or "stronger than" the Maginot Line. After the armistice, their propaganda trumpeted that the breaching of the Mannerheim Line was "a feat without parallel in the annals of war." Naturally, while the fighting was going on, the Finns did nothing to discourage the enemy's propaganda efforts on their behalf.

Since the war, however, Finnish historians have belittled the line's strength perhaps too much, insisting that it was mostly just conventional trenches and log-covered dugouts and that the real strength of the Mannerheim Line was the *sisu* of the troops manning it.

The truth lies somewhere in between. It is still possible to get a firsthand impression of the strength of the line's fortifications by examining the ruins of several of its blockhouses. These can be found within 100 meters of the main road between Viipuri and Leningrad, on the site of what used to be Summa village—that is to say, at the most critical and vulnerable point of the entire Finnish defense. The biggest and most elaborate bunkers, with the exception of the coast-defense forts on the gulf shore and on the coast of Ladoga, were located north of Summa, covering the Lähde road. These probably still exist, but they are far from any road that tourists normally travel, and the entire Isthmus is still considered a militarily sensitive area by the Russians. One would be well advised not to go wandering through the woods.

The surviving bunkers show signs of terrible damage—the author crawled around inside one that looked as though it had been beaten into the earth with a giant ball-peen hammer—but enough was left to draw some conclusions. First of all, these were not anything as big or elaborate as the multi-layered dinosaurs of the Maginot Line. They were, however, massive, thick, multi-chambered blockhouses; if manned by stubborn defenders, they would have been very tough to take and even harder to knock out with fire alone.

Just how strong was the line, then? Here, the researcher runs into considerable confusion. Every general who published a book about the Winter War gives a different estimate of the line's strength. Mannerheim, in his *Memoirs*, states that the entire line contained only sixty-six "strong points," of which about forty were too old or thin to withstand much modern artillery fire.

General Öhquist, distinguished commander of the Finnish Second Corps, which bore the brunt of the Isthmus fighting, offered a different breakdown of figures. From the Gulf of Finland to the Vuoksi Waterway, the line had ninety-three "strong points," of which Öhquist judged forty-nine to be of inferior quality and durability; along the Vuoksi Waterway, north to Lake Ladoga, Öhquist counted some twenty-six "strong points," all of them old, but many of them modernized in the months before the war.

Perhaps it depends on how one defines the term "strong point." Mannerheim was apparently listing only those positions that were "strong" by the standards of 1939—bunkers made of reinforced concrete. Öhquist's figures seem to include a number of the stronger field fortifications—log-roofed bunkers or elaborate earthworks. The Russians, for their part, added to the confusion by the flat claim that they captured more than "300 forts," whatever that may mean; the total is exaggerated even if it includes the coastal defense works in the Koivisto sector, on the gulf islands, and those in the secondary defense line manned by the Finns after the Mannerheim Line was breached in February.

Finally, in the early 1960s, a Finnish historian tried to settle the matter once and for all by the simple method of counting the strong points listed on contemporary maps. He came up with a total of 109 reinforced concrete positions for the entire eighty-mile length of the line.

The line was strongest on its flanks, where fixed coastal defenses mounted cannon whose calibers ranged from 120 mm. to 254 mm. Even in midwinter the ice on that part of Lake Ladoga is too treacherous to bear the weight of heavy equipment; too many underground streams feed into the lake from the Finnish shore. Nor is the much thicker gulf ice usable until February, after several weeks of hard freeze. The line could not, therefore, be turned by an outflanking maneuver, at least not in the first weeks of fighting.

The most dangerous sector of the line was astride the shortest route between Viipuri and Leningrad, where two major roads went through the village of Summa and toward the village of Lähde. This ten-mile stretch, between the Summajoki River and Lake Muolaanjärvi, also ran through some of the poorest defensive ground on the Isthmus—rolling, stumpy, comparatively open farmland—and the ground was quite hard by December. Good tank country.

To plug this gap, the so-called "Viipuri Gateway," the Finns had constructed thirty-five reinforced concrete positions, including some of the biggest and most elaborate they had ever built. Only about fifteen of them, however, a ratio of about one per kilometer, were of modern construction.

The approaches to the line were heavily fortified. Vast fields of barbed wire entanglements had been erected, and thousands of mines had been seeded on all likely avenues of approach. The entire Karelian Isthmus was belted as well by a line of antitank obstacles, five to seven rows deep: granite monoliths that had been sunk into the earth, at the cost of much sweat, during the final summer of peace. It came as a very nasty shock to the Finns to discover that most of these rocks were too short to actually stop Soviet armor; the Russians knew what they were doing when they adopted the Christie suspension design, for it made their vehicles agile and gave them good climbing traction. Still, the rocks did help; if a tank hit one at the wrong angle, it would throw a tread and just hang there, a veritable sitting duck. Also, when climbing over the rocks, the tanks' lightly protected underbellies would be exposed, and a lucky grenade toss, or even a burst of heavy machine-gun fire, could do damage.

All things considered, then, the Mannerheim Line was no pushover. Manned by stubborn troops, it was a formidable defense line, even if it fell far short of André Maginot's monument to militarism's Age of High Baroque. But it had glaring weaknesses: the pillboxes were sited too far apart to give mutual fire protection to one another. As soon as the Finnish infantry on either side had been killed or driven out, there was nothing to prevent Red infantry from swarming over isolated strong points, or Russian tanks from simply driving up and parking in front of the firing ports, a tactic that would prove devastatingly effective in many battles. Most of the modern bunkers had firing chambers large enough to accommodate a Bofors antitank gun, but there were too few of these precious weapons to go around and none to tie down in static defensive roles. Most of the bunkers, therefore, were armed with nothing heavier than Maxim guns.

Perhaps even more critical was the lack of Finnish artillery to back up the line; heavy guns were so few, and ammunition so limited, that many Russian attacks that could easily have been broken up by shell fire were allowed to proceed without interference. When Red infantry swarmed over the pillboxes, the men inside could not call down shrapnel barrages to clean them off. And, in the final days of the struggle for the line, when the Russians wheeled up dozens of flat-trajectory field guns, in plain sight, and fired massed salvos at the bunkers' firing slits, there was nothing heavier than mortars to fire back at them with.

Naturally, when the Russians started inflating the line's reputation to fabulous proportions, it was not in Finland's best interests to issue disclaimers. The problem was that the Finnish public, too, believed that the line was impregnable. Old soldier that he was, Mannerheim knew there was no such thing as a truly "impregnable" defense. He flatly predicted, even before the first battles were fought, that the line that bore his name could be shattered whenever the enemy decided he was willing to absorb the enormous losses it would require.

Before the war there had been heated debates among the Finnish generals about the final configuration of the line. Mannerheim and many of his staff believed the defenses should be placed so as to incorporate all of the older fortifications. A different theory was propounded by General Öhquist, who believed that if some of the more exposed older positions were abandoned, the other strong points could be improved by earthworks in such a way as to increase the overall depth of the defenses. Had his suggestions been followed, the Russians would at least have been denied certain advantages of cover and observation that they later enjoyed. Over Öhquist's objections, however, the final configuration of the line was drawn so that the defenses bent inward to form a sort of elbow near the village of Summa. This salient would be the greatest danger zone on the entire Isthmus because a Russian penetration there, or at any point for ten kilometers north or south of Summa, would open up the rear of the entire Mannerheim Line. Ideally the line should have been laid out so that Summa formed a reserve position, a backstop. As finally conceived by the high command, the line would have been satisfactory only if Finland had possessed sufficient trained reserves to launch big counterattacks against the Russians drawn up before it; and Finland did not.

After the war, Marshal Timoshenko, who masterminded the cracking of the line, showed Nikita Khrushchev proof that Soviet intelligence had all along been in possession of detailed maps of the Mannerheim Line; but nobody had bothered to consult the intelligence service before starting the war. "If we had only deployed our forces against the Finns in the way even a child could have figured out from looking at a map, things would have turned out differently." *

*Crankshaw, ed., 301.

Baron Carl Gustav Mannerheim, commander in chief of the Finnish armed forces—*Photographic Center of the General Headquarters, Helsinki*

Mannerheim at work at headquarters at Mikkeli, eighty-five miles northwest of Viipuri—*Photographic Center of the General Headquarters, Helsinki*

General Harold Öhquist, commander of the Finnish right wing on the Karelian Isthmus—*Photographic Center of the General Headquarters, Helsinki*

Granite antitank rocks stretched across the Karelian Isthmus—*Photographic Center of the General Headquarters, Helsinki*

Taipale Peninsula, across which Russians launched massed frontal assaults—*Photographic Center of the General Headquarters, Helsinki*

Flanks of Finnish position at Taipale (photo taken in summer 1941)—*Photographic Center of the General Headquarters, Helsinki*

Finnish Maxim machine gun at Taipale—*Photographic Center of the General Headquarters, Helsinki*

Trenches on the Mannerheim Line—*Photographic Center of the General Headquarters, Helsinki*

Finnish troops in action on the Kollaa front—*Photographic Center of the General Headquarters, Helsinki*

Finnish arctic frontline dugout, large and well heated—*Photographic Center of the General Headquarters, Helsinki*

Finnish defenders of the Kollaa River line—*Photographic Center of the General Headquarters, Helsinki*

Finnish coastal-defense cannon, near the mouth of the Gulf of Viipuri—*Photographic Center of the General Headquarters, Helsinki*

Boat-shaped sledges pulled by reindeer, used by Finns in central and northern forests—*Photographic Center of the General Headquarters, Helsinki*

Gunner firing a Lahti automatic rifle at attacking Soviet infantry—*Photographic Center of the General Headquarters, Helsinki*

▲ CHAPTER 7 ▲ ▲

The Karelian Isthmus: Round One

There were ten separate campaigns developing in the early days of December, from one end of Finland to the other. To try to describe all of them in strict chronological order—recounting events on each front day by day—would be to create a most unwieldy and confusing narrative. Therefore, whereas the reader should bear in mind that all of these battles were evolving simultaneously, some sort of arbitrary order must be imposed for the sake of clarity. Since the threat to Finland was most critical on the Karelian Isthmus, and since the military operations there in December form a coherent narrative unit, that theater will be examined first. Subsequent chapters will work northward from Fourth Corps's zone to the Arctic.

General Meretskov stormed across the Isthmus frontier with 120,000 men, 1,000 tanks, and the supporting fire of about 600 guns. Before the border area could be turned into a combat zone, however, the Finns had to move the civilians out. During the interval between the collapse of the Moscow negotiations and the start of hostilities, thousands of Karelian families were evacuated. The Finnish border troops who organized this exodus were deeply moved by the toughness and patriotism of the farming families they dealt with. They were simple people, few of them educated, and they lived poor, marginal lives close to the earth. But they had *sisu* in abundance.

In one village, a detachment of border guards came up to the home of an aged peasant woman and sadly informed her that she must prepare to leave her home, possibly forever, with only the belongings she could carry on her back and in the horse-drawn sled tethered near her cabin. In the morning, they would return and burn her house to the ground, so that the Russians could not sleep there. When the soldiers returned the next morning, they found the sled parked by the old woman's door, piled high with her possessions. When they entered the farmhouse, they were startled to see that the entire dwelling had been scrubbed and whitewashed until it sparkled. Stuck to the wall by the door, the woman had left a note saying that she had gone to fetch something at a neighbor's house and would return in time to drive the sled away in the soldiers' company. In the meantime, the note concluded, if the soldiers would look by the stove, they would find enough matches, kindling, and petrol to burn the house quickly and efficiently. When the old woman returned, the soldiers asked her why she had gone to so much trouble. Pulling herself upright with all the dignity she could summon, she looked them in the eye and replied: "When one gives a gift to Finland, one desires that it should be like new."*

In another border village, covering troops roused an old farmer from his sleep—a gentleman who had refused earlier evacuation—and informed him that there would probably be fighting here by morning. They had come to burn his house tonight, they said, because when the battle started, they would be too busy. Grumbling, the old peasant gathered his few personal belongings, hitched up his horse, and rode eastward. Later the next morning, even as the first sounds of skirmishing could be heard in the distance, the same Finnish border troops were astonished to discover that the old man had returned and was wandering amid the ruins of his former house, prodding the ashes with a tree branch and muttering to himself in the thick dialect of the Karelian Finns. Several soldiers went over to the old fellow and asked him what he was doing back here, especially with the fighting now in earshot. The farmer's gnarled features twisted into a grim smile and he said: "This farm was burned down twice before on account of the goddamned Russians—once by my grandfather, and once by my father. I don't reckon it'll kill me to do it either, but I'll be damned if I could drive away without first making sure you'd done a proper job of it."

The abandoned villages were not hospitable even in ruins. Booby traps had been placed with such cunning and imagination that *Pravda* was moved to complain about the Finns' "barbaric and filthy tricks." Everything that moved seemed attached to a detonator; mines were left in haystacks, under outhouse seats, attached to cupboard doors and kitchen utensils, underneath dead chickens and abandoned sleds. The village wells were poisoned, or, if time and chemicals were lacking, fouled with horse manure. Liberal use was made of cheap pipe mines—steel tubes crammed with explosives, buried in snowdrifts and set off by trip wires; the charge went off at waist level and caused very nasty wounds. A colonel named Saloranta invented a type of wooden mine, impossible to detect with electronic devices, that was powerful enough to blow the treads off a tank. Soon the Russians had to detach patrols to clear the roads with sharp prods before the tanks could advance.

*Langdon-Davies, 126.

Under the newly frozen lakes, mines were strung on pull ropes; only partly filled with explosives so they would retain buoyancy for several days, the charges were not designed to blow up the tanks but rather to shatter the ice beneath them. When word got around about this tactic, the Russian tank drivers began to avoid the lakes altogether, which was precisely what the Finns wanted, since it was much easier to ambush the vehicles in the countryside than out on the lakes, where their guns could sweep the terrain all around. At several locations the Finns unrolled enormous sheets of cellophane over frozen lakes so that, from the air, they would look unfrozen, and the enemy would not even bother trying to cross them.

Almost from the opening minute of the war, traffic began to back up on the Russian side. Mechanized columns were jammed bumper to bumper, with vehicles slewing off the roads into the morass of snow, weeds, and half-frozen bogs on either side. Sporadic but heavy snowstorms lashed the advancing columns, immobilizing some and slowing others to a crawl. And even a token show of Finnish resistance caused delay and confusion far out of proportion to the size of the force doing the resisting.

Between the frontier and the Mannerheim Line was a buffer zone between twelve and thirty miles deep. In this border area, Mannerheim had deployed about 21,000 men, organized into four "covering groups." Each was designated by a letter of the alphabet corresponding to its commander's name. Under control of Second Corps (Öhquist), were Groups U, M, and L; under control of Third Corps (Heinrichs) was the northernmost covering force, Group R. Strategic command of the overall Isthmus battle was under command of Mannerheim's chief of staff, a tough-minded, intelligent general named Hugo Östermann. The general line along which the covering troops were positioned ran through a string of small Karelian villages: Uusikirkko, Kivinapa, Lipola, Kiviniemi. A large part of the First Division was held in reserve between the covering troops and the line, between Lakes Suulajärvi and Valkjärvi. Mannerheim wanted to disrupt and pin down at least one large Russian formation out in the open and then bring up the First Division to attack it, but things didn't work out that way, and most of the division appears to have been withdrawn back into the line before it saw much action.

General Östermann had always thought the plan too ambitious for untried troops. More than Mannerheim, he seems to have appreciated the fact that the "wild card" in this strategy was the Russians' tanks and the effect they might have on troops who had never faced armor before, even in training. Östermann had envisioned a strictly delaying role for the covering troops, while the Mannerheim Line was being manned. Of course, as it turned out, the line already was manned when the war began. Since this was

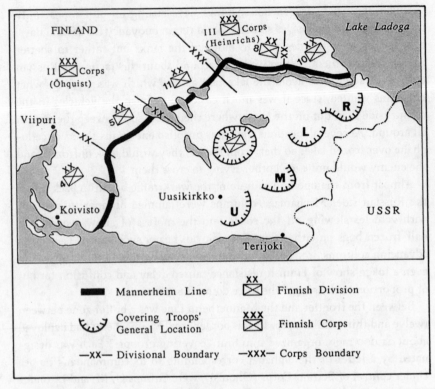

3. Actions of Covering Groups on Karelian Isthmus

the case, Östermann felt it was folly to risk good troops in front of good defensive positions rather than behind them. The net result of this command uncertainty was furious resistance at some places, token displays at others, and a spotty effort rather than a concerted defensive strategy in the buffer zone as a whole.

By the end of the war's first day, the Russians had pushed back elements of Group U to the eastern edge of Terijoki village. Finnish resistance was fierce, and about half the village was torched either as a result of shell fire or as part of a "scorched earth" effort. The covering troops hit the Russians with four counterattacks on the first night, causing considerable casualties and confusion. When the Finns finally yielded the field, early on December 1, they blew up a railroad bridge in the invaders' faces and halted all mechanized pursuit for about ten hours.

Enough reports had come up the chain of command by the end of December 2 for Mannerheim's generals to have a roughly accurate picture of the

Russians' advance. Clearly they were operating in such a way as to leave themselves vulnerable for the sort of quick-jab tactics Mannerheim had originally envisioned. Demolitions and booby traps—and the *fear* of booby traps, which was just as effective—were delaying the Reds' advance. Token Finnish resistance, even a single sniper shot, had halted vast columns for hours. The enemy was sticking to the good roads, which caused its formations to bunch up and become harder to deploy. Under those conditions, the army was very vulnerable to flank attacks. Moreover, most of the Red columns were out of touch with each other. Columns that had crossed the border moving parallel to one another were now sometimes heading in divergent or even opposite directions, exposing one another's flanks and rear more dangerously with each kilometer they advanced. Some tempting opportunities seemed to present themselves, but by the time Östermann got his plans drawn up, the situation had changed. Things would not hold still long enough for the Finns to take advantage of the enemy's awkwardness.

It was mainly the tanks that were causing the confusion. No Finnish soldier had ever confronted a rolling wave of armor before, or, for that matter, even a single modern tank in a training scenario. Officers had briefed their men on the psychological effect of massed armor, trying to build them up for that particular experience, but talking about it in a training class and actually facing roaring, clanking, fire-belching steel monsters were two very different things. The Russians' armored tactics, at this stage of the war, were pretty crude—straight-ahead cavalry charges, mostly—but their effect on the Finns was shattering.

At one sensitive juncture, two alarming reports reached Östermann's headquarters stating that the enemy had gained a beachhead on the Baltic coast and that a major armored breakthrough had occurred just a few kilometers in front of the Summa sector of the Mannerheim Line. Both reports proved false, but by the time the truth was learned, it was too late to halt the withdrawals they had caused. A great deal of terrain was given up without a fight, and Mannerheim was furious.

He ordered Öhquist to turn his men around and retake the ground that had been lost. Öhquist had the backbone to refuse, and to assume personal responsibility for the consequences. He told Mannerheim that the lost ground was not worth the cost of recapturing. Öhquist had spoken to his field commanders, and they had all expressed resentment at the situation. Their men were tired, confused, and resentful that headquarters was sending them all over the Karelian Isthmus on half-cocked missions whose objectives seemed clear to no one. Mannerheim backed down.

Finnish historians have made a determined attempt to track down the

origin of those two alarms, but without success. Most likely the disorganized state of Finnish communications was to blame, along with the confused
nature of the fighting. Add to those factors the raw, inexperienced reflexes
of midlevel staff officers, and the result was a situation that permitted a pair
of wild, unverified rumors to penetrate all the way to Isthmus Headquarters
disguised as fact. Any and all such rumors could, and in a more experienced
army would, have been either squelched or verified at a local level before
entering the chain of command. Those same chaotic conditions, of course,
also made it easy for Finnish-speaking Red Army personnel to tap phone
lines, break in on radio frequencies, and otherwise interpose themselves inside the fragile net of Finnish communications. The reports may have been
simple ruses; if so, they were spectacularly successful, and the men who
thought them up deserved the Order of Lenin, for each rumor had the effect
of handing the Russians a sizable battlefield victory at no cost to themselves.
Certain Finnish commentators, however, do not rule out the possibility of
treason, although if any tangible evidence exists to substantiate that charge,
it remains classified to this day.

On December 4 Mannerheim came storming down to Östermann's
headquarters at Imatra. Öhquist—who had plenty of better things to do—
was ordered to attend. If we are to believe Östermann's account, Mannerheim gave him a cruel dressing down, blaming the collapse of his cher-
ished "forward zone" strategy on Östermann's halfhearted compliance with
orders. Östermann offered his resignation; according to Östermann, so did
Mannerheim. Having vented their tensions, however, both men backed off
from this angry confrontation, realizing what a deleterious effect such an
occurrence would have on the Finns' morale. Mannerheim still seemed to
believe that some of his strategy could be salvaged.

And by December 4 there were signs that the Finnish Army was steady-
ing down. After the initial shock had worn off, the Finnish soldiers began
to figure out ways to handle the tank problem. It was soon discovered that
the tanks could be dealt with at close range in a number of ways. Logs, even
crowbars, jammed into their bogie wheels often stripped a tread and immobilized them. Once an attacker on foot got really close to a tank, the attacker
had the advantage. The problem still remained, however, of surviving long
enough to get that close.

By now, too, a cheap, effective, homemade weapon had appeared in great
quantities. It was the "Molotov Cocktail." The Finns did not invent these
devices—that honor apparently goes to the Republicans in Spain—but they
did christen them with the name that has stuck like glue ever since, and in
the first week of the war the Finns manufactured vast quantities of them.

When the supply of bottles ran short, the State Liquor Board in Helsinki rushed 40,000 empty fifth bottles to the front.

In its crudest form, the cocktail was no more than a bottle full of gasoline with a rag stuck in its mouth; but the puny fireball that resulted from this device was rarely enough to do more than scorch paint. The Finnish version was far more powerful, consisting of a blend of gasoline, kerosene, tar, and chloride of potassium, ignited not by a dishrag but by an ampoule of sulfuric acid taped to the bottle's neck. Other, more potent versions included a tiny vial of nitroglycerine. Clusters of stick grenades, held together with tape, were also effective against treads. Twenty-pound satchel charges were used as well, although it took nerves of iron to get close enough to sling one of these weapons. Casualties among the tank-hunter squads were in fact very high—70 percent in some units—but there was never a shortage of volunteers. Eighty Russian tanks were destroyed in the border-zone fighting.

Heavy fighting continued in scattered locations on December 4, as some of the covering troops took positions in the Mannerheim Line. On December 5, part of the Fifth Division left the line and moved up to cover the left of Group U. The Fifth Division's men were shaky, and none of them had faced tanks before. As they were moving into position, their advance element, a dismounted cavalry unit, suddenly began to scream "Tanks!" Panic ripped through the ranks. Whole companies took to their heels; men leaped out of trucks and left them with their engines running; gunners abandoned their weapons; wounded men were left on the field by their attendants. Most of the Fifth Division troops didn't stop running until they were back in the line, where officers who had witnessed the debacle cursed and punched and in some cases threatened to shoot them. A few hours later, it was learned that the cause of the panic was a lone *Finnish* armored car that had been scouting in advance of the infantry.

Mannerheim's display of pique seems to have lit a fire under Östermann because Finnish activity in the forward zone became much more aggressive on the night of December 5–6. A number of ambitious raids were launched against exposed Russian salients. A couple of these actions stung the Russians badly and inflicted several hundred casualties on them. By December 6, however, there really wasn't much of a "forward zone" left: only a few shallow strips in front of parts of the Mannerheim Line. Virtually all of the still-committed covering troops had withdrawn back into the line by the end of the day.

If, on the one hand, there had been no smashing Finnish victory, at least there had been no Poland-style breakthroughs, either. And if many units had performed badly in their first encounters with tanks, most of them had rallied quickly and mastered their panic. If the Finns had possessed even a single brigade of modern armor, they could have cut several Soviet formations to ribbons; but tanks were costly items, and Finland's military priorities were strictly defensive.

It is also possible, as some Finnish historians have suggested, that Mannerheim, old cavalryman that he was, had something of a blind spot about armor. He kept up with modern military theory, he knew all about the blitzkrieg, and he encouraged imaginative tactics for use against tanks. But tanks can also serve in a defensive capacity—as mobile reserves that can be used to add weight and power to local counterattacks, as artillery, as mobile antitank units. Given the constricted area of the Karelian Isthmus, the number of tanks needed was not prohibitively large; thirty or forty would have been a great help.*

Most important of all, however, by actively engaging the enemy from the first instead of passively waiting behind their fortifications, the Finns gained valuable experience. The most precious datum was the knowledge that the Russians were not supermen—far from it; they were slow, ponderous, unaggressive, and unimaginative. They *could* be beaten.

The Finns who had fought them in the border zone took that message back into the Mannerheim Line, and as they told their stories, there was a discernible stiffening of resolve along the entire defensive front. The defenders were going to need that resolve because there was a firestorm coming down on their heads like nothing any of them had ever imagined.

So congested and confused were the advancing Russian columns that it took an additional thirty-six to forty-eight hours after the covering troops had disengaged for the Soviet artillery to catch up and dig in. During those first days, a number of local probing attacks were sent against the line, but they were not seriously threatening.

The Russians were, in fact, curiously lethargic and followed a predictable workaday routine. Russian infantry, often riding in trucks, would arrive at their jumping-off points at first light and then move out, not very energetically, in the general direction of Finnish lines. Sometimes by simple weight of numbers they forced the Finns to withdraw from exposed or unsupported positions, but thereafter they did nothing to exploit these little victories. In

---

*Mannerheim may have learned a lesson from the Winter War, however, because when the Finnish Army went into action again, in 1941, it had lots of tanks, most of them, in fact, reconditioned Russian vehicles captured in 1939–40. They were augmented by some Czech models handed down by the Wehrmacht.

the afternoon, when the light began to fail, the Russians would withdraw a kilometer or two to the east, dig in behind a wagon circle of tanks, parked with their headlights and machine guns facing out, and build huge campfires. The Finns would then creep forward and reoccupy their positions, usually without interference and often reaping the bonus of discarded Russian equipment or bits of thrown away paper that proved useful to the intelligence staff.

Mannerheim was still unsatisfied. He wanted the Finns to do more, to press forward under cover of darkness and attack the enemy while he was warming himself at his campfires. Most Finnish soldiers lacked either the confidence or the experience to try a night attack, at least at this stage of the fighting. Moreover, early December marks the beginning of the period of maximum winter darkness in these latitudes, and very few flare pistols, star shells, or searchlights had reached the line as yet. One cannot blame the Finnish officers for not wanting to risk shaky troops on nocturnal operations without such things.

The first major Russian blows did not fall on the "Viipuri Gateway" at Summa but, rather, on the extreme left flank of the Mannerheim Line, in what would come to be known as the Taipale sector, after the small Ladogan fishing village that anchored its right flank. Meretskov knew the Finns would expect him to hit Summa first, and the reasonable assumption was that the defenders had concentrated both their strongest fortifications and their tactical reserves in that part of the line. He therefore resolved to launch a strong feint attack at Taipale, in hopes of drawing off those reserves and softening up the Summa sector.

But the Finnish Tenth Division, dug in at Taipale, knew it could count on no significant reinforcements. Mannerheim and his generals knew exactly what Meretskov was up to, and they were not going to shift a single company from Summa if they could help it. The line at Taipale followed the outline of a long, tapering, blunt-ended promontory, bounded on the south by the Suvanto branch of the Vuoksi Waterway and on the north by Lake Ladoga itself. Between the wide Suvanto and the lake ran the narrow Taipale River.

Along the Suvanto sector the Finns enjoyed a slight advantage of elevation and had some dry ground to dig in. Across the base of the promontory, however, the water table was very close to the surface and the entrenchments there were little more than augmented drainage ditches. The narrow tip of the peninsula, called Koukunniemi, was no-man's-land. The Finns had voluntarily given it up because it was low, marshy, and utterly barren of cover. This was a sensible step to take, for it enabled them to streamline their positions and concentrate their limited strength. They also hoped that, by leaving the cape undefended, they could tempt the Russians into attacking

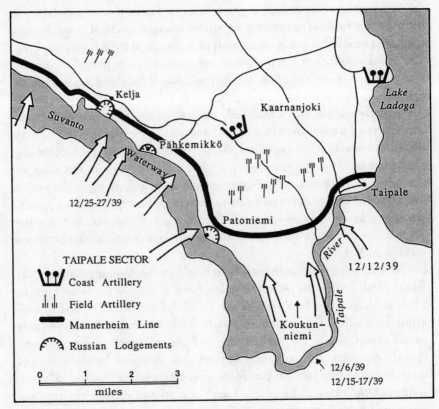

4. Russian Attacks on Taipale Peninsula, December 1939

there in strength. The open tongue of land was a killing ground. Every millimeter of it had been ranged by Finnish artillery and a fire plan worked out to bring down destruction on any force that gained a foothold there.

As soon as their first artillery batteries caught up with them, late on December 6, the Russians moved against Taipale. Their attack began with heavy artillery preparation, a foretaste of what was to come all along the line. After a four-hour bombardment, the Red infantry swarmed forward. They attempted a crossing at the Lossi ferry landing but were thrown back. Just as the Finns had hoped, the enemy did swarm on to the vacant promontory of Koukunniemi, and once they were in the bag, the Finnish artillery plastered that exposed ground with devastating effect. The Russians sustained hundreds of casualties, and the survivors of the barrage fled at the first sign of a counterattack by Finnish infantry.

Skirmishing and artillery duels now flared constantly along the entire

Taipale sector as the Russians probed, tested the defenders' strength, and brought up more guns. The next major Soviet effort against Taipale came on December 14, and by that date patrols and aerial photographs had given the Finns a clear idea of what sort of odds they faced. From December 6 to December 12, only one Russian division was engaged on this front; now a second division was deployed. Russian artillery strength had risen, during that same interval, to fifty-seven batteries, as opposed to the nine motley batteries the Finns could call on.

Under cover of predawn darkness on December 14, the Russians mounted a strong attack, preceded by a bombardment of unprecedented weight and fury. Crouching in their trenches under this thunderous flail, the men of the Tenth Division began to curse their own artillery, which fired not a shot in reply. The division was unaware that the Finnish gunners were under strict orders not to expend ammunition in counterbattery fire but to conserve their shells for more economical targets. They soon had plenty.

At about 11:30, the barrage suddenly lifted. The defenders looked to their front and saw thirty Red tanks rolling toward the southern end of Kou-kunniemi. Moments later another force of about twenty tanks was spotted advancing against the northern side. Behind the armor, in large, closely packed formations, was an entire infantry division. A nerve-grinding silence settled over the scene as the last shell fire tapered off. The stillness and ten-sion were screwed to a terrible pitch by the growl and clank of the tanks' treads, steadily increasing in volume. The infantry formations advanced with a steady, parade-ground gait. The tanks opened fire, their shells rippling across the neck of Koukunniemi. Casualties grew, and so did the Finnish infantry's impatience with their own cannoneers.

Then with a startling crash all the Finnish guns opened up. Once again they had held fire until the enemy had reached a preplotted killing ground, and now their gunners fired with the methodical, steady rhythm of pro-fessionals—careful, unhurried salvos that dropped cluster after cluster of high explosive and shrapnel into the middle of those dense, screaming for-mations of Red infantry. The attack melted away in about five minutes, leaving the snow dotted with 300 or 400 casualties and the burning hulks of eighteen tanks.

A third Soviet division now entered the fight at Taipale, and the disparity of artillery strength grew even greater: nine Finnish batteries against eighty-four Russian. The newly arrived Red infantry performed poorly, however. They panicked under shell fire, and in attack after attack they were seen milling around under the bombardment like a herd of sheep. Nevertheless the attacks continued, establishing another trait that would prove characteristic of all the Mannerheim Line battles: the Russians' willingness to take needless, hideous losses and still keep coming. Besides field and coast artillery, the Finns repulsed them with massed rifle fire and hundreds of machine guns and automatic rifles, with mortars and mine fields, and with grenades. Whole platoons of Russian infantry would become entangled in barbed wire hidden beneath snowbanks, like bugs in a spider web, and would be picked off one by one. Perhaps the deadliest weapons in the Finnish arsenal were the six-inch coast-defense rifles at Kaarnanjoki and Jariseva, which subjected the advancing Russian columns to airbursts of shrapnel, scything them down like giant shotgun blasts. One typical Russian attack during this period, lasting just under an hour, left 1,000 dead and twenty-seven burning tanks strewn on the ice.

Just before Christmas, the three Russian divisions operating in front of Taipale, the Forty-ninth, 150th, and 142d, were joined by yet another, the Fourth, on the eastern side of the Suvanto. Finnish reconnaissance planes revealed that the ratio of artillery was now nine batteries against 111. On Christmas Day, under cover of a thick ground fog, the Russians crossed the frozen waterway and established beachheads at Patoniemi and Pähke-mikkö. When daylight burned off the fog, the Finns counterattacked furiously, killing 500 Russians at Patoniemi alone. The attacking force that had crossed at Pähkemikkö was betrayed by the very same fog that gave it cover. Unknowingly, the Russians had established their beachhead on a piece of terrain that was exposed to several flanking Finnish machine-gun nests, some of them only 100 meters away. When the mist evaporated, the Finnish gunners were surprised to see an unprotected swarm of enemy troops right in their sights. Eyewitness accounts of the battle state that the piles of Russian dead grew visibly larger each time the machine guns sprayed fire back and forth over the exposed landing spot.

Farther north along the Suvanto, another Russian battalion had taken advantage of the fog and established itself at Kelja. This unit dug in and signaled for reinforcements. If reinforcements had been able to cross in strength before the fog burned off, it is possible the Russians could have cut off the entire Taipale promontory. They were well behind the Finnish right and close to some lateral roads that would have facilitated such a move.

But by the time reinforcements began edging out onto the ice, the mist was lifting. Several machine guns and two old quick-firing field guns, probably "French 75s" from World War I, took the crossing under heavy fire. This checked the Russian buildup for a precious interval of time but obviously could not hold it permanently. Pressure was building and the danger was grave. Every Finnish gun that could be brought to bear was swung around to fire on the Kelja salient, and every available man, including headquarters' and other noncombatant personnel, was organized to storm the beachhead after the guns finished working it over.

The battle seesawed all day and into the night, when the fighting continued under the hard white glow of a winter moon. At the same time the Finns tried to wrest Kelja from the Russians who were dug in there, they also had to repel repeated attempts by fresh forces of regimental size to cross the ice and reinforce the beachhead. The last Soviet troops were ejected from Kelja only at 9:15 the following morning, almost twenty-four hours after their initial crossing. It had been close and bloody work. Within the Kelja perimeter, and scattered over the ice leading to it, lay more than 2,000 Russian dead.

By mid-December the main weight of the Russian attack had shifted to the Summa sector; the Christmas crossings were the last massive effort aimed at Taipale. Even so, this never became a "quiet" sector. There were numerous Russian probes between January 1 and the start of the Russians' all-out offensive in February, when the tempo picked up considerably. The Finnish Tenth Division held its line for the entire duration of the war, however, even though the same exhausted men manned these positions, without relief, during every single day of that ordeal. In December alone the Tenth suffered 2,250 casualties, and by the end of the war it was stretched very thin indeed.

Taipale was a slaughterhouse for the Russians. The land surrounding the promontory was either flat or lightly rolling, with few trees. The last half kilometer of any approach to Finnish lines had to be made across wide sheets of open ice. The Russian attacks formed in the open, approached in the open, and were pressed home in the open, against an entrenched defender well supplied with machine guns. Moreover, at this stage of the war, the Russians had no snowsuit camouflage for their men and no whitewash for their tanks. The tanks moved in ungainly clumps, and the infantry attacked in dense, human wave formations. It was the Somme in miniature. To the Finns who witnessed these attacks, it seemed beyond belief that any army, no matter how fatalistic its ideology or inexhaustible its supply of manpower, would continue to mount attack after attack across such billiard-table terrain.

In some battles the Finnish machine gunners held their fire until the range was down to fifty meters; the butchery was dreadful. In a number of cases Finnish machine gunners had to be evacuated due to stress. They had become emotionally unstable from having to perform such mindless slaughter, day after day.

Manning the center of the Mannerheim Line, in the Summa sector, was the Finnish Fifth Division. Except for a small number of men who had been involved in the last hectic stages of the border-zone fighting, its troops were untried. Before the Russian assaults began, the division's commander went on record to express his own lack of confidence in his men's ability to withstand a massive armored onslaught, or to plug Russian breakthroughs with counterattacks of their own.

The first big Soviet push against the Summa sector came at 10:00 A.M. on December 17, after a five-hour artillery barrage and tactical strikes by approximately 200 aircraft. There were two major thrusts: one against Summa itself and one against the Lähde road defenses, about two kilometers northeast of Summa village. The village of Lähde was situated several kilometers behind the line itself and was the site of a vital road junction. It was here, between these two tiny villages, that the Russians would push the hardest and here that the Mannerheim Line would finally break. But not this time.

Russian sappers led off the attack. They had crept close to the antitank rocks under cover of their own barrage, and when the shell fire lifted, they set off enormous charges that opened rubbled paths through the rocks and wire entanglements. Out of the smoke came a wedge of fifty tanks. These advanced to the gaps, crawled through and over the broken monoliths, crushed the wire, and thrust into the trench network held by the Finnish infantry.

To counter this tactic, the Finns had ordered their infantry not to withdraw but to stay in position and fight off the Red infantry that came after the tanks, in the hope that, unsupported, the tanks would eventually withdraw. It was a fairly desperate stratagem, and costly, but it worked. The Finns took galling fire from the milling Soviet tanks, but as long as they stayed put and cut down the infantry, no really dangerous breakthroughs occurred.

It would not have worked if Soviet tank/infantry tactics had not been such a botch. Coordination between the two arms was virtually nil: they attacked together, in the same general direction, but that was all. The tanks would surge forward, seize a patch of ground, and then churn around aimlessly on that ground, waiting for the infantry to catch up to them. When the tankers realized their infantry were not coming, whether because they had been repulsed at the wire or just never showed up at all, they either withdrew on their own accord or else formed defensive wagon-train circles and tried to hold their gains through the hours of darkness. And when the sun went down, the Finnish tank-killer teams came out to stalk.

Nailing tanks at close range was always dangerous, but it was especially so in the Lähde sector, where the trees were thin and the ground relatively flat. As always, there were too few Bofors guns, and the open landscape did not favor their deployment. Casualties among the antitank gunners were high.

To the south, on the same day, a similar attack was launched at Summa itself. Here either the Russian commander did not use sappers or they were knocked out by their own barrage, for relatively little damage was done to the antitank rocks. And if they did not actually stop the charging tanks, the rocks did force them to climb at a steep angle, rendering them momentarily vulnerable. Soviet designers had sacrificed all-around armor protection in their vehicles in favor of heavier firepower: below the turrets each type of Russian tank had its weak spots, which the Finns quickly learned to aim for. When a tank nosed up to climb over the rows of boulders, daring individuals could scuttle forward and slide mines on to the spot where the treads would soon come crunching to earth; and they could do it in relative safety, since the target tank and most of its neighbors would be unable to depress their machine guns low enough to hit the ground immediately around them.

In the Summa attacks the Russians tried to use the thick surface ice of the lakes as avenues of approach to Finnish lines. From the Russian side, the tactic seemed logical; there was plenty of room for a dozen or more tanks at a time to deploy and to advance swiftly across those surfaces. But if the middle of the lakes gave plenty of maneuvering room, the Finnish side did not; there, the rough shoreline terrain would close in again and offer, at most, four or five exits off of the lake that were suitable for tanks. And of course the Finns had covered those exits with ambush parties or antitank guns. In the first attacks against Summa and Lähde, the Russians lost thirty-five tanks, about one-third of the number engaged.

During that same twenty-four-hour period, the Finnish high command knew next to nothing about what was happening in the Summa sector. Russian shell fire had cut most of the telephone lines, and before the battle was an hour old, the Finns' old-fashioned radio sets broke down, one by one, from exposure, concussion, and overwork. Even worse, frontline communications on the company and battalion level were a hodgepodge of improvisation. Many of the radio and switchboard operators had not been given codes to use, and it was obvious, early in the fighting, that the Russians were eavesdropping. So the frontline signalmen improvised, in classic Finnish style. They began to converse in a slang-riddled mixture of Swedish and regional Finnish dialect and started referring to friendly commanders by picturesque and frequently scatological nicknames. One pities the Russian interpreters who, with commissars observing closely, strove to make something rational of those conversations.

An even heavier blow was aimed at the Lähde positions on December 18, when sixty-eight tanks attacked behind heavy artillery and aerial preparation. The Finnish artillery, firing from their pinpoint prewar maps, destroyed ten vehicles before they could get within a mile of the line, taking the steam

out of the attack. Another fifteen tanks were disabled in close combat. The
Russian infantry never got through the boulders. At Summa an unsupported
Russian infantry attack failed, leaving 500 bodies on the fields in front of the
Finnish wire.

On December 19 the Summa positions were battered by continuous
attacks. Heavy pressure was also felt east of Summa, along all the line defenses up to Lake Muolaanjärvi, where the monstrous heavy K.V. tanks
appeared for the first time in the line fighting. Combat spread into Summa
village itself. As the tanks churned through the narrow, rutted streets, Finnish infantry swarmed over them from roofs and upper stories, firing their
Suomis through observation slits, levering open hatches and stuffing grenades into turrets, drenching the tanks with showers of Molotov Cocktails.
By the time combat ebbed, on December 20, a huge tract of land in and
around Summa was littered with the hulks of fifty-eight burned-out Russian tanks. So far, in the first twenty days of fighting on the Isthmus the
invader had lost a minimum of 250 armored vehicles. One Russian tank brigade commander deserted to the Finns rather than face the consequences of
reporting his losses to the division commissar.

At Lähde, on December 19, the critical "Poppius" bunker, a major forti-
fication named for its commander, was hit so badly by close-range tank fire
that its metal embrasures jammed. Overrun, its garrison resisted Russian
infantry for forty-eight hours with grenades and small arms, until a Finnish
counterattack retook the ground around the bunker and freed them.

Although there were some new attacks on December 20, they were not
as serious as the earlier wave; the Russians had burned up their supplies as
well as lost a substantial percentage of their armor. One tank battalion ran
out of gas in front of Summa and just sat there, being picked off tank by
tank. Twenty Russian vehicles penetrated Summa village on the twentieth,
but eight of them, including three K.V. monsters, were knocked out in close
combat.

The first Russian offensive against the Mannerheim Line had failed. Seven
infantry divisions had been launched against Taipale and Summa, with two
armored brigades and large packets of divisional armor, the whole effort supported by at least 500 guns and between 800 and 1,000 aircraft. Every Soviet
unit thrown against the line had been mauled. Three-fifths of the tanks sent
against the line had been destroyed. The tank drivers faced a layered defense:
first, the ditches, bogs, and snow-covered mush of the landscape itself, augmented by extensive mine fields and tank traps; next, deadly accurate Finnish
artillery fire; up close, rows of granite boulders, log obstacles, and camouflaged pits. Once they had gotten past all of those dangers and were inside

Finnish lines, they faced gasoline bombs, satchel charges, cluster grenades, and individual Finnish madmen erupting out of nowhere to fire their rifles and submachine guns at observation slits, periscopes, and gun muzzles. If they survived all that and plunged through to the rear of the line, that was where the Finns had carefully sited their precious Bofors guns.

As for the long-suffering Russian infantry, they attacked with what Mannerheim described as "a fatalism incomprehensible to a European."[*] Their assaults had been delivered by waves or dense columns of men whose approach to Finnish lines had been screened, if at all, only by the incidental cover of scattered trees or the haphazard shield of the tanks—and these were usually too far ahead to protect the infantry at all. In one sector of the Summa battlefield, repeated attacks were delivered straight across a massive Finnish mine field by men who used their own bodies to clear the mines: they linked arms, formed close-order rows, and marched stoically into the mines, singing party war songs and continuing to advance with the same steady, suicidal rhythm even as the mines began to explode, ripping holes in their ranks and showering the marchers with feet, legs, and intestines.

A survivor of one such Russian attack recorded his experiences this way:

> The battalion commander, Popov, called all the officers together and gave us the following orders:
>
> "The attack will be repeated! And let's not lie in the snow, dreaming of our warm beds! The village must be taken! Company commanders . . . will shoot anyone who falls back or turns around!"
>
> One does not have to be a psychologist to know that the new attack, in which the soldiers would have to climb over the bodies of their own killed and wounded, would fail.
>
> Of the more than 100 men of my company who went into the first attack, only 38 returned after the second one had failed. All of us worried and wondered: what happens now? As if in answer to our question, the battalion commander, who had taken over when Popov was wounded, called all the officers to him. . . . he held a field telephone in his hand. . . . "Comrades, our attack was unsuccessful; the division commander has just given me the order personally—in seven minutes, we attack again. . . ."
>
> The rest I remember through a fog. One of the wounded, among whom we advanced, grabbed my leg and I pushed him away. When I noticed I was ahead of my men, I lay down in the snow and waited for

[*]Mannerheim, 368.

the line to catch up to me. There was no fear, only a dull apathy and indifference to impending doom pushed us ahead. This time, the Finns let us approach to within 100 feet of their positions before opening fire. . . . *

From a letter found on the Summa battlefield after the first round of attacks: "We march already two days without food. . . . in the severe cold we have many sick and wounded. Our commanders must have difficulty justifying our being here. . . . we are black like chimney sweeps from dirt and completely tired out. The soldiers are again full of lice. Health is bad. Many soldiers have pneumonia. They promise that the combat will be over by Stalin's birthday, the 21st of December, but who will believe it?" †

The strain on the defenders was almost as great. The Finns had to rebuild their defenses, string barbed wire, lay mines, and bury telephone cables at night when they should have been resting. Food was sporadic and poor. Thirst was worse; it was impossible to simply reach down and suck on a handful of snow because the shelling had contaminated the white stuff, and men who drank it suffered agonizing stomach cramps.

It had been a resounding defensive victory, but the more thoughtful Finnish officers looked beyond it and wondered what would have happened if the Russians *had* handled their armor professionally. Their defeat had been so smashing and one sided that it seemed reasonable to assume that the Russians, too, would ask that very question and, next time, do things better.

*Garthoff, Raymond I., ed., *Soviet Military Doctrine* (Glencoe, Ill.: Rand Corporation, 1953), 237.

†Engle, Eloise, and Lauri Paananen, *The Winter War* (New York: Scribner's, 1973), 63.

▲ CHAPTER 8 ▲ ▲

"A Stupid Butting of Heads"

The Russians had been stopped cold against the Mannerheim Line. From POW interrogations, deserters' reports, and captured documents, it became clear that the Soviets' morale was poor, that their supplies were not getting through from Leningrad, and that firing squads were working overtime dealing with men, officers and troops alike, who had refused to participate in still more suicidal frontal attacks.

The Finnish generals were swept by a mood of euphoria. General Östermann, who had been so cautious in his handling of the border-zone battles, now came down hard on the side of a bold and ambitious Finnish counterstroke, a kind of Cannae in the snow, designed to nip off and annihilate the three Russian divisions dug in before Summa. Even the dour and realistic General Öhquist seems to have been swept up by the concept, although it is not always easy to tell, from their postwar writings, which one had the most to do with the plan's parentage. What is certain is that Östermann forwarded a counterattack proposal to Mannerheim as early as December 11, which Mannerheim promptly rejected as premature.

The optimum date for launching such an operation would have been December 20 or 21, when the Russians were still winded and reeling from their losses. The problem was that several of the Finnish units earmarked for the counteroffensive were still engaged on those days, repelling the last, somewhat enfeebled, attacks or mopping up stubborn Russian pockets still clinging to Finnish positions. The plan was approved by Mannerheim only on December 22, about eighteen hours before H-Hour.

In his memoirs, Öhquist equivocates a bit by saying that he had to go along with the plan or possibly be relieved of his command. Evidence suggests, however, that in the beginning he was just as enthusiastic about it as Östermann. He did, however, insist that the attack plan include strong elements of the only fresh Finnish division on the Isthmus, the Sixth. But the Sixth was designated Commander in Chief's Reserve, and at the time

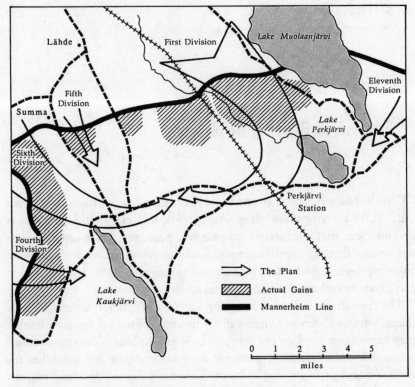

5. Finnish Counteroffensive Objectives and Actual Results

the counterattack was being drawn up, it was engaged in digging back-up fortifications around Viipuri. Mannerheim procrastinated for about forty-eight hours before agreeing to commit part of the Sixth, and by the time the green light was given, it was too late to launch the attack any earlier than December 23. It was also too close to H-Hour for the Sixth Division to move into its assigned place in any kind of order.

On the map, the plan looked exciting. It was a double-pincers maneuver: a large set of arrows inside a small set of arrows, converging on a big salient in Russian lines that corresponded to the elbow bend at Summa. The Sixth Division would attack the left flank of the salient, the First Division would attack the right. There was a bulge in the Russian salient in front of the Finnish Fifth Division, which would launch a more modest pincers attack of its own. The Fourth and Eleventh divisions would hammer the deeper flanks of the salient, tying down as many Russian troops as they could. The fresh units of the Sixth would be interposed in the line between the battle-scarred Fourth and Fifth.

The Sixth would attack in the area of Karhula, along a southeastern axis, with the objective of cutting the Russians' main supply artery east of Lake Kaukjärvi. The First Division would strike south and southeast toward the crossroads at Perkjärvi railroad station, then move westward until it linked up with elements of the First.

This was a very bold plan. If it succeeded it might knock three Russian divisions out of the Isthmus fight and certainly ruin the enemy's timetable for further offensive action. It would, if successful, win perhaps a month of time—time for the voice of world opinion to gather strength, and for military aid from the outside world to reach Finland in sufficient strength to equip two more divisions.

It was, however, utopian; there were so many things wrong with it that one scarcely knows where to begin describing them. The plan itself was vast in scope but diffuse in concentration, and so complex that even an experienced field army would have been challenged to pull it off. The Finnish Army had never in its entire history attempted an offensive operation on this scale. Except for enduring sporadic air raids on Viipuri, the entire Sixth Division was unbloodied. This kind of attack needed armor to give it speed and cutting power and massive, flexible artillery support; it had neither. Artillery support in turn required smooth and reliable communications; Finnish communications were neither. It was a plan that demanded fresh troops who had a clear concept of their roles in the operation, yet the units designated to take part in it had at best thirty-six hours to prepare, and many of them were still involved in violent skirmishing when the orders came down. Add to these factors the normal amount of confusion attendant on a complex offensive, and one has a recipe for military disaster. In the event, the operation was something less than a total debacle, but that was only due to blind luck and the usual Russian incompetence when it came to following up opportunities.

The Finnish generals seem to have forgotten that the Russian soldier is, and always has been, a much tougher proposition in defense than in offense. Dug in and well supplied with ammo, most Russian soldiers would fight to the death, as the invading Germans would soon learn. To attack such an enemy with raw and exhausted troops is risky enough. To do it without any accurate picture of the enemy's dispositions is sheer folly. And the Finns' reconnaissance was woefully inadequate. They knew more or less which Russian units were directly in front of them, but they had only the vaguest ideas of what sort of forces they might run into behind that frontline crust.

It is a wonder the attack was launched at all. A blizzard raked the Isthmus just hours before the jumping-off time, dropping temperatures to a brutal twenty degrees below zero. A fierce wind off the gulf lashed the snow into horizontal sheets that cut through snowsuits like a blade. Virtually every unit that had to change position in order to participate in the offensive got lost, delayed, or rerouted. One battery of urgently needed howitzers, attempting to follow a vague set of marching orders in the middle of a snowstorm, finally entrenched itself a mere ten kilometers from where it was supposed to be. The fresh battalions of the Sixth Division, on whom so much depended, were not ordered forward in coherent, easy-to-manage formations, but all at once, in a sprawling mass of men and equipment that straggled over a good part of the Karelian Isthmus. It finally ended up in the right slot, but hours late—its men were suffering from exposure, half its heavy equipment was missing, and its units were appallingly intermingled. Officers were commanding strange men, men were serving in strange units; everybody was cold and tired and rapidly getting exasperated. On viewing this anarchy, several officers on the spot immediately tried to call headquarters and beg that the attack either be postponed until things could be sorted out, or abandoned altogether. The calls never got through. The shooting hadn't even started yet, but already the fragile Finnish communications net had collapsed under the strain. Telephone communications in most places did not survive much longer than the radio system. Two hours into the battle General Öhquist had lost all contact with two entire divisions.

Ready or not, the attack jumped off at 6:30 A.M., December 23, behind a pathetic artillery barrage lasting ten minutes. The fortunes of the attacking units varied wildly. One battalion of the First Division passed easily as far as the Perojoki River, vigorously attacked a fortified Russian encampment there, killed forty enemy troops and a large number of transport animals, and retired to Finnish lines with only light casualties. The battalion next to it, however, ran into serious resistance from the start, took heavy losses, and had to be rescued by a reserve battalion.

The Sixth Division, to its credit, attacked with surprising élan, broke through a crust of spotty frontline resistance, and penetrated about two kilometers into the Russian rear. There the attackers encountered a large and previously undetected enemy tank park. They were also brought under heavy and accurate shell fire, directed from two large, out-of-range captive balloons. This part of the Sixth's advance was halted, for good, as early as 10:00 A.M. Two other battalions of the Sixth, part of infantry regiment JR-17 (JR = *jalkaväki rykmentti*, or "infantry regiment"), pressed onward until early afternoon, then they too encountered stiff resistance. There was no hope of further progress without artillery support. Miraculously, they were able to contact the battery that had been assigned to support them; a barrage was requested on the proper map coordinates. "I'm sorry," the battery commander replied, "we can't shoot over there—it's out of range."

Only then did the Finnish infantry commander learn that the code word he had been issued had been switched, at the last minute, to another artillery battery, one located far out of range. He attempted to use his organic mortars as field artillery, only to discover that the fresh supplies of shells, delivered just before the attack, would not fit the tubes. By late afternoon, every battalion in the Sixth Division was demoralized by that kind of incident, and the soldiers were shaken by their first experience of heavy shelling. Clearly there was not much more the Sixth could do.

The Fourth Division's attack encountered strong resistance from the start, and its advance gradually angled away from a direction that would have taken it into position to hit the Russian tank park from the rear. New Russian units were now being rushed into the battle zone from nearby sectors, and by midafternoon the Fourth Division, too, was stopped in its tracks.

There was a bitter irony taking shape amid all this confusion. In dealing with the Finnish attacks the Russians were exposing the locations and strength of all their forward reserves of men and armor. The fire control observers accompanying the Finnish infantry were presented with incredibly choice and vulnerable targets—battalion headquarters, truck depots stacked with petrol and ammunition, powder magazines, radio stations, unguarded gun batteries—and were unable to call down a single coordinated Finnish barrage on any of them.

By 3:00 P.M. the Finnish high command had heard enough to know that, instead of a brilliant counterstroke, it now had the makings of a first-class debacle. The order went forth to cancel further offensive operations and withdraw to the Mannerheim Line. The order was ancient history by the time it filtered down to the front. Most local commanders, acting on their own responsibility, had already called off their attacks and were now desperately trying to extricate their men.

By the time the operation was over, the attackers had suffered 1,300 battle casualties and 200 cases of frostbite. It had certainly been the most unimpressive Finnish effort of the war. Considering the scope of the operation, the rotten weather, the inexperience of the men involved, and the hopelessly bad communications, the time that had been allocated for mounting the attack was absurd. The Sixth Division's troops had been shoved forward in one great ungainly mob; horses' hooves and sled runners had severed telephone lines, artillery support had been weak and unreliable, and the enemy's dispositions had been an utter mystery.

In short, the counterattack revealed just how raw, even amateurish, the Finnish Army was at large-scale conventional warfare. The oversights and false optimism, the slipshod planning, the brushed-off details, the euphoric assumptions that characterized both the plan and its execution, were the symptoms of sheer inexperience.

General Öhquist makes a valiant attempt to defend the operation in his postwar writings. He argues that the attack *did* gain time for the Finns to prepare for the next big Russian push, and he claims that the effort gave "valuable experience" to the officers and men who participated. Perhaps so, but since the Finns never again dared to launch a major counterattack on the Isthmus, it is difficult to see what good all that experience did them. The most discernible result of the operation was gloom in the ranks; the men knew they had made a game try out of a rotten plan, and their opinion of the high command's competence took a nose dive. The men nicknamed the operation with a Finnish idiom that defies exact translation but that can be roughly and appropriately rendered as "a stupid and misbegotten butting of heads."

At the time, the Finns had no idea of what sort of losses they had inflicted on the Russians. Postwar evidence, however, does suggest that the enemy suffered at least as many casualties as the attackers and that the confused nature of the fighting, plus the fact that it was taking place up to two kilometers behind Russian lines, really did alarm the Soviet command and throw them off balance. But even if the counterattack did delay the start of the big Isthmus offensive, it was only by a matter of a week or so. The whole curious and abortive business seems to have made very little difference, one way or the other.

▲ PART II ▲ ▲

Uncommon Valor: Battles in the Fourth Corps Zone

The Red Army possesses all the advantages over the armies of other states in its ability to operate in the harsh conditions of the winter period. . . .

—*Red Army Manual of Winter Combat,* 1939 edition

CHAPTER 9

Tolvajärvi: The First Victory

The sheer number and potency of the Russian attacks came close to overwhelming the Finns during the war's first frantic days. Mannerheim was especially worried about his frontline officers. Most of them were reservists, under fire for the first time, facing enormously daunting odds, and for at least the first few days they were more concerned with just keeping their units from disintegration than they were with launching fancy counterattacks. Mannerheim's first priority was to intervene decisively on at least one front—to do something, appoint somebody who could stop the passivity and fatalism that was clearly spreading through the ranks of the outnumbered defenders. But where should he make that move, take that gamble?

The decision was made somewhat easier by the priorities of geography. Danger to the overall Finnish cause increased dramatically in a north-to-south direction. It was annoying to lose Petsamo, of course, but that loss was neither surprising nor alarming, given its remoteness from Finnish population centers and its proximity to the Soviet bastion at Murmansk. The attacks on Salla, Kuhmo, and Suomussalmi were dangerous, but they were developing slowly. Far graver danger loomed in Ladoga-Karelia, to the north of Fourth Corps, where the situation was growing more desperate with each passing hour. And nowhere was the situation unraveling faster than on the Tolvajärvi road. It was there that Mannerheim chose to take drastic action, and it was there, in a battle that is still virtually unknown outside of Finland, that the Finnish Army would find its first Winter War hero, fight one of its most impressive battles, and win its first significant victory.

By the end of the war's first day, Mannerheim's headquarters was inundated with alarming reports about the intensity of fighting in the Suojärvi area, north of Fourth Corps's flank, an area where little activity had been anticipated. The northernmost prong of the Russian drive had been launched by the 155th Division, advancing against token resistance toward an impor-

tant road junction at Ilomantsi. Next, forty-odd miles farther south, the
Russian 139th Division had been identified, moving through the Suojärvi
lakes along the axis of the Tolvajärvi road, obviously making for an important interior road that ran through Värtsilä and Korpiselka. Both of these
advances seriously threatened the critical rail line that ran from Joensuu
through Sortavala, then skirted the western shore of Ladoga, and thence ran
down to the Isthmus. In other words, the Finns' main lateral supply line for
the whole Ladoga front, the artery they had planned to use to send reinforcements to the Isthmus after the long-planned Fourth Corps counterattack,
was imperiled.

The Russian Fifty-fifth Division was on the move, parallel to the railroad
line between Suojärvi and Loimola. If it got beyond Kollaa, Mannerheim
knew, the planned Fourth Corps counteroffensive would become compromised, perhaps rendered impossible. In the meantime, while all these surprise attacks were knifing through spotty resistance, the Russian Eighteenth
Division was proceeding slowly but steadily along the Uomaa road, while
the 168th Division, on the Ladoga shore road, was advancing from Salmi
through Pitkäranta to Kitelä. By midday December 1, it was clear that the
worst danger was above Suojärvi on the Tolvajärvi road, where the defense
looked to be on the verge of disintegration. Some of the reports reaching
Mannerheim were in fact exaggerated, but their panicky tone was an accurate
reflection of the way things were going.

Opposing the Russian 139th Division was a force of about 4,000 men designated "Task Force R," for their commander, Lieutenant Colonel Räsänen.
It was an ad hoc formation comprised of four independent infantry battalions of varying strengths and states of equipage, and a "bicycle battalion"
designated "PPP-7." The "PPP" stands for a Finnish designation too lengthy
and eye glazing to warrant its full reproduction here; the "bike battalions"
were not uncommon in European armies at this time, and, of course, they
did not fight on bicycles but merely used them for transportation. PPP-7,
by this time, had traded its useless two-wheelers for skis, although photos
of the Tolvajärvi campaign indicate that at least they rode to the front on
wheels, before the snow got too deep.

A shaky patchwork force to begin with, Task Force R suffered as well
from the absence of a strong hand at the helm. The "R" himself, Lieutenant
Colonel Räsänen, seems to have been stunned by the crisis pitch of the whole
tactical situation, a series of interlocking threats that must have looked, both
on the map and on the ground itself, quite overwhelming. Räsänen lost
his grip on things about twenty-four hours after the fighting started. The
situation was one that demanded vigorous personal example, and frontline

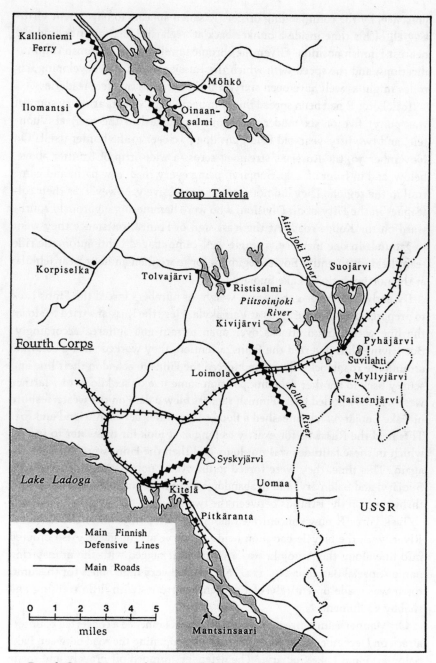

Kallioniemi
Ferry

Möhkö

Ilomantsi

Oinaan-
salmi

Group Talvela

Aittojoki River

Korpiselka

Tolvajärvi

Ristisalmi
*Piitsoinjoki
River*

Suojärvi

Kivijärvi

Pyhäjärvi

Fourth Corps

Suvilahti

Loimola

Myllyjärvi

Kollaa River

Naistenjärvi

Syskyjärvi

Lake Ladoga

Uomaa

Kitelä

USSR

Pitkäranta

◆◆◆◆◆◆ Main Finnish
Defensive Lines

Main Roads

0   1   2   3   4   5
miles

Mantsinsaari

6. Fourth Corps Sector and Events at Tolvajärvi and Ilomantsi

presence, by the commanding officer. Räsänen appears to have spent virtually all of his time inside a bunker back at Äglǎjǎrvi, six miles behind the nearest Finnish position. Given the chronic unreliability of Finnish communications, and the speed with which the Russian threat was developing, six miles might as well have been sixty. The defense was in effect leaderless.

Task Force R had been spread thinly to begin with, and its artillery support was puny: five or six modern weapons husbanded in the rear, at Vuontele, and two fifty-year-old field guns dug in closer to the border itself. On November 30, the Russians streamed across a wide strip of frontier above, below, and in front of Lake Suojärvi, using every road, cow path, and game trail in the region. They did not move as aggressively, however, as their colleagues in the Fifty-sixth Division, who were hammering vigorously southward on the Kollaa road. At the least sign of Finnish resistance they went to ground. In one instance, a single well-camouflaged Lahti automatic rifle team held up an entire Soviet regiment for more than an hour near Jehkila, at the northeast tip of Lake Suojärvi.

By early December 1, however, weight of numbers forced the Finns back to prepared delaying positions at Varpakyla. Here the Russians tried to storm the line with frontal attacks over open terrain and suffered accordingly. But having thus diverted the Finns' attention, they worked strong columns around the roadblock's flanks and forced the Finns to abandon their line and scurry back to another delaying position some five or six kilometers farther west. As they pulled back, Finnish sappers blew a dam on the western shore of Lake Suojärvi and unleashed a flood of icy water between friend and foe. This held the Russians for exactly as long as it took for the water to freeze, which in these latitudes was not long, and then the Finns were pushed back again. This time, they were forced to uncover a north-south road between Suojärvi and Salonjärvi and to abandon a stout little roadblock that had been thrown up on the isthmus between the two lakes.

Task Force R now concentrated along the western bank of the Aittojoki River, with the bicycle battalion held in reserve at Äglǎjǎrvi. Also ordered into line along the Aittojoki was a virgin unit tagged with the uninspiring name "Special Battalion No. 112." No one had very high hopes for this unit, for it was made up entirely of rear-echelon troops with little training and shabby equipment.

On Mannerheim's direct order, Task Force R launched a concerted counterattack on December 3, with the objective of reopening the road between Lake Salonjärvi and Lake Suojärvi. The defenders jumped off bravely and made considerable progress; the attack seems to have taken the Russians by surprise. The appearance and deployment of Soviet tanks then worked its usual havoc, stalling the attack in its tracks; at this juncture, with the outcome wavering, a large Soviet force was spotted moving across the ice of Lake Salonjärvi, obviously intending to encircle the Finns battling along the main road. The situation was saved by the 112th Special Battalion, which launched a mettlesome counterattack against this outflanking force, halted it, and even pushed it back into the forest. This vigorous little action allowed the main Finnish force to disengage and withdraw, in surprisingly good order, to the prepared defenses along the western bank of the Aittojoki.

They were not there for long. Before dawn the next morning, December 4, the Russians came against them in great strength in the gloomy darkness. The Aittojoki line held for three hours, during which time the invaders launched repeated and costly frontal attacks.

One such attack finally broke through and erupted into a rear area where the bicycle battalion had established its headquarters. There was chaotic fighting as officers, quartermaster troops, clerks, medics, and walking wounded fought the attackers with side arms, knives, weapons grabbed from the dead. The defense rallied around the battalion commanding officer, a major, whose example steadied the men and brought some coherence to their resistance. He might have been able to stabilize the situation, but he was seriously wounded about midway through the battle. With the telepathic speed peculiar to battlefield rumors, the word spread that he had been killed. That threw the impromptu defensive perimeter into disorder, and rumors quickly traveled to the Aittojoki positions that there were Russians running wild in the rear. That did it: the Aittojoki line caved in, and Task Force R withdrew in disorder. This time, Räsänen's headquarters retreated all the way back to Tolvajärvi, arriving there about noon.

At Äglajärvi lay strong natural defenses; there the weary men of Task Force R tried to make a stand. They had regrouped and dug in by the morning of December 5. Spurred on by angry signals from Mannerheim, Räsänen's staff formulated a risky and overly ambitious plan: they positioned the bicycle battalion forward, in a rather exposed position, and braced it on the flanks and rear with Special Battalion No. 112. These two units were expected to absorb the Russian attack and hold it in place while the rest of Task Force R, now being assembled out of sight in the dense forests north of the road, pounced suddenly on the Russians' flank.

It would have been a sound plan for a force that was rested, well led, and graced with good communications. But the strength and fury of the Russian assault undid the entire scheme; the bicycle battalion broke under the pressure in a quarter hour. The irony of the situation was that, during that period of time, the Russians were so embroiled breaking through PPP-7 that a sudden attack from the woods on their right would have struck them like an avalanche. The reasons why the maneuver was not started are unclear: Räsänen may have issued orders that never got through, or he may have lost his nerve and either canceled them or never issued them at all.

A general retirement was ordered, and this time it was conducted in some order, thanks to a stubborn rearguard action fought by Special Battalion No. 112—fast becoming the fire brigade unit of the whole front. The Finns were now close to Tolvajärvi itself. They had been battered for nearly a week by superior forces, they had been overrun time after time by tanks without being able to defend themselves effectively, and they had been shelled heavily every single day without being able to reply with anything more than museum pieces. When not in combat they were marching or digging. They were exhausted, hungry, cold, scared, depressed, and whipped. Räsänen felt that he had no choice but to signal headquarters that his men were beyond the point where they could be counted as effective troops.

Mannerheim had already reached that conclusion, not just about the Tolvajärvi road, but about the whole Suojärvi front in general. The same day he had ordered Task Force R to retake the ground east of the Aittojoki, he had also ordered a general counterattack up the Kollaa road, against the Fifty-sixth Division, with the objective of recapturing the railroad station at Suvilahti. This operation, too, had failed, and the Russians were now dangerously close to the Kollaa River line.

The momentum clearly belonged to the enemy. Up on the Tolvajärvi axis, the Finns had retreated under fire for a distance of almost forty miles. The men's nerves were frayed: there were instances of Finnish troops firing on each other, and units that had taken to their heels at the sight of Russian tanks now ran away at the mere rumor of tanks. By the end of the war's first week, the enemy had covered without undue difficulty one-half of the distance to the rail junction at Värtsilä. If the Russians took that city, the entire Finnish front in Ladoga-Karelia would collapse, and the Mannerheim Line itself would then be open to attack from the rear.

Mannerheim had reserves, of course, and the main function of strategic reserves is to counter such unforeseen threats. His problem lay in the size, the multiplicity, and the far-flung disposition of these Soviet thrusts. Once his two reserve divisions had been committed, there was nothing else left; he could not afford to make a mistake. His original strategy had called for husbanding all the reserves and then using them as a single powerful instrument on the Isthmus, where, in his opinion, the war would either be won or lost.

Now he was forced to parcel out smaller batches of men to various flashpoints in the wilderness north of Lake Ladoga. Even if those reinforcements could turn the tide in every battle to which they were committed, those victories could not, in and of themselves, alter very much the odds against them on the Isthmus. But the potential danger from those invading columns, should they penetrate the wilderness zone and spread out through Finland's internal communications, was too great to be ignored. Moreover, the threat was immediate in nature, while the Isthmus situation was still fluid, still developing.

In reserve, Mannerheim had the Sixth Division at Luumäki in southern Finland and the Ninth Division encamped at Oulu, both understrength and not yet fully equipped. He could also draw upon a few battalions of reservists, sketchily trained and lightly armed, and nine battalions of quartermaster troops who had recently been earmarked as combat reserves—there being not enough quartermastering to do, thanks to all the shortages of clothing and equipment. They were thoroughly unprepared for a combat role.

Nevertheless, it was time to make the hard decisions, and Mannerheim acted decisively: on December 4, he ordered JR-25, of the Ninth Division, to entrain for Kuhmo, to serve there as the nucleus for a newly formed brigade. He dispatched JR-27 toward Suomussalmi on December 7. The third and last remaining part of the Ninth Division, JR-26, had already been deployed on the Isthmus.

On December 5, JR-16 of the Sixth Division was placed under Mannerheim's personal command and sent to Tolvajärvi, to put some backbone into the crumbling defenses there and, it was hoped, act as the vanguard for a counterattack. JR-17 and JR-19 were sent to the Isthmus, where they joined the scratch units already feverishly constructing an "intermediate" and a "final" line of fortifications behind the Mannerheim Line.

Having made these decisions, Mannerheim took comfort from the fact that the Soviet columns north of Ladoga were isolated and unable to support one another. If they could be destroyed quickly, most of those precious reserves might be redeployed to the Isthmus before the new year. Mannerheim was taking a bold, calculated risk. Given field commanders of sufficient aggressiveness and imagination, it just might work.

The Marshal was fortunate enough to have such officers. First, he cleared out some dead wood by sacking the commander of Fourth Corps, Major General Heiskanen. To replace him he brought in one of his best officers, Major General Woldemar Hägglund. An alumnus of the 1918 class of the Twenty-seventh Jaegers, Hägglund was a Finn of the dark, stocky type—touched, as it were, with the Mongol brush. Hägglund proved a good choice: with two divisions and a far-flung array of hodgepodge outfits, he would successfully check, and fight to a standstill, an eventual total of ten Russian divisions.

In Colonel Paavo Talvela, Mannerheim would find his strong right arm on the battlefield itself. A battalion commander during the civil war, Talvela had also led a regiment of border guards during the uneasy years following independence. He was a success in civilian life as well, serving as vice president of the national film company and president of the State Liquor Board.

It happened that during the civil war Talvela had led troops in the Ladoga-Karelia region; he knew that landscape intimately. Later he had war-gamed extensively over maps of that area during his stint at the Finnish War College, where he had graduated at the top of his class. On the day that Suojärvi fell, Talvela went to Mannerheim and requested that he be given a combat command in that threatened sector. He also begged Mannerheim to release to him a regiment of the Sixth Division, JR-16, whose commander, Aaro Pajari, was both a friend and another respected veteran of civil war battles in that area.

Mannerheim was not yet ready to make that decision, but in the next twenty-four hours the situation at the Tolvajärvi front deteriorated badly. Task Force R's counterattack came to grief, the defensive line along the Aittojoki crumbled, and on December 5, Ägläjärvi fell to the Russians, putting them halfway between the border and their objective, the railhead at Värtsilä. North of Tolvajärvi, the Russian 155th Division was making steady progress in its drive on Ilomantsi. If Ilomantsi fell, the enemy would have a clear route to Korpiselka, twenty-five miles to the south. And if Korpiselka fell, all the Finnish troops around Tolvajärvi would be cut off. The key to these campaigns was the possession of roads, and the Russians were closing in on too many sensitive arteries.

Mannerheim decided to wait no longer. He summoned Talvela back on the evening of December 5 and sent out the orders to shift regiment JR-16 from Oulu to Värtsilä; a single artillery battery was also earmarked for additional support. Talvela arrived at Mannerheim's headquarters in Mikkeli on Finnish Independence Day, December 6, at about 4:00 A.M. Mannerheim was up; indeed, he was in full dress uniform.

He explained the situation to Talvela, outlining the failures and frustrations of the past forty-eight hours. In his opinion, the threat was most dangerous in the Tolvajärvi/Ilomantsi sector, although things were still chancy between Ladoga and Suvilahti, where Fourth Corps was trying to cope with developments there. What had begun as a single eruptive thrust had now shaped up into two discrete campaigns: the one on Fourth Corps's northern flank, along the road from Suvilahti to Kollaa, and the one that had now reached crisis condition on the roads to Tolvajärvi and Ilomantsi. Mannerheim had therefore decided to detach all the troops on that front from Fourth Corps and make that sector operationally independent, its commander reporting directly to Mannerheim's headquarters. All Finnish troops in the Tolvajärvi/Ilomantsi sector would henceforth be known as "Group Talvela."

Now that Talvela had been put in command, Mannerheim listed his objectives: halt the enemy drives on Tolvajärvi and Ilomantsi, throw them back, and recapture Suojärvi's road network, cutting off the supplies of the southern Russian column, on the Kollaa road. Even when all possible reinforcements arrived, Talvela would still have less than one-half the known manpower of his opponents, no armor whatsoever, no air support except for reconnaissance flights, and so few mortars and guns that the disparity in firepower was, on the face of it, quite absurd. Even so, Talvela was ready and eager to give it a try.

The Marshal had picked his man well. Paavo Talvela was another veteran of the legendary Twenty-seventh Jaegers and had first seen action as an ardent young patriot on the Russian front in 1917. He volunteered for the Jaeger program in Germany and returned to Finland with that unit in 1918. During the civil war campaigns, he rose to the rank of major. During the republic's early years, Talvela had been politically active, working tirelessly to consolidate the influence of the clique of ex-Jaeger officers in opposition to the anti-German senior officers. Promoted to colonel in 1928 at the relatively young age of thirty-one, he resigned his commission two years later as a political gesture. He held several executive positions in civilian life, with considerable success, but he remained keenly concerned with matters of national defense. He was also one of the few men to become personally close to Mannerheim himself and visited the Marshal numerous times at his private home, a sure sign of high favor. Mannerheim had his failings as a general, though fewer than many more famous commanders one could name, but bad judgment of men was not one of them. In Talvela he saw a man who could stabilize a seemingly impossible situation: fiercely patriotic, energetic, imbued with boldness and resolution, physically tough, Talvela was an imaginative tactician and was thoroughly familiar with the terrain his forces would be operating in.

Talvela's first action was to telephone Pajari, who had reached Värtsilä with his troops on December 6. Drive to Tolvajärvi, Talvela ordered him, find out what was going on up there, then drive back to Värtsilä, where Talvela would meet him late that night. Pajari moved fast: he arrived on the Tolvajärvi front by car at about 10:00 P.M. He spoke to the commanders on the spot, interviewed a random sampling of their men, encouraging them to speak freely, studied the ground, scanned the latest intelligence reports on the enemy's strength and intentions, then left. He had seen all he needed to see.

He met with Talvela in Värtsilä at about 3:00 A.M. His situation report was grim: the defenders of Tolvajärvi, he told Talvela, were right on the edge; they were physically exhausted, and discipline was being maintained only by a thread. One more Russian push would probably snap that thread. These men had been retreating, or engaging in uniformly futile delaying actions, for a week, pounded by artillery they could not reply to and overrun by tanks they could oppose only with machine guns and hand grenades. The enemy, the Russian 139th Division, was well led and evidenced a high degree of training and tactical cohesion. Time and time again they had executed bold flanking attacks, unhinging the Finns' defensive positions.

Furthermore, the weather had not been in the Finns' favor: snowfall had been both light and spotty, which meant that the off-road snowdrifts were not yet large enough to seriously hamper Russian infantry, and the ground covering was not yet deep enough for the Finns to make full use of their ski mobility. In terms of manpower, the odds against Group Talvela were something like five to one. The Russians' superiority in artillery was overwhelming, and of course they enjoyed an absolute monopoly on armor. To halt such an attack, Pajari concluded, a near miracle would be needed. To wrest the initiative from the Russians and actually throw them back seemed beyond the realm of the possible.

Talvela also had to be concerned about the secondary threat at Ilomantsi. There the Russian 155th Division had rolled unchecked in a southwesterly direction until it was only ten miles or so from Ilomantsi. A ragtag force amounting to two Finnish battalions was delaying them as best it could, but the only thing that really kept the enemy from smashing through and taking the Tolvajärvi positions from the rear was the lack of aggressiveness being shown by the 155th Division's commander, General Gusevski. As long as there was no sudden eruption of Russian activity, however, Talvela felt he could concentrate his attention on Tolvajärvi.

The first thing he had to do was stop the disintegration of the defenders. The terrain on the western shore of Lake Tolvajärvi was well suited for defensive action, and it was there, Talvela decided, that the Finns should turn and make their stand. He sent Pajari back to the front armed with full authority to take charge. Pajari arrived at dusk on December 7 and relieved Lieutenant Colonel Räsänen of his command.

It was almost too late. In the brief period of time since Pajari's first nocturnal inspection, the Tolvajärvi front had crumbled. The sorely tried PPP-7, for example, had retreated five miles since daylight from its positions at Ristisalmi, on the eastern shore of Lake Ala Tolvajärvi, to Lake Hirvasjärvi, north of Lake Tolvajärvi.

On the affirmative side, a second battery of artillery had arrived on December 6, and two more were known to be en route. Fourth Corps was sending a fresh battalion from its reserves (ErP-9; "Er" standing for "independent" or "detached"). Most heartening of all was the fact that Pajari's own regiment, JR-16, began to reach the Tolvajärvi front on December 7.

That unit's first battalion (1/JR-16) arrived at the front early that morning and at once dug in to the north and west of a bridge that spanned the narrows between Lakes Tolvajärvi and Taivaljärvi, a location known as Kivisalmi. The Third Battalion (3/JR-16) arrived later and took up defensive positions along the western shores of Tolvajärvi and Hirvasjärvi. Talvela himself arrived late in the day and immediately undertook a personal reconnaissance.

What he saw was not encouraging. Before the First Battalion had finished digging in at Kivisalmi, it had been hit hard and had abandoned its positions in a state of panic. Some of its men fled as far west as Korpiselka before regaining control of themselves. The resultant gap in Finnish lines allowed the enemy to gain control of Kottisaari Island, as well as a tactically important peninsula known as Hirvasharju, a long narrow finger of land that extended to the northwest and split Lake Hirvasjärvi off from Lake Tolvajärvi. Located there was a newly built two-story tourist hotel, constructed chalet-style with its second floor overhanging the first. The marvelous view it afforded of the lakes and their surrounding hills, impressive enough to warrant such a tourist facility, was to prove of inestimable value to the Russians in the days to come. Now they truly held the high ground. The commander of the Russian 609th Regiment inspected the captured building, savored its qualities as both an observation post and a ready-made bunker, and promptly turned it into his own headquarters.

The Finns would pay a heavy price for the ground they lost on this day. Talvela arrived on the scene in time to try personally to rally some of the fleeing men of 1/JR-16, but they were too dispersed for his efforts to make much difference. The panic simply ran its course until the fleeing men grew ashamed of themselves and drifted back to the fold.

Some of the panic-stricken men of 1/JR-16 ran through, and almost infected, the arriving formations of 3/JR-16, under personal command of Lieutenant Colonel Pajari. Pajari did what officers are supposed to do in such situations: he sauntered casually along the line his men had been fortifying, admonishing them to hang on and do their duty. His calmness, his firm but reasonable tone of voice, kept the panic from spreading to his own men, and for the moment they appeared steady enough.

In truth, however, Pajari had some basis for misgivings about this unit. The Third Battalion of JR-16 was comprised almost entirely of working-class men from the factories of Tampere, an industrial city that was in 1939, as it had been in 1918, a center of left-wing political power. And in 1933, during celebrations marking the fifteenth anniversary of Tampere's capture by the Whites, Pajari had been involved in an incident. On that occasion, some of the local Social Democrats had hoisted red flags underneath the Finnish colors to protest a ceremony that in their opinion commemorated the crushing of a genuinely spontaneous workers' uprising. Pajari had personally organized and led a force of 200 Civic Guardsmen, mostly officers and noncoms who were by all accounts unarmed, to rip down the red banners.

In the weeks of press attention that followed the incident, working-class resentment focused on Pajari, and a lot of unpleasant old wounds were reopened in the Tampere area. Memories of that incident certainly loomed large in Pajari's mind as he paced the rows of freshly dug foxholes near Tolvajärvi, trying to set an example for soldiers, at least a few of whom might have wanted him dead only five short years ago. In any event, the Third Battalion stood firm throughout the day, aided by the fact that the enemy, no doubt fortunately, contented itself with consolidating its gains on the far shore of Tolvajärvi. Through field glasses, Pajari could see the Russians industriously fortifying the tourist hotel.

By the time Talvela conferred with Pajari early that night, the situation appeared to have stabilized. Both men had seen enough to know that the virus of defeat was spreading throughout their entire force, veterans and replacements alike. They agreed that some sort of dramatic action was necessary to curb the panic, regain some measure of initiative, and prove to the men that the Russians could be beaten.

Talvela formulated a bold scheme for a raid-in-strength against a sensitive position behind enemy lines, across the ice of Lake Tolvajärvi and against one of the Russian units known to have bivouacked along the road that led to Ägläjärvi. Talvela wanted to lead the attack himself, but his officers talked him out of it. Pajari volunteered, in spite of the fact that he had already put in a full day.

The raiders would be drawn from Pajari's own JR-16, specifically from its Second Battalion, which had passed a quiet day in reserve. Two companies set out just before midnight, moving across the ice south of Kottisaari Island. A feint attack, to draw the Russians' attention in the opposite direction, was launched about an hour later against Kottisaari itself. But the unit that mounted the attack was the already shaky Seventh Bicycle Battalion, and when its commander, a major named Ericsson, was killed early in the skirmishing (the second battalion commander to die in five days), the attack faltered, and PPP-7 soon faded back to the Finnish side of the lake.

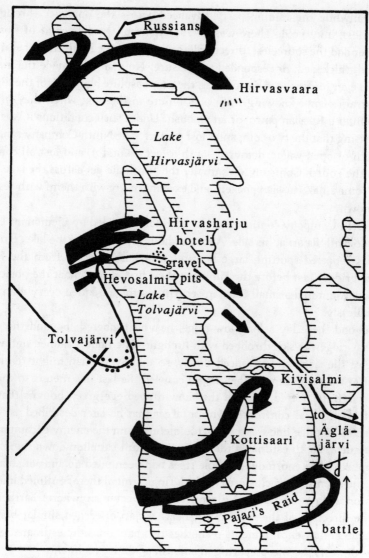

7. Pajari's Raid and Climactic Battle of Tolvajärvi Campaign

Meanwhile the raiding party advanced across the open ice through a moonless, inky void. There was no sound except the soft chuff of skis on powder and the sourceless, directionless whisper of the ice itself as it shifted, settled, thickened, or responded to pressure. No man who made the march would ever forget the eerie stillness, the near absolute blackness of the night, the strain of not knowing from one minute to the next when they might encounter a Russian patrol or an ambush. Under such conditions it was not surprising that the two companies lost contact. The Ninth Company ran into a patch of open water, detoured south to get around it, and lost all contact with the Fourth Company. Eventually the Ninth did get across the lake, ran into some small Russian pockets, and exchanged fire with them, with results unknown.

Fourth Company continued on its original route, led by Lieutenant Urho Isotalo, with Pajari at his side. About an hour after crossing the lake, Finnish scouts reported spotting large bonfires in a gully not far from the Kivisalmi bridge. Just before the Finns got their first clear look at the objective, they encountered a small Russian security patrol and killed every man in it soundlessly.

Beyond there lay a long low ridge, heavily timbered; beyond the crest of that ridge the sky throbbed with firelight. The raiders fanned out at the base of the ridge and advanced slowly, so that every man might reach the crest at the same time. When Pajari crawled the last few meters to the top and carefully peered through the snow-draped evergreen boughs that hid his force, he was confronted with a target that he later described as "delicious." The ridge line was a scant 100 meters from the enemy encampment. At a guess, Pajari estimated that there was a full battalion down there. The campfires were enormous—whole trees had been piled up and set ablaze—and the enemy stood clustered in thick rings around them, outlined like targets on a shooting range. No sentries were visible anywhere. Farther off, in the direction of the road to Äglä järvi, Pajari discerned similar bonfires around similar encampments—another two battalions, he estimated. With one company, he was preparing to ambush an entire regiment.

It took time to spread the ambush out properly along the ridge line, and while Pajari's men were getting settled, they heard strong volumes of fire over their left shoulders—the feint attack on Kottisaari Island. Using this noise as cover, the company quickly finished taking its positions. The Russian battalion below them merely looked up at the sound of the distant firing, shrugged, and returned to their bonfires.

By 2:00 A.M. 140 riflemen and sixteen automatic weapons were spread out in a semicircle along the ridge crest, under good concealment in the snow and brush. Every man had his targets lined up in advance. Pajari himself fired the first shot as a signal, and the ridge line on either side of him crashed and flamed as volley after volley smote the fire-lit gully. The effect on the enemy was instantaneous. So great was the shock of the ambush that Pajari, writing about the battle later, could not recall seeing or hearing a single shot fired back at them. After three or four minutes' firing time, there were no more standing targets; the dead lay in heaped-up rings around their campfires.

The Russian units encamped farther along the road responded with wild outbursts of fire in all directions, while Pajari stealthily led his men out through a gully quite close to one of the encampments, in order to confuse any pursuers. From the volumes of fire and the patterns of muzzle flashes, it was obvious that two of the Russian battalions had gotten locked into a fire-fight with each other; they were still exchanging fire when the Finns passed out of earshot, two hours later.

The return march was more tiring and more nerve-racking than the approach. The excitement of the ambush was wearing off. And half way back to Finnish lines, Pajari collapsed and had to be transported back in an improvised litter—the only Finnish casualty of the raid. Pajari, it turned out, had a serious heart condition; he had known about it for some time, yet he had volunteered to lead the raid anyway. Word of the raid's success, the first Finnish victory anywhere on the crisis-plagued Fourth Corps front, spread quickly and had a bracing effect on the defenders' spirits. The Russians could not only be beaten, they could be made fools of. The enemy seemed to have been stung badly by the raid, too, for it attempted no large-scale actions for the next two days, December 9 and 10.

Still, the front was not exactly quiet. Snipers were active on both sides, patrols clashed in the deep woods, and there were artillery duels: small packets of fire from the Finns, sudden massive eruptions from the well-stocked Soviet batteries. One such barrage drove Pajari's raiders out of the farm buildings where they had been resting after their nocturnal exertions.

With things simmering rather than boiling at the Tolvajärvi front, Talvela decided to absent himself long enough for a quick inspection of the secondary front at Ilomantsi, some twenty-five miles to the northwest. Up there, the enemy 155th Division was still advancing, albeit at a slow pace, and it was still powerful. A sudden breakthrough here would imperil the big counterattack Talvela was already planning at Tolvajärvi.

The situation he found at Ilomantsi was this: by December 7, the Russians had reached a point only twelve miles from the Ilomantsi-Korpiselka road junction. The Finns had opposed them from a dominant terrain feature called Möhkö Hill. Talvela had ordered Möhkö held at all costs, and its weary defenders, Battalion ErP-11, under Major Nikoskelainen, had managed to hang on, repulsing several attacks before finally being forced to withdraw to Oinaansalmi on December 9.

All Finnish forces in the Ilomantsi sector were now grouped under the command of Colonel Per Ekholm, another Twenty-seventh Jaeger veteran who had once been Talvela's superior officer during his stint with the Civic Guard. Designated "Task Force E," this group was now at peak strength: four battalions, two of whom, however, were poorly trained ex-quartermaster troops. On December 8, the Ilomantsi defenders received their first new "artillery support": a single battery of mortars. A day and a half later, Task Force E received a battery of real artillery, such as it was: two old "French 75s," one of which was later discovered to be inoperable. Add these new weapons to the four turn-of-the-century pieces the Finns already possessed, and Ekholm now had a handful of 81 mm. mortars and five light field guns, the most modern of which barely qualified as "obsolescent," to wage war against a full division armed with at least forty modern cannon.

Nevertheless, Ekholm turned on the Russians and struck them hard. One of his patrols discovered an understrength enemy battalion, about 350 men, wandering behind the Finnish left flank about five miles northeast of Ilomantsi, near a bog called Tetrilampi. Ekholm organized a strike force, ordered that it be heavily equipped with automatic weapons, and quickly surrounded the curiously apathetic enemy force. He laid an ambush during the last hours of darkness, and at first light the Finns opened a murderous cross fire. The Russian force was annihilated; not a single man escaped. To the commander of the 155th Division, it seemed as though the forest had simply swallowed up one of his battalions. Russian tactics, from that day on, became noticeably more cautious.

Talvela thought the omens looked good. On both fronts his men had stopped retreating and had struck the invader with stinging jabs. The effect of those actions had been to throw the Russians off balance and slow them down. Now, Talvela believed, was the time to strike, with concerted, all-out attacks on both fronts. He completed his plans on December 10, briefed his officers, and selected December 11 as the time to attack.

But the Russians, at least on the Tolvajärvi front, were not as passive as they seemed, and before Talvela could launch his counterattack on the eleventh, he suffered a nasty surprise on his own left flank. An entire Soviet battalion had marched, undetected, through the tree-choked wilderness north of Lake Tolvajärvi. Without any warning, they erupted from the trees and fell upon Pajari's only supply line, the road to Korpiselka, at a point about two miles northwest of Tolvajärvi village.

There were no defensive works here, and few combat troops either, just field kitchens, some artillery personnel, quartermaster and medical units, and the headquarters company of JR-16. At about 11:00 P.M. on the night of December 10–11, the Russian battalion struck from the forest. The Finns were taken completely by surprise and by all rights should have been routed from the field in short order.

But something strange happened. The first target overrun by the enemy raiders was a field kitchen where large vats of sausage soup were simmering. After scattering the handful of panic-stricken cooks who stood in their way, the attackers caught a whiff of the soup and the majority of them paused and began to eat. The momentum of their original attack, which had been devastating, vanished, and the startled Finns received a priceless interval of time in which to recover.

And recover they did, rather quickly. As chance would have it, Colonel Pajari himself happened to be in the vicinity when the Russians struck. He put together a makeshift force of some 100 cooks, clerks, medics, supply sergeants, and artillerists and led them personally in a vigorous counterattack. He controlled his improvised company by the simple expedient of shouting orders in a fierce parade-ground voice and limiting them to five or six words. What followed, an engagement promptly dubbed the "Sausage War" by the Finns, was one of the few recorded instances of bayonet fighting in the Winter War. It was close, brutal, and without mercy.

Two of Pajari's men formed a hunter-killer team: one man carried a powerful flashlight, the other a Suomi submachine gun. These two prowled the woods, locating small isolated groups of Russians or individual stragglers. When the prey was spotted, the light was switched on, and the Russians invariably froze like deer, just for an instant, and that instant was all that the Suomi gunner, Sergeant Miinalainen, needed. With short bursts of 9 mm. slugs, he cut down man after man.

While the hand-to-hand melee was raging, two hastily summoned companies of frontline troops arrived and attacked the Russians from the east. By 4:00 A.M. the Russians were in full retreat, and by dawn the fighting had petered out entirely. Exact Russian casualties were hard to estimate, for many men died unseen and uncounted in the forest. Out of the entire battalion, only a few dozen men are known to have made it back to Russian lines. Daylight revealed at least 100 frozen corpses strewn around the bullet-riddled soup pots of the field kitchen, some with hunks of sausage still stuck to their gray lips.

During the height of the fighting a war cry was sounded from Finnish lips that had not been heard since the Thirty Years' War: "Hakkaa Päälle!" It translates literally as "Cut them down!" but has the more vicious connotation of "No quarter!"

While the "Sausage War" was raging in the rear, another battle erupted on the southern flank. A Russian battalion moved out from Kottisaari Island across the ice, evidently hoping to fall on Tolvajärvi village from the south. The Finns had listening posts out on the ice, and the Russian move was spotted. Word was passed to Lieutenant Eero Kivela, whose company, a part of JR-16, was closest. Leaving two platoons and his heavy machine guns to guard the village, Lieutenant Kivela outflanked the outflankers with three rifle platoons. At first light, the Russians were just across the lake, still in the open. Kivela's men picked their targets and killed scores with their first volley. The Russians panicked and fled back across the open ice, where they made superb targets. Kivela's men kept firing until the last of them had vanished into the predawn gloom. About 200 Russians lay dead on the ice. Kivela's men helped themselves to sixteen light machine guns before retiring.

There were several other, less threatening, Russian probes during the first half of December 11, all successfully repelled, and by the time the shooting had died down, so many Finnish troops had been in firefights that Pajari recommended to Talvela that the counteroffensive be postponed for twenty-four hours, so that everyone could get his wind back. Talvela agreed. On the whole, the actions of December 10–11 had gone in favor of the Finns, and it did not seem prudent to launch a do-or-die counterattack with worn-out men, however much improved their morale might seem.

Talvela's plan for the counterattack of December 12 also took into consideration the fact that many of Pajari's men were still tired. The initial operations were therefore detailed to the freshest units: battalion ErP-9 and two companies of First Battalion, JR-16. Talvela thought that if these fresh troops could only unlock the Russian defenses, then the other units could be put into motion to add weight and flexibility to the attack. This two-tiered tactic was risky, and only a commander with absolute faith in his men could have developed such a plan with any realistic hope of success.

This was the plan: one strong pincer would cross the northern end of Lake Hirvasjärvi, then pivot to the southeast and strike the Hirvasharju peninsula from the rear. It was there, on the high ground surrounding the new tourist hotel, that the enemy had centered his strongest defenses. Only when he was sure that this northern pincer had made some progress would Pajari lead a frontal assault on the peninsula. In addition to the troops he had originally brought with him, Pajari was able to deploy some reinforcements that had just arrived on the Tolvajärvi front: one company from JR-37 and the Tenth Independent Battalion (ErP-10). At the same time the northern attack went in, a southern pincer comprised of two companies of ErP-112 would also assault Kottisaari Island. If the high ground on Kottisaari were taken, the

Russians' one and only supply line, the road over the Kivisalmi bridge, could be brought under fire. Talvela hoped that the two initial northern-flank/southern-flank attacks would cause the enemy to weaken its center, perhaps commit its reserves. If Talvela's timing and luck were good, he could then hit the tourist-hotel sector with some hope of success. Like most such elaborate battlefield plans, however, this one survived intact for only a few minutes.

Plans were also laid for the counterattack up at Ilomantsi. On December 11 the Russians had attacked at Oinaansalmi and at the ferry crossing at Kallioniemi and had been thrown back at both places, with moderate casualties. At the former location, Ekholm's men had knocked out two Red tanks with Molotov Cocktails and satchel charges; at the ferry, the Russians left 134 dead on the ice. The plan for December 12 called for three of Ekholm's battalions to tackle the Russians at Möhkö, both from flanks and frontally, while his fourth battalion remained on the defensive at the ferry crossing.

December 12, then, was to be the day of decision for both sectors of Group Talvela's front. Talvela had done well since his arrival. He had imparted vigor and resolve to the defense, and his two strong right arms, Ekholm and Pajari, had scored impressive tactical victories against isolated enemy detachments. But the bulk of both Russian divisions remained intact and very strong; the Finns had purchased their victories so far at a considerable cost in men and a much higher cost in energy. The odds remained desperately stacked against them. It is one thing to defend, or even to counterattack from within a defensive context, and another thing altogether to launch a complex offensive against an enemy with a distinct advantage in numbers and a crushing advantage in firepower. That enemy, moreover, was well dug in, was well supplied with ammunition, and had a tradition of being much tougher on the defensive than in the attack. But the Finnish Army believed in intangibles, and on December 12, that faith, together with the courage, resilience, and initiative of a handful of officers and men, would be just barely enough to tip the scales.

Pajari's northern pincer maneuver went wrong almost from the beginning. Major Malkamäki's two companies of JR-16 (Second and Third companies) were hampered by foot-deep snowdrifts and did not reach their jumping-off points until well after daylight, thus losing all hope of tactical surprise. Worse, while the Finns thought they were sneaking up on the Russians, two battalions from the Russian 718th Regiment were doing the same thing to the Finns, from the opposite direction. The result was a frantic meeting engagement that took both sides by surprise. Malkamäki's Third Company, on the extreme Finnish left, took the full impact of this encounter and was badly knocked about by Russian machine-gun fire. Most of that

company withdrew, and some of its men did not stop until they got as far
as the Tolvajärvi road. The Second Company slipped out of the meeting
engagement and did manage to get across the lake and execute a southward
turn, but was stopped cold at about 11:00 A.M. when it ran into heavy fire.
It lost contact with the unit on its right flank, ErP-9, at about the same time.

Contact was lost because one company of ErP-9 had gotten mangled in
the meeting engagement and had retreated all the way back to Tolvajärvi
village by 10:30. Two companies of ErP-9 did manage to join 2/JR-16 at
the Hirvasvaara ridge, about a half hour after that company had gone to
ground. Even with three companies, the Finns at Hirvasvaara could make
no progress. They were drawing heavy Russian fire from two directions. At
noon Major Malkamäki judged the whole venture to be hopeless and ordered
a withdrawal. Most of the Finns then executed a wide-swinging retreat to
the northwest, around the upper end of Lake Hirvasjärvi. Part of 2/JR-16
also withdrew at this time, but part of it, perhaps 100 men or so, did not and
stayed dug in at Hirvasvaara. Although they were unable to advance any
farther, they kept fighting.

Whether this determined little stand was the result of platoon-level initiative, or whether these soldiers simply didn't get the word to pull out, is
not clear. What is clear is that by staying at Hirvasvaara, they tied down a
large number of Red troops who otherwise would have been free to oppose
Pajari's attack on the peninsula. Their contribution to the outcome of the
battle was far out of proportion to the number of men involved.

While the Finn's northern pincer was coming to grief, the southern pincer, the assault on Kottisaari Island, was not faring a whole lot better. Two
companies of ErP-112 attacked the southern end of the island at 8:00 A.M.,
supported by heavy machine guns and three or four pieces of artillery. Elements of ErP-112 penetrated as far as some rocky islets near the Kivisalmi
bridge but were forced back shortly after noon because their supporting
company (9/JR-16) never showed up. That happened because regimental
headquarters never managed to give its commander a jumping-off time; by
the time he got his orders, the designated hour was long past and he had to
wait for further instructions. Once again the lack of reliable field radios had
sabotaged a Finnish operation.

Pajari's main thrust, against the Russian center, also fared poorly at the
start. The initial attack was assigned to the Second Battalion of JR-16, but
Pajari did not wish to send his men against fortified positions over open
ground without artillery support, and the guns didn't get into position until
two hours after they were supposed to. When they finally did open fire, the

effect was so paltry that Pajari cursed himself for having bothered to wait for them.

Throughout the bitter struggle for the Hirvasharju peninsula, the Finns tried, with some success, to compensate for their lack of artillery support by employing their Maxim heavy machine guns *as* light artillery. Finnish machine-gun teams were trained to advance in close coordination with the infantry and often deployed their weapons to engage specific targets with pinpoint fire at dangerously close ranges. Since the weapons, with full water jacket, weighed more than forty pounds even without a tripod, it took strong men as well as brave ones to handle this job in combat. Casualties among Finnish machine gunners were high in every offensive engagement. Time and time again during the blistering fight around the hotel, the Finns used their Maxims the way a better-equipped army would use bazookas, grenade launchers, or light mortars. This tactic provided yet another example of the Finns making the most of their limited resources, but it was a costly expedient.

The attack went in with two companies abreast. Lieutenant Isotalo led his Second Company (2/JR-16) across the straits on the southern side, with surprisingly light casualties, thanks in part to the enormous volume of fire put out by his supporting machine guns. On the northern side, Sixth Company was not so lucky. Pinned down by intense but wildly inaccurate artillery fire and, more seriously, by much more accurate fire from Russian light automatics, most of its men drifted south out of the worst of it and mingled with the platoons of Fourth Company. Fifth Company, under command of Lieutenant Aarne Heinivaho, attacked somewhat later than the Fourth and Sixth, more or less right into the middle of things. The result was that for a time all three companies were hopelessly intermingled, and command control became difficult.

There was still some momentum behind the Finnish attack, however, and intense firefights erupted all along the peninsula. Several machine-gun squads crossed the straits and began firing in close support of the infantry. First they silenced a number of Russian foxholes and gun pits on the western end of the peninsula, then they began dueling with the Russian heavy MGs that had been galling the infantry from the direction of Hirvasvaara.

As the Finns fought their way forward, the tourist hotel loomed ahead as a dramatic, magnetic objective. Fire blazed from its windows and from the loopholes that had been cut into its thick log walls. The engagement became one of individual efforts, of platoon leaders organizing private little battles, using whatever small forces they could control, friends and strangers alike.

Several platoon leaders were hit. Lieutenant Isotalo was shot in the hand; he paused long enough to have it bandaged, then went forward and took control of his men once more. The worst fighting occurred at a line of gravel pits about 200 yards west of the hill where the hotel loomed. Here the Russians had emplaced ten heavy machine guns and at least as many Degtyarev automatic rifles. The fighting was close and savage, but the Russians gave way first, and the survivors of the gravel-pit line retreated to the hotel.

At this juncture, three Soviet tanks were spotted advancing on the road that led from the hotel to the Hevosalmi straits. The road was so narrow, however, and the terrain on both sides so jagged, that they were compelled to advance slowly and in a single-file line. Pajari had sited his 37 mm. Bofors guns in anticipation of just such a contingency, and all three tanks were destroyed before they could really intervene in the battle.

The men of 2/JR-16 had now fought their way to the foot of the hill leading to the hotel. Disorganized and winded, they were stopped cold by shelling and by withering automatic fire. At noon a general retirement was ordered back to the line of the gravel pits. Once this had been accomplished, the Finns sorted themselves out again into proper companies, platoons, etc. During a brief lull, the Finns were able to grab a smoke, eat, and replenish their ammunition. A mortar platoon also crossed the straits and dug in behind a low ridge west of the gravel pits—just in time, as it happened, to disrupt an attempted Russian counterattack from the direction of the hotel.

While this midday lull was taking place, Pajari received his first hard news about what was happening on his right flank. Predictably it came not by radio but from the lips of an exhausted runner. When he had listened to the man's tale, Pajari knew he could expect no real help from that direction. Reports from the stalled Second Battalion on the peninsula indicated that they had run out of steam: it would be hard to get these men to leave the relative safety of the gravel pits and advance once more into the heavy fire coming from the hotel and the high ground around it. Pajari had no reason to doubt the pessimistic reports he was getting. With his own eyes for the past hour, he had seen the steady flow of wounded men coming back from the peninsula, and he had been dismayed to see the proportion of platoon-level officers and noncoms on the stretchers.

Pajari had now come to the leadership crux of the battle. There was clearly a dangerous threat on his northern flank, for a strong Russian force there had routed one of his companies and blunted the attack of all the others in that pincer. As far as he knew at that moment, there was not a single Finnish soldier on the eastern side of Lake Hirvasjärvi. That part of his plan had become a shambles. And if he had not been hurt as badly on the southern pincers, at Kottisaari, neither had he gained very much ground. The only place where even a partial degree of success had been gained was in the center. So far it didn't look like a propitious day for making a gamble. Pajari had only the most limited reserves, and to achieve anything he would have to commit them all at one point. But where? How serious was the threat up on his northern flank? How realistic were his chances of crashing through a position as strong as the hotel?

While Pajari was mulling over this decision, he received a new message. Contrary to the first reports, there *was* a Finnish force still fighting on the northern flank. There were, it transpired, scattered pockets of Finnish resistance in the woods north of Lake Hirvasjärvi, and the two or three isolated platoons still clinging to their perimeter in the Hirvasvaara area. That news, modest though it was, tipped Pajari's decision. Some portion of his original plan had survived, after all; there was at least enough of a Finnish demonstration on that northern flank to divert some of the enemy's attention to that direction.

Pajari ordered the Third Company of ErP-10 to reinforce the men at the gravel pits, and he sent the Second Company straight across Lake Myllyjärvi to attack the base of the Hirvasharju peninsula, where it had a wishbone configuration, the idea being to increase pressure on the hotel from the northwest.

At 1:30 P.M. the attack against the hotel resumed. It was by far the toughest objective the Finns had yet assaulted. The building was centered atop a sixty-foot hill. Designed chalet-fashion, the bottom story was built of logs and granite walls, and the second story, also massively walled with logs, overhung the first. Its walls had been loopholed and its windows sandbagged. There were rifle pits scattered around the building, and the entire position fairly bristled with machine guns and Degtyarevs. Given a few medium-sized field guns or some reliable air support, the Finns could have sat back and pounded the place to matchsticks in relative comfort. But lacking that kind of firepower, it would be an infantryman's battle, and it would be bloody.

For an hour the fighting seesawed. The Finns fought their way through the Russian foxholes one at a time and hurled grenades through the hotel windows. Sometimes the Russians hurled them back. One Finnish company commander was killed, another badly wounded. What tipped the balance was the timely arrival of Pajari's reserve, Second Company, ErP-10, on the northern arm of the peninsula. As Pajari had planned, this force now brought the hotel under heavy fire from a second direction, forcing the defenders to return fire in two directions at once, and weakening the overall volume of fire.

A few Finns who had managed to get fairly close to the hotel building worked their way to its southern side and began to snipe at the windows from there, thus bringing the position under fire from yet a third direction. To the hotel's defenders, it looked very much as though they were in danger of being surrounded. At first a few, then more, Russians in the vicinity began to give ground and withdraw in the direction of the Kivisalmi bridge. Sensing the letup in resistance, the Finns closed in on the hotel, throwing dozens of grenades into the bottom-floor windows and rapidly silencing all resistance.

The Russians still held the top story, however, and from that vantage point they were firing on everything that moved. Clearly there could be no general Finnish advance as long as the hotel was still holding out. Lieutenant Siukosaari, commanding the Sixth Company, thought that the easiest way to eliminate the problem was simply to pour petrol into the building, torch it, and shoot down any Russians who tried to flee. He was overruled by a major standing nearby, who ordered a more conventional assault. Whether this was done out of squeamishness or out of respect for the hotel itself, which had been a source of intense local pride before the war, is unclear.

In any event, Lieutenant Siukosaari led the attack, armed with a Lahti pistol. In a scene reminiscent of a western movie, he ran head on into a similarly armed Russian officer at the doorway leading to the hotel's kitchen. Both men "slapped leather" at the same time. Lieutenant Siukosaari fired first, at a range of about three feet, then led his men charging into the hotel over the Russian's crumpled body.

Once inside, Siukosaari's men made short work of the second story. They tossed dozens of grenades upstairs, then rushed up the stairway. They found twenty-eight Russians still alive, most of them wounded and none of them in any mood to continue the fight. They also found the corpse of the commander of the 609th Regiment, together with a great many valuable documents that were promptly sent back to the intelligence experts. Of more immediate value were eighteen usable automatic weapons and thousands of rounds to feed them; Lieutenant Siukosaari's platoon instantly doubled its own firepower.

Pajari, meanwhile, had thrown in his last "fresh" unit, Bicycle Battalion PPP-7, again, in hopes of giving even more impetus to the attack. The defense around the hotel had crumbled, and the Finns had enough energy to mop up as far as the Kivisalmi bridge. Pajari ordered them to keep going as far as Ristisalmi, another four miles, but they were too weary to advance another meter beyond Kivisalmi.

December 12 was also the day of decision up at Ilomantsi. The ambitious double-pincers attack on Möhkö, from north and south, failed to accomplish much. Another breakdown in battlefield communications apparently was the main reason for the failure. Up near Kallioniemi, however, the Finns scored a defensive victory by knocking out four more Russian tanks on December 12.

December 13 saw several Soviet infantry probes repulsed at Kallioniemi and a renewed Finnish effort against Möhkö. By day's end it seemed clear that a stalemate had been reached along the whole Ilomantsi front. Task Force Ekholm, though bravely and skillfully led, simply did not have the firepower or manpower to throw the Russians back; and as for the Russians, the 155th Division still did not have any skis, nor did it receive any, until the last few weeks of the war, and it was just about paralyzed. The cold was severe, down to twenty-five degrees below zero, and the snow was more than a foot deep, with more falling every day. Ekholm's men held good defensive ground. As long as weather conditions made deep flanking movements impossible, the Russians would not be able to budge them.

At both Oinaansalmi and Kallionsalmi, position warfare became the norm. Ekholm waged an active defense, however, staging raids and probing attacks throughout the remainder of the war. Once, in mid-December, the Russians tried to slip a battalion around to threaten Finnish communications, and there was a virtual replay of the "Sausage War" incident, with Colonel Ekholm personally rallying a company of clerks, supply officers, and other rear-echelon types and counterattacking vigorously. Although the Ilomantsi front never really became "quiet," it had become quiescent by the end of December, with both sides almost literally frozen in place. If there were no dramatic Finnish victories at Ilomantsi, it could still be said that Ekholm and his men performed their primary task very well: they prevented a Russian breakthrough, guarded the backdoor for the Finns at Tolvajärvi, and thereby contributed mightily if indirectly to Group Talvela's great victory.

On December 13, Battalion PPP-7 advanced as far as Ristisalmi, while the rest of Pajari's weary force took the day off. In retrospect, Pajari regretted this decision. There was plenty of fight left in the Russian 139th, and events proved that the best way to deal with the situation was to launch constant relentless attacks before the enemy had a chance to recover and dig in. Once dug in, the Russians proved themselves to be stubborn fighters, and the Finns always suffered more losses when attacking them under those conditions. After the breather of December 13 Pajari drove his men mercilessly. Some of them hated him for it at the time, but since the war many of those same men have admitted publicly that his tactics were the right ones for the circumstances.

What the Finns did not know on December 14 was that a fresh Russian division had entered the battle. The Seventy-fifth Division, from Eighth Army reserves, had been sent in to replace the badly mauled 139th. Pajari first learned of this ominous development from intelligence reports reaching him on December 16. Aerial reconnaissance from the morning of December 17 confirmed heavy enemy traffic moving in both directions along the Ägläjärvi road. Fresh troops of the Seventy-fifth were moving up and survivors of the 139th withdrawing toward the border. There is some evidence that the spectacle of the retreating 139th, its men half frozen and burned out, burdened with hundreds of wounded, had a marked effect on the morale of the new men moving west.

Pajari's response was to push his men even harder. The attack was resumed on December 14, with ErP-9 as the leading element. Its attack was stopped cold when two Russian tanks appeared, driving back and forth with impunity and firing at will on the Finns, who were pinned against a thin ridge with nothing stronger to throw at the tanks than hand grenades—not even a gasoline bomb. Word of the holdup reached the battalion's sole antitank gun, a mile in the rear. One of its gunners, an enterprising corporal named Mutka, hitched his 37 mm. gun to a big farm horse and moved it to the front lines in true Napoleonic style, himself riding bareback on the animal for part of the distance. Once he reached the front, Mutka unlimbered quickly, drew a bead on the tanks, which were offering themselves as splendid targets, and knocked them both out with three or four shots. The sudden destruction of both tanks had a demoralizing effect on the Red infantry, and the Finns were able to surge forward for about a mile before encountering heavy resistance again, at Metsanvaara ridge.

Talvela was able to send forward about 350 replacements on December 15. Pajari could replace some of his losses, but the fresh troops were over-age reservists, willing enough to fight but sketchily trained and wretchedly armed.

On December 16 the Finns pushed beyond Metsanvaara and made good progress until they ran into a stone wall of resistance at a roadblock just west of Lake Hietajärvi. Dug in there were 200 men from a Russian officer-candidate school: they were young, well trained, physically tough, heavily armed, and fiercely motivated. Survivors of the Tolvajärvi campaign all seem to agree that these were the finest Russian soldiers they faced during the entire affair. Finnish casualties were high; one platoon from the Sixth Company of ErP-9 lost six out of twenty, including its commander, in the first hour of fighting. The defenders stood their ground until killed; only two of the young officers are known to have survived, so intense was the fighting.

Meanwhile, to avoid an incessant series of such engagements, Pajari was trying to outflank the main road. He sent one company from ErP-10 on a wide end run to the south, through Vieksinki, and from that direction its men launched a number of guerrilla strikes against the Russians on the Äglajärvi road. Two companies of ErP-10 performed a symmetrical and complementing maneuver in the north, moving through Ylajärvi, hoping to strike Äglajärvi by surprise from the northwest.

To revive the attack, Talvela gave Pajari operational command of all Finnish reserves in the Tolvajärvi sector on December 17. His order of the day stated the situation plainly: "The last energies of the troops must be used. . . ." A quick check was made to see if any of the overrun Russian armor could be salvaged, but Pajari's ordnance men radioed back to Talvela that the vehicles were "junk" and would have to be reconditioned thoroughly before anyone could use them. Pajari was also promoted, an overdue gesture one might think, to full colonel on December 17.

A new danger faced the Finns on December 18. Soviet tactical air strikes were launched for the first time on this front, with results that were more disturbing than damaging. Pajari's flanking attacks made little dent on the strong Äglajärvi defenses. The one from the north did not achieve surprise and was stopped by a roadblock at Valimaki, a couple of miles above the main Russian perimeter at Äglajärvi. Five miles to the southeast Pajari slipped another unit, ErP-112, through the forest south of the main Russian position and ordered it to cut their supply lines at Pojasvaara. Here, too, the enemy was dug in and seemingly waiting for the Finns. ErP-112 had no artillery support, and by the time it made contact with the enemy its men were exhausted from a forced march through dense forest. After a day of desultory skirmishing, it withdrew.

On December 19 Mannerheim promoted Talvela to major general. Mannerheim was also on the verge of calling off the whole Finnish counteroffensive. The casualty lists were appalling, and he had begun to question whether Talvela's men were capable of much more. Talvela, however, was fired up, and he insisted that his men still had enough drive to break through the Russian defenses and roll them back far enough to stabilize the front. Mannerheim agreed to give him a little more time to try but was ready to call a halt if casualties seemed excessive.

In the predawn darkness of December 20 the Russians made a vigorous sally from the Äglajärvi perimeter, using a battalion of infantry and nine tanks. The leading tank made straight for the Finns' antitank platoon and rammed the first gun it came upon. The formidable Corporal Mutka thereupon closed with the tank, while it was still grinding metal with one of his precious Bofors guns, and blew it up with a satchel charge, blocking the road for the rest of the enemy's armor. When daylight arrived, Mutka bore-sighted his one remaining Bofors gun and hit the last Russian tank in the column, setting it afire. He then worked forward with deadly accuracy, knocking out two more vehicles. The crews of the surviving tanks, seeing what was coming, abandoned their vehicles, which the Finns captured intact and with their motors still running. The Russian attack evaporated. The Finns tried to follow it up with their own attack on Ägläjärvi but were unable to penetrate its defenses.

On this same day, Pajari reached the end of his physical endurance. That a man with a serious heart condition had managed to lead such a battle, and indeed, taken up a gun and fought in it more than once, seems incredible. Talvela ordered him to the rear, and command passed to Lieutenant Colonel Kaarlo Viljanen, yet another of the Finnish officer corps's seemingly inexhaustible supply of Twenty-seventh Jaeger veterans.

Fighting continued on December 21, 22, and 23, without discernible gains but with increasing casualties. Russian air attacks on the Tolvajärvi-Ägläjärvi road grew heavier, but by now the Finns had moved in some light flak batteries to deal with them, and three Russian planes were shot down on the twenty-first alone.

Late on December 21, 2/JR-16 and two companies of ErP-9 attacked Ägläjärvi from the north, while two companies of ErP-10 and all of ErP-112 struck from the south. It was a night attack, and at first it went well. The Finns managed to cross the ice and close on the village without heavy losses. Russian fire, though heavy, was mostly wild. Once inside the village, however, it was another matter. The Russians had fortified every barn, cellar, farmhouse, and outbuilding. Automatic weapons, sited for converging fire, raked every open lane and pasture. Casualties among Finnish platoon leaders and NCOs were heavy. One battalion lost all three of its company commanders. A battalion commander, a middle-aged reservist who had no business being in the middle of such a fight, went berserk, ordered his machine guns to fire on friendly troops, and threatened to shoot any man who disobeyed him. Several Finns were wounded before the man could be restrained and disarmed. When the officer came to his senses and saw what he had done, he went to pieces. He was led from the field, sobbing and wailing.

Each building had to be reduced as a separate strong point. "The houses were shot full of holes like sieves," remembered one participant.* The Finns grenaded each building, but even the wounded Russians kept fighting. There were vicious firefights inside the riddled buildings, nasty close-up work with pistols, grenades, bayonets. One detachment of Finns managed to set up a

*Chew, 55.

roadblock west of the village and cut it off from reinforcement. Finally, the northern arm of the attack, ErP-10 and ErP-112, entered the village from a new direction. The fighting now became so close that neither side could use its mortars. It was simply a matter of who broke first. By noon the balance shifted in favor of the Finns, when the Second Company of the once-forlorn PPP-7 gained a foothold in the center of the village and knocked out a number of interlocking machine-gun nests that had been galling the Finns for hours. By 2:00 P.M., the Russians were in retreat.

At nightfall, December 23, the Finns had reached the banks of the Aittojoki River, and there the entire Finnish effort simply ran out of steam. Mannerheim wisely called off the attacks. There was good defensive terrain along the Aittojoki, and it seemed clear that the original Soviet threat to Tolvajärvi and the important roads beyond it had been decisively checked.

In proportion to the numbers engaged, the Tolvajärvi campaign was for the Finns the bloodiest of the war. Fully one-third of Talvela's officers and noncoms were killed or wounded, and one-quarter of his rank and file: a total of 630 men killed and 1,320 wounded.

Russian losses will never be known accurately; an unknown number—certainly at least 1,000—perished unseen and uncounted in the snowy wastes. Between Tolvajärvi and the Aittojoki, 4,000 Russian bodies were counted; their wounded probably numbered 5,000, and almost 600 were taken prisoner. Russian armor was virtually wiped out: fifty-nine tanks and armored cars were destroyed. The Finns welcomed into their arsenal 220 usable Russian machine guns and light automatics.

Talvela's accomplishment was remarkable. He had eliminated the direct threat to the entire Ladoga-Karelia front, and he had also burned up a good part of the Eighth Army's reserves, thus improving Fourth Corps's chances closer to Ladoga.

Psychologically, the victory at Tolvajärvi was like a shot of adrenalin to Finnish troops everywhere. The enemy at Tolvajärvi had not been composed of second-rate troops, either, for the 139th Division had been tough, aggressive, and boldly led. But its morale was not good: the Russians didn't know why they were fighting and the Finns did. Yet the Finns' morale had also been very low before Talvela and Pajari arrived. As Task Force Räsänen, the Finns were actually beaten, and their entire front was on the edge of collapse. If the Tolvajärvi campaign proved anything, other than the toughness of the Finnish soldier, it reaffirmed the power of a commander of strong will and personality to materially change the course of battlefield events, even at the eleventh hour.

Back at Fourth Corps headquarters, General Hägglund no longer had to worry about being outflanked from the north. For the rest of the war, Group Talvela's front was the scene of only limited ground activity, although Russian air raids in this sector were heavy from time to time. On Christmas Day, for instance, General Pajari's headquarters at Aittojoki was severely bombed just as Christmas services were being held. The regimental chaplain, among others, was killed where he stood. Finnish fighter patrols were quickly sent to the vicinity and arrived in time to shoot down four of the bombers.

In late December the first American-Finnish volunteers to reach the front were put into the line in Talvela's sector. This was a token force only, about a platoon's worth, but it saw more or less constant patrol action until the war's end and seems to have acquitted itself well.

Late in January the Russians in the Tolvajärvi-Ägläjärvi sector escalated the scale of combat by launching a number of effective probes, this time using ski troops, that caused the Finns some temporary problems. There was much small-scale skirmishing in the forest, rather complicated for such small battles, usually involving one side or the other making wide flanking loops with their skiers. Each side won engagements and lost some, but the Russians never quite managed to get anything going on this front that might have significantly altered the basic stalemate. Although company-sized detachments came fairly close on several occasions, they never again reached the Tolvajärvi-Aittojoki road with anything bigger than a reconnaissance patrol.

▲ CHAPTER 10 ▲ ▲

The Kollaa Front: They Shall Not Pass!

Mannerheim had not expected a serious Russian threat to materialize either on the road to Tolvajärvi or the road south from Suvilahti. When the Russians struck hard along the axes of both roads, they came close to upsetting the entire scheme of defense in the Finnish Fourth Corps sector, north of Lake Ladoga. The original plan for that sector had been to pin the enemy against a strong line of prepared positions anchored on Lake Ladoga and stretching north to Syskyjärvi, and then strike them on the right flank from the lake-spattered wilderness to the north.

Now that very wilderness had become a crisis spot. By the end of the second day's fighting, Finnish intelligence realized that the lightweight border forces in that sector were facing two full Red divisions, both well supplied with artillery and armor. While the Russian 139th was systematically pushing back Task Force Räsänen on the Tolvajärvi road, its sister unit, the Fifty-sixth Division, came storming across the border north and east of Suvilahti. If the Fifty-sixth continued its drive along the road from Suvilahti to Loimola, it would completely disrupt the planned counteroffensive on the north shore of Lake Ladoga. Even worse, it might take the main defensive line— Ladoga to Syskyjärvi—from behind and open the vulnerable "back door" to the Isthmus itself.

As it was, the unforeseen power of the Russian thrust at Suojärvi drew off a dangerous percentage of Fourth Corps's strength and tied down many troops originally earmarked for use in the planned counterattack north of Ladoga. Not only was Suojärvi a junction for good roads leading to the north, west, and southwest of Finland's interior, it was also the hub of a region of some economic importance to the Finns, home to a sizable complex of paper and lumber mills.

The national border east of Suojärvi, as it was drawn when Finland became independent, was a strange protuberance, shaped roughly like a hammer's head and jutting into the Soviet Union like a peninsula thrusting into the sea. Surrounded on three sides by enemy territory, the place was patently indefensible, so when the Russian advance nipped off this little outcropping of Finnish soil, the only Finns caught by the encirclement were a few small groups of border guards. Many of these men were able to take advantage of their familiarity with the landscape to slip through enemy lines and rejoin friendly troops farther west. Those who did not make their escape suffered varying fates. Some were killed by the Russians; others succumbed to exposure and hunger. Incredibly, a few men managed to survive in that tiny pocket until the end of the war more than 100 days later, hiding out in remote farmhouses and logging camps and using their skills as woodsmen to elude enemy patrols.

On the day the war started, the Suojärvi front was defended by border guard detachments totaling about a battalion's worth of troops, two regiments from the Twelfth Division (JR-34 and JR-36), a handful of light-to-medium artillery pieces, and an old armored train from the civil war days bristling with machine guns and French 75s in steel cupolas. This train proved to be quite effective in slowing the Russians' advance. Hastening from trouble spot to trouble spot, it gave the Finns at least a token measure of mobile artillery support. Perhaps even more valuable than its firepower was the psychological effect on the defenders' spirits as the train hove into sight, bellowing and roaring like some prehistoric monster, gushing angry smoke, knocking sheets of snow from the trees when it fired its main battery, its armored gunports blazing fire at the advancing Russians.

There were fierce delaying actions on all the approaches to Suvilahti, but the invaders' numerical superiority and tanks enabled them to outflank or overwhelm each Finnish position. The defenders hung on to Suvilahti by their fingernails until just before midnight, December 2, when the last roadblock detachment, some of its men weeping from exhaustion, staggered back into the perimeter. The enemy was still very cautious about fighting at night, so the Suvilahti defenders were able to slip away without serious interference. Before leaving they burned every farm, factory, house, and wagon. As they retreated down the road toward Loimola, the flames spread to the lumberyards, igniting not only vast piles of raw planking but hundreds of nearby trees as well. The sky over the forest was smeared with concentric fans of red-orange flame boiling up through heavy rolls of smoke, and on the still winter air the retreating Finns could hear not only the roar and crack of the flames but also the screams of burning livestock.

December 3 dawned in a sky still greasy with smoke. One Finnish battalion had gotten only as far as Naistenjärvi and was regrouping near that frozen lake from the rigors of its night march. All the other Finnish units were strung out raggedly some six kilometers farther south, trying to scratch trenches into the hard ground on the southern bank of the little Piitsoinjoki River. They needed time to catch their breath. Once they had done that, they would be put into motion to carry out a bold and promising plan formulated during prewar maneuvers by the commander of JR-34, Colonel Teittinen.

Teittinen was a native of this region, and he knew its topography intimately. So far nothing except the size of the Russian attack had surprised him, and the numbers were not so disparate as to render his counterattack plan invalid. Teittinen knew that the geography of this region, the interaction of lake and road and river, was such that any attacker who stayed bound to the main roads would be at a great disadvantage compared to a defender who could utilize the whole landscape. He also knew how desperate things were up on the Tolvajärvi road. He therefore planned to leave a minimum defensive screen along the Piitsoinjoki River line and concentrate every available man and gun at Kivijärvi, a point equidistant from both the Loimola road and the Tolvajärvi road. Once gathered there, his force could strike at the flank or rear of either enemy force, depending on which one seemed to offer the best prospects of success. The woods around Kivijärvi were impenetrable to anyone who did not know the hidden paths, and Teittinen was certain he could escape detection and fall on the exposed enemy like a thunderbolt. As soon as the Russians were shattered on one road, he could then turn and strike the other. He hoped to have all the arrangements readied by December 6 at the latest.

But Mannerheim's headquarters intervened on December 3. The high command wanted a strong counterattack mounted back up the Loimola road in the direction of Suvilahti. Both JR-34 and JR-36 were ordered to mount the attack, supported by a paltry two batteries of artillery. The time allotted to prepare for this operation was only five hours.

The order landed on Teittinen's command post with the impact of a howitzer shell. Both regiments had been under fire since the first day of the war, had just completed a dangerous and exhausting night withdrawal under hazardous conditions, and as a consequence were both weary and disorganized. It seemed quite unreasonable to expect these troops to reform, resupply, make plans, and launch a coordinated, controllable counterattack in the space of five hours. To make matters worse, large quantities of the Twelfth Division's winter equipment, including many of its skis and supply sledges, had only just arrived by train in Loimola and could not possibly be distributed to the troops within that space of time.

Teittinen issued the necessary orders but continued to put calls through to Mannerheim's headquarters in a vain attempt to convince the high command that the attack was hopeless. His calls were received with patronizing skepticism. Only a few minutes before the designated jumping-off time for the attack, he made one final effort to get through to Mannerheim himself, hoping that the Marshal's sense of realism would prevail and the counterattack order be rescinded. The call never got through. The last person Teittinen spoke to was a staff orderly who listened to his pleas in cold silence, then archly informed him that Mannerheim was asleep and could not be wakened for matters of less than apocalyptic urgency.

All Teittinen could do was scrape together a disorganized mob of tired, hungry, frightened, resentful men and shove them back up the road, straight into the teeth of the Soviet formations that had pursued them the night before. What transpired was pathetically predictable. Most of JR-34 simply could not make the effort. One company commander was heard to remark that Mannerheim could come up there and personally threaten to shoot everyone in the regiment, for all the good it would do. The men were punchy with fatigue and stumbled when they walked. Two battalions of JR-36, somewhat better rested than the others, were herded into a semblance of organization. Their officers begged and borrowed hundreds of pairs of skis from neighboring units. Incredibly, there were still several hundred men in these two regiments who had not yet been issued personal weapons; the rifles were still in warehouses in south-central Finland. Before the war the Twelfth Division's commander had been informed that a rifle for every soldier was a luxury Finland could not afford in peacetime. Indeed, some men in the division never received weapons; hundreds of Twelfth Division soldiers fought the remaining engagements of the war with captured Soviet arms.

To the surprise of no one on the scene, the attack finally jumped off much later than its ordained starting time of 6:00 A.M. JR-36 led the advance, its Third Battalion on the right, following the highway and rail line, its Second Battalion on the left, both being led by a reconnaissance detachment. At first it seemed as though luck was with the Finns; the enemy appeared to have withdrawn during the night. In reality the Finnish counterattack had started at precisely the time the Russians were rotating their decimated forward units and replacing them with fresh troops. The forward elements of JR-36 got as far as Liete village, about five kilometers northwest of Suvilahti, before encountering any resistance.

When the enemy did make its first appearance, it was dramatic. Soldiers from the reconnaissance detachment suddenly appeared, backs to the enemy, screaming, "Tanks, tanks, tanks!" Twenty Soviet vehicles came rumbling into view around a distant curve in the road. The sight of them was enough to disrupt the Finnish counterattack. Both battalions of JR-36 took to their heels in headlong panic.

No infantry were seen operating with the tanks, and the tankers were not very keen in their pursuit. They followed the fleeing Finns cautiously down the Loimola road, hurling desultory rounds at their backs now and again.

The rout was stopped by the reserve battalion of JR-36, which had been digging in at Lake Naistenjärvi. The broken battalions fled back through the First Battalion's line and were cursed, kicked, and cajoled into some kind of order by their officers. A small highway bridge between Naistenjärvi and the Russian armor, wired for demolition the day before, was blown up. Red infantry now hastened forward to join the tanks, but meantime the faithful armored train had arrived on the Finnish side of the blown bridge. It laid down a blistering barrage of cannon and machine-gun fire, effectively checking the Russians long enough for 1/JR-36 to finish digging in, positioning its heavy weapons, and restoring discipline to its sister units.

Tank terror still gripped the survivors of JR-36; the men's hands trembled and their voices cracked when they spoke of the armored monsters. Next time all it took was the rumor of tanks, not their actual appearance, to shatter their nerves. This time the fleeing men did not rally until they reached Loimola itself.

The fear of armor had not communicated itself to JR-34. There is some indication that Colonel Teittinen's men had their spines stiffened by the spectacle of what had happened to their sister regiment and had spontaneously resolved that it would not happen to them. With one entire regiment caved in, there was no point in trying to hold the line at the Piitsoinjoki River. Teittinen led his regiment about six kilometers back to the line traced by a small stream known as Kollaanjoki—the "Kollaa River"—and decided that this was the best defensive ground left between Loimola and the rear of Fourth Corps. JR-34 turned and dug in along the southern bank of the Kollaa, spotting its antitank guns on the main road and covering the flanks of the road with wire entanglements buried in deep snowdrifts. Until trenches, mortar pits, and log-roofed dugouts could be constructed, it wasn't much of a defensive line, but the men of JR-34 were tired of running. Here, at this insignificant subarctic river, the Finns turned to make their stand. Thus was born the "Kollaa Front." In the weeks to come the phrase "Kollaa still stands!" would inspire Finns everywhere, and the insignificant river would become a symbol of resistance against tremendous odds.

Of course there was little choice in the matter. Kollaa had to be held or else the Russians would smash into the rear of Fourth Corps, break open the "back door" to the Karelian Isthmus, and Mannerheim's entire scheme of defense would collapse. But holding Kollaa was not a spectacular defensive victory, the way the early victories at Taipale and Summa had been. It was a grinding battle of attrition. There were no dashing maneuvers through the forest, no sensational raids: just two determined armies, one of them growing steadily mightier as the other grew thinner and more haggard.

Fortunately the retreat-weary men of JR-34 were given a few days of respite, thanks to the cautious nature of the enemy's pursuit. It was not until December 7 that Russian units made their appearance on the north bank of the Kollaa.

"River" is perhaps a misleading word for the Kollaa. At no place was this obscure waterway more than a few meters wide, and no one had ever foreseen that it would become the pivotal position on which the fate of all Fourth Corps depended. In the beginning there were no prepared defenses for the men who dug in there, other than a few foxholes athwart the road itself and a screen of antitank rocks that had been emplaced on the shoulders of the road and of the railroad embankment. Beyond that, there were only the dugouts and bunkers that Teittinen and his men had to dig out of the granite-hard soil during whatever spare time they had between Soviet attacks.

At the start of the battle Teittinen could call on the support of a half dozen nondescript batteries of guns, of various calibers, ages, and states of mechanical reliability, along with the ever-faithful armored train, whose crashings and belchings always raised the defenders' spirits, regardless of what damage it might do to the enemy. Teittinen sent repeated pleas to Fourth Corps and to Mannerheim for more artillery support, and finally, a week or so into the battle, he got it: two French 3.5-inch field pieces whose barrels bore a casting date of 1871. These antiques could no longer be aimed with any accuracy; they were just pointed in the general direction of the Russians and kicked off. Their age-pitted ammunition was not very lethal, but the old black-powder shells made a very satisfying "Bang!" when they detonated.

The pattern of fighting on the Kollaa front was defined by the very first Russian attacks and in weeks to come would change little. The first Red thrust came barreling straight down the highway, a column of tanks firing on the move, with infantry formations dimly in view straggling behind them. The tanks clattered right into the cross hairs of waiting Finnish gunners, and the leading three vehicles were hit within seconds of each other. The remaining tanks retreated, and the unsupported infantry could make no progress on its own.

The struggle for Kollaa began, then, with those three burned-out tanks on the Loimola highway. As the Russians' strength grew, and the urgency of their attempts to break the Kollaa line increased, the battle spread day by day in a wider and wider arc on either side of the highway, the attackers massing at more and more points, and the defenders stretching their resources, day by day, to meet each new threat. The Russians moved, the Finns countered. It was set-piece conventional battle, except for the odds, which were not conventional at all. No matter how many men the Finns scraped up and fed into the line at Kollaa, the Russians came against them with triple or quadruple their strength. At the start, a single regiment of Finns faced a division of Russians. Then, two divisions. The Finns' strength grew to two regiments; the Russians deployed four heavily supported divisions. There were never enough Finns to meet every threat, never enough guns firing in support. Always the dreaded "big breakthrough" seemed just minutes away from happening. The image suggested by the defense was that of a rubber band being stretched tauter and thinner every day, until the breaking point must surely come at any hour.

Every day following their first probe on December 7 the Russians broadened the frontage of their attacks, called in more air strikes, and wheeled up more batteries of artillery, more tanks, and more men. And every day the importance of Kollaa grew. To the south, on the shores of Lake Ladoga, General Hägglund was risking everything on the long-planned counterstroke against the big Russian salient pinned, its left flank against the lake, at Kitelä. If the Kollaa front was ruptured while that attack was developing, Fourth Corps would surely collapse, for it would be impossible for Hägglund to disengage and wheel any significant forces to face a new threat from his rear.

In late December the Russians tried some new tactics. One day they would send their troops forward in tight clusters, bunched behind lines of firing tanks. The next day they would try to infiltrate small bodies of men equipped with individual shields of armor plate, each with an observation slit cut into it, an expedient that was curiously medieval in appearance and not very practical. Once a man was hunkered down behind that armored shield, he was not likely to come out from behind it and charge. It was very difficult to aim and fire through the small observation slit and the smaller rifle hole cut below it. Finnish snipers positioned themselves in front of the defenders' main line and shot dozens of these shield-bearing warriors in the legs and buttocks. But the Russians at Kollaa learned from their mistakes and even became good at adapting the forest to their needs. They learned, for instance, how to make "ice roads" by employing hundreds of men to trample the snow flat, then corduroying the resulting lane with sawed-down tree trunks. After the logs were in place, water was hosed over them. In a matter of hours it froze solid, and the road surface thus created would be serviceable for light tanks and field artillery.

In mid-January the Russians reinforced their artillery at Kollaa so that when they opened an all-out offensive during the week of January 21–28, they would deploy fifty batteries, almost 200 weapons, against the Finns' total of twenty guns. The January assaults were not fancy, consisting of human wave attacks all along the line—constantly, without pause—while thousands of shells rained on the defenders. Russian casualties rose to more than 1,000 men a day. Against one strong point, known to the Finns as "Killer Hill," the Russians threw a 4,000-man regiment against a defending force of 32 Finns. More than 400 Russians died; 4 of the Finns survived.

Under this kind of strain men snapped suddenly and without warning. During these January attacks one coolly professional platoon leader, who had endured two weeks of nonstop shelling and whose unit had repelled so many Russian attacks that they had lost count, suddenly went through that invisible window that marks the border of reason. He stumbled into his company commander's dugout, tears streaming from his swollen, blood-shot eyes. "My wife is coming here with more machine guns!" he babbled. "My wife is coming and bringing us more weapons, so we can kill all of the bastards, every last one of them!" With that, still gesturing and yelling incoherently, he turned and ran outside into the Russian bombardment, where he was at once killed by shrapnel.*

In late February and early March, by which time the importance of the Kollaa front had become secondary, the Russians' attacks became almost vindictive in their savagery. There were so many planes in the air over Kollaa that groups of two or three aircraft would gang up on individual Finnish soldiers caught in the open and waste thousands of rounds in strafing attacks on one man. By then, the Russians had deployed eighty batteries of artillery. The landscape around Kollaa had been pulverized. The once-dense forests had been stripped of all foliage, turned into a bleak moonscape of overlapping craters, the lacerated earth prickly with the torn, skinned stumps and trunks of blasted evergreens.

A final wave of Soviet attacks began on March 2. The defense was broken and penetrated dozens of times, but each time, the Finns somehow contained the enemy, repaired the damage, retook the lost ground, held out. So thinly stretched were the defenders during those last days of the struggle that company-sized Russian salients were counterattacked by as few as five or six Finns.

Nevertheless, Kollaa held out until the end. When the cease-fire took effect, on March 13, the defenders slowly emerged from their holes and wandered aimlessly over the devastated landscape. The silence was deafening.

*Engle and Paananen, 140.

▲ CHAPTER 11 ▲ ▲

The *Mottis* of General Hägglund

Before 1939 passed into history, Western newspaper readers had learned at least two words of Finnish. One, of course, was *sisu* (guts). The other was *motti*, a word usually seen in the context of *motti* tactics.

In Finnish, the word *motti* denotes a pile of logs or timber, held in place by stakes, destined to be chopped or sawn into convenient lengths of firewood. *Motti* tactics was the term applied to the way the Finnish Army dealt with the long road-bound Soviet columns that were surrounded and cut to pieces north of Lake Ladoga and up in the vast subarctic wilderness of north-central Finland. The textbook *motti* operation had three phases:

1. reconnaissance to get a fix on the enemy and encirclement to prevent further movement and to pin the enemy into a narrowly circumscribed area;
2. quick, sharp attacks, using concentration of force to gain local superiority or at least equality, delivered at vulnerable points along the entire length of the enemy column, the object being to split its formation into a half-dozen or more isolated fragments;
3. detailed destruction of each pocket in turn, weakest ones first, while hunger and cold worked on the stronger ones.

So it is that even today, when the Battle of Suomussalmi is taught in the military history course at West Point, the Finnish Army is credited with inventing this tactical doctrine and refining its principles for years before putting them to the test in 1939.

It may all be a myth. Even Finnish historians tend to become a little cagey when writing about the *motti* battles, and there seems to be no direct evidence that *motti* tactics by that name were ever taught as part of the Finnish Army's prewar training doctrine, although that is not to say that individual officers may not have come up with the name spontaneously and quite independently of one another, long before the Western correspondents in Helsinki got wind of it and made it briefly a household term, as they had two months earlier with the word "blitzkrieg."

Mannerheim and his commanders knew Soviet military doctrine intimately. When the war broke out, he was surprised strategically by the size of the enemy's effort in the great forests of north-central Finland, but he was not surprised tactically. On a tactical level, the Russians behaved very much as Mannerheim had expected.

The Russian civil war had been too unusual and too political in nature to have offered many military lessons. The Soviet officer corps, like their counterparts in most European states, had been trained to fight a conventional war, moving in columns along roads, with objectives of a conventional nature: cities, railroad junctions, bridges, and the like. The Stalinist purges had gutted the Red Army of three-quarters of its best professional leadership. Mannerheim had nothing but contempt for the kind of officers who had been moved up the promotion ladder to replace those killed or imprisoned during the purges, regarding them as working-class thugs in uniform, no matter what their rank. He knew them to be timid, slow, and unimaginative. If one factored into that the doctrine of blind political obedience to the "Politruks," the frontline commissars who had to approve every tactical order before it could be given to the troops, then the Red Army looked like a massive but elephantine organism: an army which, when committed to battle under Finnish conditions, was almost guaranteed to stick to the roads because to do otherwise was to risk total loss of control, the breakdown of the disciplinary system, and political malfeasance. Initiative in the Red Army of 1939 was a quality more apt to get an officer shot than promoted.

With the presumptive enemy so well understood and the terrain of Finland so intimately known, it was natural for the Finnish Army to shape its tactical doctrines accordingly. Even if *motti* tactics were not taught as such before the war, skills were taught that made such tactics the natural outcome of the conditions under which the fighting would take place. Individual and small-unit initiative, expert camouflage, rapid movement on skis, quick concentration and quick dispersal, the technique of large-scale as well as small-unit ambushes—all of these skills were honed to a fine edge in the Finnish Army. When troops so indoctrinated were turned loose against large, road-bound Russian columns, *motti* tactics were the natural result. Evidence suggests, in fact, that the Finns on some battlefronts did not even call what they were doing *motti* tactics until they read about it in the newspapers, after which of course the name stuck.

In December, when the Western press began trumpeting the successes of these dazzling new tactics, the Finns naturally did nothing to disabuse all of those sympathetic foreign journalists, making it seem even more as though Mannerheim and his staff had been nurturing these concepts for years, waiting to unleash them and dazzle the world.

The reality was that, although *motti* tactics were a dramatic tactical success, they were more often than not a strategic failure. The Finns' objective was to shatter the invading columns and either route them back over the border in disorder or annihilate them as quickly as possible. When the Russian columns broke into strong defensive *mottis*, it was in fact a setback for Finnish strategic goals, given the Russian soldiers' proclivity for defensive fighting. None of the *mottis*, including the so-called Great Motti at Kitelä, which contained an entire Soviet division, would have been too hard to reduce if the Finns had been decently equipped with artillery, armor, or tactical air power; but those were the very things the Finns lacked, and without them, each *motti* had to be starved, frozen, and finally hacked into pieces. To do that required two more vital commodities that were in short supply in Mannerheim's inventory: manpower and time. Mannerheim had hoped, in fact, to avoid the creation of strongly fortified pockets such as the bigger *mottis*. He knew how tenacious the Russian soldier could be in defense—he had commanded enough of them in his time—and he also knew that Red Army doctrine, reinforced by the severe example of the purges, dictated that any piece of terrain taken from an enemy became "Russian" soil and so must be defended to the last man and bullet.

General Hägglund, in his postwar writings, stated flatly that of the eleven *mottis* that resulted from his long-cherished counteroffensive, only the Great Motti at Kitelä was planned. The others "just happened." Hägglund likened them to "wood chips" that fell this way and that and declared that the dispersal of Finnish forces required to subdue or contain all those pockets made it impossible for his strategy to yield the sort of victory he had envisioned.

The original plan had called for halting the Russians along a strong line of both natural and prepared defenses anchored on Lake Ladoga and running through Ruokojärvi and Syskyjärvi. While they were engaged along that line, the Finns would fall upon their vulnerable right flank. Hägglund was prevented from carrying out this plan by the unexpectedly strong enemy thrusts at Tolvajärvi and down the Loimola road.

When the Russians crossed the border on the north coast of Lake Ladoga, the Finns engaged them with delaying actions, as planned, slowing them down so that the main Russian force did not reach Kitelä, just east of the main Finnish defenses, until December 10. Several heavy Russian assaults were launched against the fortified line, but all were repulsed with considerable loss. Especially valuable to the defenders were the six- and ten-inch coast artillery batteries on Mantsinsaari Island, which interdicted the main Russian supply line to the east and greatly hampered resupply and reinforcement of the spearhead up at Kitelä.

As the situations at Tolvajärvi and Ilomantsi stabilized and as the defenses at Kollaa continued against all odds to hold, General Hägglund decided to proceed with the original plan, even though it was now somewhat diluted because so many reserves had been drawn off to meet those threats to the north of Fourth Corps.

There were two Soviet divisions in the Kitelä salient: the 168th, concentrated along the coastal road ("Pitkäranta road"), and the Eighteenth, concentrated on the right flank of the salient from Syskyjärvi back along the only other decent road in this sector, the Uomaa road. Attached to the Eighteenth Division was the Thirty-fourth Tank Brigade, although the 168th, too, had attached armor formations. Both divisions were well supplied with artillery. Leading into the Russians' right flank, at a point some twelve kilometers or so behind the front, was a secondary north-south artery called the Siira road. This avenue afforded the Finns an excellent approach to the sensitive Uomaa road, the northern of the Russians' two supply lines on the Ladoga front.

Hägglund seems to have been thrown off balance by the crises up at Kollaa and Tolvajärvi. His first two moves were abortive false starts that should have alerted the Russians to what was up but do not seem to have had that effect. The first warm-up attack was launched on December 12. Hägglund was probably motivated by the good news from Tolvajärvi, where Talvela had successfully eliminated one of Fourth Corps's worst threats. Eight Finnish battalions assembled far out on the Finnish left near Kotajärvi and moved out through the woods to try and stage a surprise attack on the Siira-Uomaa road junction.

The approach march went badly. The terrain was far worse than even the Finns were used to dealing with. The infantry grew tired long before they reached enemy lines, and inevitably a quantity of extra ammunition, heavy machine guns, mortar parts, and radios were set down and marked for the reserves to pick up and bring forward later. Exhausted and disorganized by the march, the Finns attacked the road junction, but only three of the eight battalions made any headway. Russian shell fire was heavy and tank/infantry counterattacks were soon hitting the Finns from both east and west as the enemy got its reserves into motion. By the evening of December 13 Hägglund's worn-out battalions broke contact and retired back up the Siira road, unable even to hold their minimal gains. It was fortunate for Hägglund that the Russians did not pursue beyond the range of their own artillery.

Hägglund made his second effort on December 17, with a conventional frontal assault on the main Russian line between Ruokojärvi and Syskyjärvi. The attackers made little headway against the Russians' superior firepower, and when his casualties started rising, Hägglund called off the operation. This endeavor was marginally successful as a feint, however, for it did draw the enemy's attention and some of its reserves away from the sensitive right flank, where Hägglund still planned to launch his maximum effort.

In Mannerheim's opinion it was taking the general too long to work up to making that effort. He sent a personal envoy from supreme headquarters with orders to get Hägglund moving, and events thereafter unfolded with more dispatch. With the Finns victorious at Tolvajärvi and with Kollaa holding, there was no reason to delay; even the weather had turned in the Finns' favor, as massive snowdrifts piled up along the rocky shores of Ladoga, making it difficult for the Russians to keep their two supply lines open and forcing them more than ever to stay close to the roads and the villages.

Hägglund's plan was this: First, an attack would be launched against Uomaa village, to cut the northern supply line and establish a roadblock facing east and to check any Russian reaction from over the border. Next, the main attack would be carried out by two task forces designated according to the first initial of their commanders' last names, Task Force A (for Autti) and Task Force H (for Hannukselka). These concentrations would strike the Russian line along a fifteen-kilometer stretch of the Uomaa road, breaking through at multiple points and driving south to the coast of Ladoga, thereby cutting off the "head" of the Russian salient, the 168th Division, headquartered at Kitelä. From their main line of resistance between Ruokojärvi and Syskyjärvi the Finns would launch diversionary attacks to pin down the sizable Russian forces dug in there and keep them from taking any action against the flanking movement. If the plan succeeded, all military logic dictated that the Russians would respond in only two ways: by launching hasty local counterattacks, which Hägglund was confident his men could handle, or by making a complete withdrawal from the Ladoga coast, which would free at least a whole division of Finnish troops to reinforce the Isthmus front.

Offensive action began on the day after Christmas, when a feint attack was launched against Ruhtinaanmäki, a hill near Syskyjärvi, successfully pinning down a sizable Russian force in that vicinity. The Finns made sure this effort did not look like a feint. They pressed the assault hard, took heavy losses, and dug in under galling shell fire. On December 27 a raid in force swept out of the forest and attacked Uomaa village. The enemy garrison resisted stoutly, however, and fell back to fortified buildings in the center of the village, where they mounted a tenacious defense. The Finns detailed a

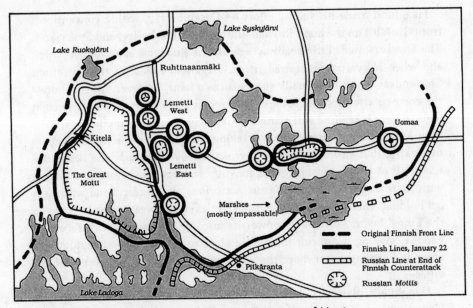

8. Development of Counterattack, Showing Formation of *Mottis*

screen of troops to keep the village surrounded and pressed on to the east, establishing their roadblock about five kilometers from Uomaa.

Having learned something from his study of the miscarried attack on December 12, Colonel Autti did not attempt to hide his force by marching through the snow-choked wilderness. He formed up his men just beyond sight of Russian lines across the Siira road and at the prearranged moment launched them behind an artillery barrage in a flat-out charge straight down the road. The attackers crashed into the Russian line, firing on the run, and broke through. By twilight they could bring the Uomaa road under small-arms fire. The road junction itself was seized the next morning, and by January 3 organized Soviet resistance had been compressed into a small figure-eight-shaped *motti* just to the west of the road junction.

Colonel Hannukselka's task force had similar success when it came storming out of the forest between Syskyjärvi and Pyhäjärvi. By the end of the first week of January the entire Russian Ladoga front had broken into pieces. Everything was going according to Hägglund's original plan, with the exception of one increasingly troublesome turn of events. Instead of being panicked into hasty counterattacks, or doing the more logical thing and staging a fighting withdrawal back to the Soviet border, the broken enemy formations were simply going to ground. When a Russian battalion was threatened with encirclement, it made no effort to break free. It simply deployed for perimeter defense and starting digging in. For the moment the Finns could only register uneasy puzzlement over this phenomenon, leave token forces to guard the bypassed pockets, and press on with the main attack elsewhere.

By January 11 Colonel Autti's force reached the village of Koirinoja and severed the supply line of the 168th Division. Task Force H was still bogged down in a series of sharp little firefights with pockets of the Eighteenth Division and Thirty-fourth Tank Brigade. Again, although these units were shattered, the fragments did not retreat or lash out wildly at their assailants; they simply dug in and refused to budge.

On the map the surrounded Russians' position now looked hopeless. But the fanatical resistance of the troops inside each of the eleven *mottis* upset every Finnish timetable. The tenacity with which the Russians defended themselves soon earned the grudging admiration of the Finns. Here was an enemy who was displaying plenty of *sisu* of its own variety. One Russian company inside the Uomaa *motti* refused an invitation to surrender even though 83 of its 85 men were dead or wounded. Most of the *mottis'* inhabitants remained peaceful unless disturbed. They were not concerned with launching sallies against the Finns, but they would fight back savagely when attacked. And the *mottis'* power of resistance was formidable. There were more than 200 tanks and armored cars inside the pockets, 100 of them in the two Lemetti pockets alone, where the Thirty-fourth Tank Brigade had been concentrated. Inside the circles of armor were hundreds of field guns and mortars that could concentrate their fire quickly on any threatened part of the defensive perimeter. Even though the tanks soon became immobilized from lack of fuel, their turrets still rotated and their guns still fired. Each *motti* remained ringed by steel and bristling with firepower. On the Ladoga front, starvation was not a major weapon in the Finns' arsenal, for there was an abundance of horse meat trapped inside the *mottis*, and the Soviet Air Force's resupply efforts, despite considerable interference from Finnish antiaircraft fire, were both determined and successful.

Not that living conditions were comfortable or that hunger was ever very far away. A diary found inside the Kitelä *motti* recorded that when an aerial food drop landed within the perimeter, the men nearby would "run like maniacs; they tear at the packages, eat, and die. Food is all in all to them. . . . a hungry human is an animal."

Inside the Great Motti at Kitelä was General Bondarev's 168th Division, dug in defending an area of more than twenty square miles. The Russians seem to have made it a point of pride not to let the Great Motti fall. In January a tenuous overland supply route was opened between the new Soviet front east of Pitkäranta and the sector of the Great Motti's perimeter near Koiri-noja. By this time, the surface ice of Lake Ladoga was frozen hard enough to bear the weight of supply sledges, even light artillery. The Russians dispatched well-armed columns out onto the ice around Finnish lines on the coast and succeeded in reopening a direct link with the trapped division.

Hägglund's men were strained to the limit just maintaining the siege of this enormous pocket. All they could spare to deal with this new threat was a handful of small guerrilla detachments. Starting about January 20, these units marched out onto the bleak, otherworldly landscape of Ladoga, where winter storms whipped waves of snow across a vast, flat, gray-black horizon. The Finns dug in on some small, bare, rocky islets that dotted the surface of the lake, close to where the resupply columns would have to pass in order to reach the Great Motti.

The enemy columns moved out from below Pitkäranta with the coming of night. There were long lines of horse-drawn wagons, trucks mounting machine guns, an escort of light tanks and armored cars, screening detachments of well-armed infantry on the flanks. The Finns' only real asset was their skill at winter camouflage and their ski mobility. Sometimes the Red columns would be smashed by fire from the Mantsinsaari shore batteries, but those positions were under increasingly heavy counterbattery and aerial bombardment and could risk exposing their positions only to fire at critical targets on the mainland. Seldom did they dare to fire at ghostly columns of horse-drawn carts out on the ice. Therefore the columns had to be stopped by ski guerrillas using for cover the rocky outcroppings on the ice desert that was Ladoga's surface.

Night after night the ski troops went out to ambush the supply columns. Eerie nocturnal firefights swirled and flickered through the murk, with men's perceptions distorted by the mirage-producing refractions of the Ladoga landscape. Sometimes the skiers would hit the same column a dozen times in one night, dashing in to open fire, hurl their bundles of stick grenades, and slide satchel charges under tank treads. Observers on the shoreline heard the hollow thud of cannon fire and saw the flash of small arms like swarms of fireflies. The strangely mirrored columns of illumination from Russian searchlights, bending and shimmering, were reflected back by the ice in weird permutations of normal light. In the morning the track of the columns would be marked by hundreds of frozen dead, who had stiffened in whatever position they were in when the bullet found them, and charred wagons, gutted horses, and occasionally a scorched and blackened armored vehicle.

About a week before the end of the war, a time when the effort was all but superfluous, the Soviets mounted an all-out offensive against Mantsinsaari and the other, much smaller clumps of stone the Finns had fortified. Overwhelming aerial and artillery bombardments literally pulverized the smaller islets, and wave after wave of Red infantry flooded the ice to finish off the surviving Finns. Only a handful of men from the Finnish garrisons survived. Hundreds perished, fighting until they were overwhelmed by waves of Soviet infantry.

In the end, thanks to airdrops, the Ladoga relief columns, and an abundant supply of horseflesh, the 168th Division survived. Its defensive position was very strong as well as large. The Ladoga coastline was a veritable rampart of granite headlands and outcroppings. Storming the *motti* from that direction would be like attacking a castle, and the inland perimeter was ringed by high wooded ridges into which the division's tanks had been buried so that only their turrets remained above ground as revolving pillboxes. The divisional artillery had been massed in the center of the *motti*, where it could bring devastating fire on any point in a 360-degree radius.

To storm such a position would require the kind of firepower the Finnish Army had learned to do without. Mortars and grenades would not do the job, and there was not enough heavy artillery to go around. What reserve guns the Finns did have were being husbanded for the Isthmus battles. Sometimes the Finnish troops were able to even the odds a little bit by using captured enemy weapons, but most of the guns that had fallen into Finnish hands were too light to make a dent in the fortified *mottis*. Occasionally, however, the Finnish soldier's talent for improvisation came into play, as happened when the Finns surrounding the "West Lemetti Motti" sneaked out under cover of darkness and penetrated the Russian lines. They then located the site of two 120 mm. mortars, tied ropes to the barrels, lashed a few dozen shells to the base plates, cut the gun crews' throats, and proceeded to drag the two weapons back to Finnish lines without being challenged. In the morning the Finns opened fire on a number of bothersome bunkers that had proven impervious to grenade and machine-gun fire and blew all of them to matchsticks.

Sometimes, either in response to Finnish pressure or to orders from higher up, the *motti* garrisons did attempt to break out. Usually this happened without much, if any, warning. The garrison of the "East Lemetti Motti" made their move against the greatly outnumbered Fourth Jaeger Battalion, which had been surrounding them and keeping up the pressure for several weeks. The Jaegers' commanding officer, a colonel named Aarnio, had just that morning received an intelligence update that confirmed a state of total quiescence within the *motti*. No enemy movement had been discerned in the last twenty-four hours. Aarnio's men were strung out in a thin ring around the *motti*, and his guard was down. Then, about 100 meters away, a mass of Soviet infantry, personally led by a general and his headquarters staff, was just suddenly *there*. Aarnio rounded up a scratch defense line of clerks, cooks, drivers, and supply and medical personnel and radioed for help. The sudden outburst of firing alerted the rest of the battalion to the fact that a breakout was being launched, and small groups of skiers were already hurrying to the sound of the guns.

For more than an hour, a confused, point-blank firefight crackled through the woods, with the heaviest action along the Uomaa road. When the firing subsided, Aarnio's patrols counted more than 400 dead Russians in the first 250 yards between his headquarters' dugout and the *motti's* outer defenses. Among them was General Stepan Ivanovich Kodratjev, commander of the Thirty-fourth Tank Brigade, who had bravely led the assault. All of his staff lay sprawled around him, including four female typists carrying rifles. A body count revealed that more than 3,000 Russians died in the breakout attempt, including 310 officers.

These were not the low-caliber officers the Finns would kill by the hundred in the great forest battles, but well-fed, smartly dressed professionals who died wearing clean white shirts, members of the Leningrad and Moscow elite. About 600 Russians survived the breakout attempt only to find themselves trapped in another *motti* identical to the one from which they had fought clear. The booty captured inside the now-deserted East Lemetti position was substantial: 105 tanks, 12 armored cars, 237 trucks, 31 civilian-pattern automobiles, 10 tractors and prime movers, 30 field kitchens, 6 usable pieces of artillery, and enough ammunition to fill 200 truckloads.

Eventually all the *mottis* except three were wiped out: the Great Motti centered at Kitelä, the Uomaa village *motti*, and the hourglass-shaped *motti* near the Siira road junction. Hägglund's counterstroke had been well planned, bravely executed, and nearly pointless in the sense that his whole purpose was to eliminate the threat in the Ladoga sector in time to send a division or more to reinforce the Isthmus. Instead, Mannerheim finally had to reinforce Hägglund at the end of January with a half dozen miscellaneous reserve battalions and a full regiment from the newly formed Twenty-third Division. It was a curious situation, this standoff between Fourth Corps and the *mottis*, and a major disappointment to the Finns. Still, despite the failure to eliminate the Ladoga salient altogether, Hägglund's men had performed remarkably. At the crux of the campaign, just before Mannerheim decided to send him additional troops, his two divisions were containing numerically superior forces at Kollaa, along the Pitkäranta line facing east, and along the original fortified line west of the Great Motti, and simultaneously besieging ten heavily fortified pockets. Like every other successful Finnish commander, Hägglund got the maximum performance from his men.

PART III

The White Death

An Arctic war . . . like an endless showing of
underexposed film.

> —Carl Mydans, *Life* magazine, after
> a walking tour of the Kemijärvi
> battlefield

▲ CHAPTER 12 ▲ ▲

The Winter Soldiers

No aspect of the Winter War so stirred the emotions of the outside world as did the Finnish victories in the great forest battles north of Fourth Corps's sector, especially that Tannenburg-in-miniature at Suomussalmi. In part it was the landscape in which those battles were fought: vast, dense deciduous forests carved by prehistoric glaciers into a patchwork of 10,000 lakes, often channeled by raw, thin evergreen-clad ridges of reddish gray granite. In part it was the fantastic disparity of numbers between the two armies involved, the whole David-and-Goliath nature of the struggle, combined with the numbing viciousness of the fighting itself, the dash and brilliance of Finnish tactics, and the staggering one-sidedness of their victories. Indeed, the first reports of Suomussalmi were greeted with skepticism, until eyewitness reports began coming back from reliable correspondents, along with photos that haunt the imagination of anyone who has ever seen them.

These victories in the northern wilderness were the most spectacular achievement of Finnish arms. Reading about the obliteration of two whole Soviet divisions by a few battalions of intrepid skiers, the American or English citizen could savor a moment of idealistic rejoicing. For the first time in many years, free men had triumphed. It does not detract from the Finns' accomplishment, however, to state that the psychological effect of these lopsided victories was not wholly positive, in that they led the outside world to expect a miraculous Finnish victory and may therefore have taken some urgency from the efforts of those who might otherwise have expedited the dispatch of military aid to Finland. The sad fact of the matter was that all of those spectacular victories combined had only the most marginal influence on the really crucial campaign: the struggle for the Karelian Isthmus. Mannerheim and his staff knew that cruel truth, even if most people in Helsinki or London did not.

One of the more curious things about the wilderness battles is that they ever came to be fought at all. The concept of "cutting Finland in two at the waist" may look inviting on paper, but the reality is much different. To be sure, an invader able to debouch from the frontier wilderness into the heavily farmed, more piedmont-like western half of Finland would be in a position to ruin the country's internal communications, as well as choke off one of its main points of contact with Sweden. The problem lay in getting that far, in successfully crossing the vast tract of virgin forest that protected the developed regions of Finland.

About all that the Soviet attacks had going for them was the fact that they were unexpected. Mannerheim had reasoned that the Russians would never send large conventional forces into such terrain. But once the Finns recovered from their shock and realized that the invaders had done just that, it was imperative that the enemy columns be stopped as quickly as possible. In many respects, the Finns charged with fighting these forest battles saw their tactical situation as being the reverse of that which obtained for their comrades down on the Isthmus. Up there in the wild and trackless forest was a perfect chance to exercise an offensive defense, to put into practice the most imaginative and free-wheeling tactical maneuvers devised during the long prewar years of austere budgets, when Finland's professional soldiers tried to compensate for their lack of numbers and technology by creating an indigenously "Finnish" style of war making.

One of the main factors that enabled the Finns to destroy forces much larger than their own was surely rooted in the differing psychologies of the men engaged on either side. To the Finnish soldier, the cold, the snow, the forest, the long hours of darkness were all factors that could be turned to his advantage. To say that the Finns were on intimate terms with winter is to voice an understatement. In Finland winter is *the* fact of life, and all else— the economy, the culture, the national psychology—is colored by, or derived from, that single overriding reality. The relationship between the Finns and winter constitutes something of a contradiction. On the one hand, winter makes life harsh and lonely and sometimes crude. It is this aspect of living with winter, the cumulative effect of endless subarctic nights, the unearthly silences of the winter landscape, the harsh and marginal quality of rural life, that imparts to the Finnish character that dour and brooding quality that is so hard for foreigners to penetrate.

Yet the Finns' relationship to winter is more symbiotic than antagonistic. Every percentile of economic growth, every pound of grain, every foot of paved highway, every new rural electrification line represented a hard-won victory, a small symbol of progress, wrested from the unyielding flint of the landscape. The Finns, by 1939, were proud of these small but cumulative victories over nature, of the way they had made the snows bloom and brought light to villages where the sun lay hidden from December to March.

When Finns are not brooding about the grimness of nature, they are apt to exult in their mastery of it. Finnish children still barely able to toddle joyfully waddle about on stubby baby-sized skis. Most adults are excellent cross-country skiers. Even the most cosmopolitan city-bred Finn is apt to leave the urban scene at every opportunity and in every season to camp, hike, or practice the recondite sport of orienteering out in the forests and fells.

Finns know how to *listen* to the stillness in the great forest; for them it is never absolutely silent, and they can read considerable information about their environment from sounds of which outsiders are not even aware. Finns, in short, can adapt to their environment because they feel a part of it. And if this was so in peacetime, it was intensified in time of war.

Arctic conditions rewrote the procedures for waging combat. Hands and feet were especially vulnerable. A man whose feet or fingers had blackened from frostbite was as effectively *hors de combat* as a man with a bullet in his leg. Diet and nutritional requirements change in arctic conditions. Troops need hot, heavy, plentiful food to fuel their body chemistry. The standard Red Army fare of black bread and unsweetened tea were simply not enough to keep men going. If a man rested his ungloved hands, even for a second, against bare gunmetal, he left blood and skin behind when he tried to pull away. If tanks and trucks were not run for fifteen minutes out of every two hours, their batteries died and could not be recharged. The Finns cleaned their rifles with a mixture of gasoline and gun oil, their automatics and artillery pieces with a mixture of alcohol and glycerine. The invaders used conventional petroleum lubricants, which not only did not lubricate at subzero temperatures but sometimes actually prevented the weapons from firing at all. There were special problems involved in tending the wounded, too, for the same cold that immobilized a man with low blood pressure also tended to freeze drugs solid. Finnish medics went into battle with ampoules of morphine tucked inside their mouths or taped to their armpits. The cold did help stanch the blood flow from many types of wounds, but it also promoted the onset of gangrene. Wounds had to be disinfected very quickly.

The winter of 1939 was one of the most brutal the northland had ever known since meteorological records started being kept in 1828. Temperatures of −30°F were not uncommon. At Sodankylä in February the thermometer dropped to a savage 42.7 degrees below zero.

Finnish soldiers knew how to dress for arctic warfare: in layers, which could be added to or peeled off as required. In addition to his regulation uniform, the ski trooper was likely to be wearing heavy woolen underwear, sweaters, several pairs of socks, boots lined with reindeer fur, and a lightweight snow cape of about the same texture and heft as a bedsheet, complete with cowl and drawstring. Snow-camouflage discipline among the ski soldiers was superb. A good man could wrap his snowsuit around him and hunker down in such a way as to be invisible to a Russian patrol passing ten meters away. Incredibly, none of the Russian columns that entered the forests had any snow camouflage at all. The tanks were painted olive drab and the men wore regular khaki uniforms, overcoats, and helmets. Not until late January did the Red Army get around to painting its equipment white and issuing snowsuits to its infantry.

Finnish soldiers accepted the forest on its own terms, whereas the invaders never lost their fear of the wilderness. When the Russians did venture into the trees, they usually went in large, clumsy formations. Mostly they preferred to huddle in the deceptive and dangerous psychological warmth of their road-bound formations.

In the forest the Russian soldiers had to face what they called *Belaya Smert*: the White Death. It came silently, when men became so numb with cold and fatigue that they just lay down in the snow and went to sleep, or it came violently, in the form of a sniper round fired from an invisible Finn hundreds of meters away. In the diary of a Russian captain named Shevenok was found the following typical response to forest conditions:

> No, the Finnish woods are altogether unlike our Ukraine. Tall pines stand all together in the snow, like paintings. Above are branches and down below it is bare, as if you were standing not in groves but in some sort of grotto with pillars. The stars wink—frigid, still. The snow falls silently, straight in the eye. The firing of the guns sounds like a long drawn-out echo from afar, as if from a tube.*

The Russians' style of bivouac was hopeless. They lugged with them huge, cumbersome field kitchens, instead of the small multi-purpose stoves the Finns used for frontline units. These highly visible Russian devices were the invaders' only source of hot food, and in arctic conditions, a hot meal could literally mean the difference between life and death. The high-hat stovepipe chimneys of these kitchens were hard to disguise. They gave off telltale plumes of smoke and were high-priority targets for Finnish snipers and mortar crews.

Aside from the field kitchens, the invaders' only source of warmth was campfires. The Russians were addicted to great roaring tree-trunk blazes around which they habitually gathered, even though the soaring flames outlined them like rifle-range targets and never failed to attract the attention of every Finnish sniper within range.

*Chew, 28.

No Finnish unit, however small, went into battle without sufficient arti-
ficial warmth for every man. Frontline dugouts were equipped with small,
efficient stoves that burned with a hot, steady flame and gave off the merest
whisper of smoke. Just behind the front lines the Finns lived and worked in
shellproof dugouts roofed over with layers of logs and earth and completely
camouflaged. Inside these dugouts the walls were lined with furs and skins.
Men could rest in snug comfort when they returned from patrol duty or
a period of combat. When a Finnish soldier was wounded, he was usually
back in the comfort of a warm aid-station bunker within the hour, while his
wounded Russian counterpart knew only an intensification of misery, cold,
and pain.

Just before their departure for the Suomussalmi campaign, the soldiers
of the Soviet Forty-fourth Division were issued thousands of brand new
manuals on the subject of ski warfare. What good this was supposed to do
is unfathomable, since the Forty-fourth Division had not been given any
skis. Nor would the manuals have done the Russians much good if they had
been so equipped. The diagrams in the manuals showed skis attached to the
cartoon soldiers' feet by means of conventional civilian bindings, with tight,
secure heel straps. The Finns, however, knew that the cardinal rule of ski
fighting is never to fight on skis if you can possibly avoid it. Finnish ski
boots, *pieksu*, had turned-up toes and no heel straps so that a man could hop
out of his skis, or back into them, in a matter of seconds.

Other worse-than-useless schematics in the Soviet ski combat manual
showed men attempting to throw hand grenades in the conventional over-
handed manner while still strapped in their skis. The Finns had perfected
a method of dropping down into a tight crouch and hurling their grenades
with a side-arm pitch. Anyone following the diagram in the Russian manual
could expect his grenade to land anywhere except the intended target.

Quite the silliest series of drawings in the Russian booklet depicted the
"proper" technique for bayonet fighting on skis. In order to bayonet an opponent, a soldier must work up a high coefficient of friction between his feet
and the ground beneath them. Since skis are designed for the express purpose of eliminating such friction, the very idea of bayonet fighting on skis
quickly reduces itself to an absurdity.

When the Russians attacked through the great central forests, they did so
in spearhead formations. Most of their units had marched from their rail de-
barkation points on the Murmansk line, in some cases a distance of 200 miles,
and had already lost up to 10 percent of their manpower from frostbite even
before they crossed the Finnish border. Snow drifts up to twenty feet high
had to be dug through and tramped down along the route of march. With
every mile they crawled westward, the columns became more strung out,

until a single division might be straggling over twenty to twenty-five miles of road. First came the advance guard, reconnaissance troops, and a packet of armored cars, then the forward elements of infantry, then a packet of armor, then some support troops—sappers and medics and quartermaster troops—and finally the main body of armor, infantry, and cannon, all followed up by a rear-guard detachment. There were no flanking roads. Flanking screens of infantry, if the terrain permitted them to be used at all, wallowed through the woods a few hundred meters from the sides of the column. As Finnish guerrilla raids intensified, this distance decreased, casualties mounted, and the pace of the invader's march slowed to a crawl and finally stopped altogether.

So one-sided were the Finnish victories, and so uniformly wretched was the human material of whole Soviet divisions, that a myth arose after the war that many of these units were made up of various political "undesirables," recalcitrant peasants from the Ukraine or minorities from the troublesome Asian republics, for example, whom Stalin had dispatched into the wilderness for the express purpose of "liquidating" them cheaply while simultaneously causing trouble to the Finns in the bargain.

Stalin was certainly capable of such bloody-minded calculations, but a close examination of the historical facts suggests a less satanic thought process. Stalin's military advisers began the war confident that they could knock Finnish resistance aside by simply hurling across the border whatever troops were on hand, whether they were any good or not. Some Russian soldiers were, of course, accustomed to harsh winters; others were not. One division was comprised mainly of Uzbeks, Tartars, Tadzhiks, and other tribal minorities from Turkestan. A large number of its men simply keeled over in the cold or just sat apathetically in their foxholes until they froze to death.

Most of the Russians, however, no matter what their province of origin, went into battle believing that Finland (or at least Finland's bourgeois government) had started the war and that the Finnish masses would welcome them as liberators. That illusion was one of the first things to die; the Finnish masses were never glimpsed, and some of the most ruthless ski guerrillas were loggers and pulp-factory workmen who had voted Communist in the last elections.

It is not uncommon to read accounts of the forest battles in which Finnish veterans voice their pity and compassion for the poorly led, ill-clad Russian conscripts they were called upon to slaughter in these campaigns. It is also common to read of instances where these same pathetic, third-rate Soviet units, half-starved and frozen to the bone, fought back with rabid ferocity even in the last extremity of their wretchedness.

For many of the encircled Soviet troops, just staying alive, for one more hour or one more day, was an ordeal comparable to combat. Freezing, hungry, crusted with their own filth (while the besieging Finns, a thousand meters away, might be enjoying a sauna-bath), for them the central forest was truly a snow-white hell. They fought because they had no choice—if they did not fight, the Politruks would shoot them; if they tried to sneak home through the forest, they would freeze to death. Surrender to the Finns was a last, desperate resort; they had been told, in lurid detail, about how the Finns tortured prisoners to death. Most of them had only the vaguest notion of where they were; many of the men who died at Suomussalmi and the Kemi River actually thought they had been advancing on Helsinki, hundreds of miles to the south. Their despair was recorded in the thousands of never-mailed letters to home they had scrawled before dying, letters they had sealed, for lack of anything better, with bits of black bread that had been chewed to a paste and dabbed onto the paper like blobs of rubber cement.

CHAPTER 13

Suomussalmi: A Military Classic

No battle of the Winter War captured the public's imagination like the Battle of Suomussalmi. The campaign continues to be taught in military academies as a "classic," an example of what motivated, well-led troops can do, with innovative tactics, against even a much larger adversary.

Suomussalmi was a provincial town of 4,000 inhabitants, made up mostly of loggers and hunters, although there was good seasonal fishing in the long, narrow, twisty lakes that radiated out from the road junction where the town had grown up. As was true with the other Soviet thrusts into the central and northern wilderness, the Finns were startled that the enemy would even bother to attack here and flabbergasted when Stalin committed two entire divisions to the operation: the 163d and Forty-fourth.

Under the command of Major General Zelentsov, the 163d Division moved from its base at Uhkta, on the Murmansk Railroad, along one of those top secret forest roads that made it possible for Stalin to mount the forest offensives. The Russians' objective was to knife through the wilderness and capture Oulu, the major rail connection with Sweden, and effectively cut Finland in two at the "waist." There were two roads leading to Suomussalmi from the frontier: The northern one, called the Juntusranta road after the first Finnish settlement inside the border, ran southwest, then joined a major north-south artery that led through Suomussalmi to Hyrynsalmi in the south and Peranka to the north. The southern track, called the Raate road, intersected the Peranka-Hyrynsalmi road in the middle of Suomussalmi and then meandered toward the more populous interior of the country. The southern route was a much better road, and if the Russians were going to try anything in this sector, the Finns expected them to use it.

Zelentsov put two of his three regiments across the border, however, on the Juntusranta track, enabling him to enjoy complete tactical surprise and massively one-sided weight of numbers. To oppose his crossing, the Finns initially deployed a border guard company of fifty men. Brushing aside the delaying actions of the border troops, the two Soviet regiments pressed on and reached the Palovaara junction sometime during the night of December 5–6. Meanwhile, their sister regiment was rolling into Suomussalmi itself, via the Raate road. Resistance on the Raate road had initially been feeble: two platoons' worth of border guards and a couple of improvised roadblocks. Even so, the invading Soviet regiment only made six miles in the first twenty-four hours of the war. Finnish reserve companies were hastily rushed down from Kajaani, and these served to stiffen the defense and slow the invaders' progress. By the morning of December 7 the inhabitants of Suomussalmi had been completely evacuated and most of its buildings put to the torch. It was a hasty job, however, and not all the fires caught. Enough dwellings were left to shelter a few hundred men and to present the counterattacking Finns with some street-fighting problems in the days to come.

Of the two Soviet regiments that had come in by the northern road, one turned north at the Peranka road junction and advanced toward Lake Piispajärvi; the other turned south and headed for Suomussalmi itself. Late on December 7 it linked up there with the regiment that had come in on the Raate road.

By companies and battalions, Finnish reinforcements began hurriedly to converge on this remote location. The enemy thrust along the Juntusranta road appeared to Major General Tuompo to pose the more significant threat, so he dispatched his meager forces to that sector first. Independent Battalion ErP-16 began arriving in Peranka at 1:00 A.M. on December 6. By midday the entire battalion had spread out on good defensive ground near Lake Piispajärvi. No sooner had the Finns taken position than elements of the Soviet 662d Regiment, which had been ordered to take Peranka by nightfall, began probing attacks. After twenty-four hours of vigorous skirmishing the initiative passed to the Finns, outnumbered though they were.

All Finnish forces operating above the Palovaara road junction were now grouped under the designation "Task Force Susi," under the command of Lieutenant Colonel Paavo Susitaival, a reserve officer who had just been granted leave of absence from his position as a member of Parliament. Susitaival's force was able to contain the Russians with surprising ease, due partly to the fact that Zelentsov, making the first of several costly mistakes, had stripped the 662d Regiment of one of its battalions, retaining it as his divisional reserve. Task Force Susi therefore found itself engaging only about 2,000 enemy soldiers. Nor was the 662d in good shape in other ways: its commander, Sharov by name, had sent a message of complaint on December 11, promptly deciphered by Finnish radio intelligence, bitterly lamenting that his men lacked boots, snowsuits, and sufficient rations. From other radio intercepts the Finns soon learned that one of the divisional Politruks had been "fragged" by some of his men. Another transmission, decoded on December 13, spoke of forty-eight frostbite cases and 160 battle casualties in the 662d alone—10 percent of Sharov's force, and he had done nothing more than skirmish with the Finns so far. Clearly this was not an elite formation.

Paradoxically for such a technologically primitive army, Finnish radio intelligence was highly developed and would prove invaluable during the Suomussalmi campaign. Mobile vans prowled the back roads, eavesdropping on Russian radio traffic and feeding the signals to data-collection centers where cryptanalysis was speedily performed. Local commanders usually had decoded enemy radio signals in their hands only four hours after they had originally been sent; a slow pace, perhaps, by the standards of today, but by the standards of 1939 a very smart performance indeed, and one that greatly aided the Finns in making their tactical decisions.

On December 14 and 15 Sharov tried to regain the initiative and was able to score a temporary advance from Haapavaara to Ketola, where he was stopped cold by heavy mortar and Maxim fire. The Finns once again employed their heavy machine guns in the role of light artillery. Sharov's lead battalion took 150 casualties. With 20 percent of his regiment out of action from fire or frostbite and the rest of his men rapidly approaching the limit of their physical strength, Sharov and his remaining troops went over, permanently as it turned out, to the defensive.

Meanwhile a much more serious threat was developing from the stronger, southern arm of the Russian offensive. With two of the 163d Division's regiments and most of its heavy weapons and armor concentrated close to Suomussalmi village, it seemed clear to the Finns that the main push would probably be in the direction of the road junction at Hyrynsalmi. An otherwise insignificant logging town, Hyrynsalmi offered the region's best road connection to Puolanka, an important stepping-stone on the route to Oulu, and was also the terminus of the sector's only railroad line. It was vital for the Finns to retain control of the place.

A major reinforcement was now on its way, in the form of a single man, an officer who would galvanize the Suomussalmi defenders in much the same way as Talvela had done at Tolvajärvi. On the same day the Russians linked up at Suomussalmi village, December 7, Mannerheim ordered JR-27, the only remaining uncommitted regiment of the Ninth Division, to entrain for the new crisis spot. The commander of JR-27, Colonel Hjalmar Siilasvuo, was yet another veteran of the fabled World War I Jaeger Battalion. The son of a newspaper editor, Siilasvuo was in peacetime a lawyer. A short, blond, blunt-speaking man, he was about to prove himself one of Finland's greatest tacticians.

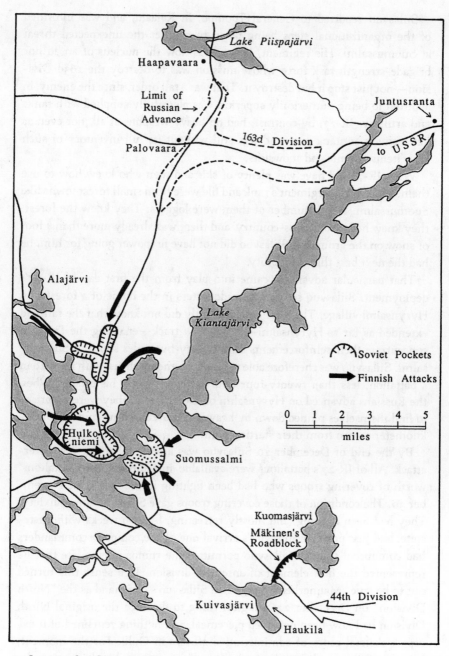

Lake Piispajärvi

Haapavaara

Limit of
Russian →
Advance

Juntusranta

163d Division

to USSR

Palovaara

Alajärvi

Lake
Kiantajärvi

Soviet Pockets

Finnish Attacks

0 1 2 3 4 5

miles

Hulko-
niemi

Suomussalmi

Kuomasjärvi

Mäkinen's
Roadblock

44th Division

Kuivasjärvi

Haukila

9. Suomussalmi Campaign: Destruction of Soviet 163d Division

Siilasvuo reported to General Tuompo, in Kajaani, and was informed of the organizational steps being taken to counter the unexpected threat at Suomussalmi. His regiment, JR-27, was now the nucleus of an ad hoc brigade-strength task force whose mission was to destroy the 163d Division—not just stop it but destroy it. That was a tall order, since the enemy, in addition to being numerically superior, was plentifully supplied with tanks and artillery. JR-27, by contrast, had no heavy weapons at all, not even as yet a single antitank gun, and was still without its full inventory of such basic items as tents and snowsuits.

What JR-27 did have was plenty of skis and men who knew how to use them. Most of the regiment's rank and file were from small forest towns like Suomussalmi. A fair number of them were loggers. They knew the forest, they knew how to ski cross-country, and there was already more than a foot of snow on the ground. If Siilasvuo did not have firepower going for him, he had the next best thing: mobility.

That particular advantage came into play from the first day of JR-27's deployment. Siilasvuo set up his headquarters in the home of a forester in Hyrynsalmi village. The Russians apparently did not know that the railroad extended as far as Hyrynsalmi—it was new track—enabling the Finns to concentrate their reinforcements only twenty-five miles south of Suomussalmi. Siilasvuo was therefore able to block the enemy thrust with more than a battalion, less than twenty-four hours after receiving his orders. When the Russians advanced on Hyrynsalmi on December 9, they were surprised to find themselves pinned down by heavy, accurate machine-gun fire only a kilometer or two from their starting point.

By the end of December 10 Siilasvuo was already planning a counterattack. All of JR-27's battalions were available, in addition to two battalions' worth of covering troops who had been fighting in the area since November 30. The condition of those covering troops gave Siilasvuo some anxiety. They had been fighting, and mostly retreating, for two weeks without respite, and just prior to Siilasvuo's arrival one of the company commanders had committed suicide. Siilasvuo permitted the rumor to circulate that he represented the first element of an entire division. In a sense this turned out to be true; Mannerheim designated Siilasvuo's command as the "Ninth Division" on December 22, a logical thing to do since the original Ninth Division had now been deployed piecemeal, and nothing remained of it except a skeletal cadre of administrative officers in Oulu. For the moment, however, Siilasvuo did not know that was happening, so his claim was quite an exaggeration. But its effect on the covering troops' morale was bracing and far-reaching. No longer did they feel abandoned to their fate, or that their enormous exertions had been for nothing. In the days to come they would give a good account of themselves.

Siilasvuo thought he could deal with the Soviet 163d Division. Its commander, Zelentsov, had showed himself to be neither very aggressive nor very imaginative. His northernmost regiment, up near Piispajärvi, had become entirely passive, and the division as a whole lay stretched out in a vulnerable road-bound column almost twenty-five miles long, from Piispajärvi all the way back to a point east of Suomussalmi village. Before dealing with the 163d, however, Siilasvuo wanted to make sure it was truly "in the bag," so he launched a road-cutting operation whose ultimate goal was to seal off the Raate road against any reinforcements coming across the Soviet border.

On the night of December 10–11 Siilasvuo moved the bulk of JR-27 to an assembly area southeast of Suomussalmi, about five miles below the Raate road. He also put his engineers to work laying down an "ice road" network that would further increase his mobility, enabling the Finns to hustle their few pieces of artillery from point to point, unlimber and fire a few rounds, pack up again, and vanish into the wilderness, all so quickly that the enemy rarely had time to reply.

The attack Siilasvuo launched on the morning of December 12 would be the first of numerous road-cutting operations his men would conduct in this sector. A typical such attack went like this: The combat team selected to make the actual cut would move into preselected assembly areas just beyond reach of the enemy's reconnaissance patrols. Finnish patrols, meanwhile, had already established the most concealed routes of approach to the road from the assembly area and secured them by positioning pickets of ski troopers on the flanks. Each combat team made its approach according to a timetable that allowed the commander on the spot to gauge the pace so that his men would not arrive at their jumping-off point too tired to do the job. At the final assembly point, usually within earshot of the road, heavy winter garb was discarded and left under guard along with the other heavy equipment. The assault teams wore only lightweight snowsheets and carried as much firepower as possible: Suomis, Lugers, grenades, and satchel charges.

Speed and shock were the ingredients of a successful road-cutting attack. While the assault team was deploying, scouts would creep as close as possible to the point of impact and would bring back last-minute coordinates for the mortars and Maxim guns, which would put down suppressive fire on either side of the raiding party.

At the signal, a short, sharp barrage of mortar and machine-gun fire would crash into the intended point of contact. After a few moments, the supporting fire would be shifted 100 meters or so to the right and left of that point, in effect sealing off a narrow corridor across the road. That was the moment to launch the assault.

A flurry of half-invisible men would erupt from the forest incredibly close to the Russians, grenading everything in front of them, raking the nearest foxholes, trucks, and tents with Suomi fire. Demolition teams would peel off and race parallel to the road, hurling their explosive packs into vehicles, open tank hatches, field kitchens, and mortar pits, with each team accompanied by a few sharpshooters who were under orders to kill the officers first. It was at this stage of the operation that enemy resistance was most fierce, as desperate Soviet troops leaped from their vehicles onto the skiers' backs, or came up out of their holes to meet them with bayonets, pistols, or rifle butts. To men watching the operation from the woods on the Finnish side, it often appeared as though the roadway were convulsed by spasms of flame and smoke with khaki and bedsheet-white figures knotted together.

The main purpose of the raid was not to wipe out every Russian soldier along a given piece of the Raate road. It was to sever the column by overwhelming localized impact and knife through to the woods on the other side. Once a breach had been torn in the Soviet column, no matter how narrow, fresh reserves would swarm out of the forest to consolidate and widen the gap, including combat engineers who would immediately, under fire, start fortifying the sides of the original breach. Eventually, in the *motti* operations to come, each road-cut was 300 to 440 meters wide, with strong barricades and earthworks sealing it off at both ends. The ramparts were often made stronger by incorporating overturned Soviet trucks or captured pieces of armor, some of them with their guns and turret mechanisms still operable. Siilasvuo and his men became virtuosos of this road-cutting technique, and on their best days they could mount two or three such operations simultaneously at widely separated points along the road, making it almost impossible for the Russians to mount an effective defense.

For his first road-cutting attack, and as the site of his vital roadblock to the east, Siilasvuo chose a natural choke point near the easternmost end of the 163d's column, a mile-wide isthmus between Lakes Kuivasjärvi and Kuomasjärvi. The task of setting up the roadblock was given to two companies of JR-27 under Captain J. A. Mäkinen. Siilasvuo may already have had inklings, thanks to the Finns' radio intelligence system, that a new Soviet division was forming up across the border to come to the aid of Zelentsov's stalled offensive. With the roadblock in place, he figured that division would do only two things: either dig in and try to bulldoze its way through the roadblock, which he estimated would take them several days to do, or else try to outflank the roadblock. But because Siilasvuo had chosen ground that was flanked on both sides by wide-open frozen lakes, any Russian commander who tried to outflank the roadblock would incur very heavy casualties from Mäkinen's numerous machine guns. Of course a really deep flanking movement, a wide end run through the deep forest, would easily nullify the roadblock, but Siilasvuo was gambling that the enemy would not do that. The Russians would have to abandon all their heavy equipment and overcome their demonstrated fear of the deep woods. As it happened, Siilasvuo was right. The gamble worked and permitted Mäkinen and 350 men to close the road to an entire reinforced Soviet division.

While the roadblock operation was successfully developing, Siilasvuo launched a battalion-sized probe against Russian positions west of the village near Hulkoniemi. This met with only limited success; the defenders were too well entrenched and too heavily supported by artillery for a single battalion to make headway against them. At least the Finns were now able to bring that section of road under harassing fire, virtually isolating Suomussalmi from that direction.

Methodically Siilasvuo tightened the noose on Suomussalmi, launching numerous quick, sharp raids against the road leading north from Hulkoniemi and against the western outskirts of the village itself. In one such skirmish two Red tanks attacked a Finnish squad caught in lightly wooded terrain near the village. A lieutenant named Huovinen taped five stick grenades together and crawled toward the tanks; his friend, First Lieutenant Virkki, intended to provide covering fire, despite the fact that he was carrying only his side arm. At a range of forty meters Virkki stood up and emptied his 9 mm. Lahti automatic at the vehicles' observation slits. The T-28s replied with a spray of machine-gun fire, and Virkki went down. Those watching felt sure he had been killed. But he had only dropped down to slap another magazine into the butt of his weapon. That done, he jumped up and once more emptied his pistol at the tanks. Altogether this deadly dance step was repeated three times, at which point the Russian tankers seemed to become unnerved. They turned around and clanked back to the village. Meanwhile, Lieutenant Huovinen had been crawling closer to them from the rear and now had his arm cocked to throw the grenade bundle. Just at that moment the tank nearest him put on speed and retreated. He lowered his grenades in astonishment. Surely there were not many instances in modern warfare of tanks being repulsed by pistol fire.

Finnish officers were trained to lead from the front, and a great many of them died at Suomussalmi. A day or two after Virkki had driven off three tanks with a handgun another lieutenant named Remes took a Russian bullet in the hand. He turned over his command, deprecated the seriousness of his injury with a few jaunty remarks to his men, and went off on his own to find an aid station. He never arrived. Just before dark the following day his body was found in the deep woods, where he had apparently run into an enemy patrol. Around him lay six dead Russians.

On December 16 Siilasvuo received his first artillery support, a four-gun battery of 76.2 mm. weapons dating from before the Russo-Japanese War, followed forty-eight hours later by a second, more modern battery, and four days after that by a pair of urgently needed Bofors antitank guns. On December 22 Siilasvuo learned that he was now officially in command of a division rather than a task force. Mannerheim sent him a Christmas present in the form of infantry regiment JR-64, a newly organized battalion of ski guerillas designated "P-1," and one additional independent battalion of infantry. With a total of 11,500 men, Siilasvuo was now as strong as he was likely to get.

Task Force Susi, still containing the enemy up in the direction of Peranka, also received a welcome reinforcement in the form of bicycle battalion PPP-6, which was given the task of clearing out some Russian cavalrymen who were operating along a primitive road that ran between Lakes Alajärvi and Kovajärvi a couple of miles northwest of Suomussalmi village. This they did successfully in a series of firefights that raged from December 17 to December 22, by which time the battalion had moved out of Task Force Susi's zone and was brought under Siilasvuo's direct command. This unit would provide much-needed extra punch on the northern end of Siilasvuo's sector.

At about the same time PPP-6 was clearing its piece of road, the main force of Task Force Susi, ErP-16, sent about two-thirds of its men on skis on a wide flanking march to Tervavaara. From there successful raids were launched on Russian positions near the Palovaara road junction. The noose was tightening.

On December 23 Task Force Susi received a sizable reinforcement, Mannerheim having decided it was time to redouble his bets in this theater, in the form of regiment JR-65, a newly formed unit that had ridden all the way from Oulu, more than 100 miles, aboard trucks in twenty-five-below-zero weather. Positioned first on the north shore of Lake Piispajärvi, JR-65 rolled the enemy back as far as Haapavaara by Christmas. The effect of this action was to pin what was left of the Russian 662d Regiment firmly in place. Sharov was unable to send so much as a squad to reinforce the more important sector near Suomussalmi itself. His unit's powers of resistance were in fact rapidly waning, as Colonel Susitaival learned on December 27, when his task force recaptured the Palovaara junction against palpably weakened resistance.

By Christmas Day, however, a new and potentially very dangerous factor had entered the tactical picture. Siilasvuo's "air support," one ancient and lumbering reconnaissance aircraft, reported on December 13 that a fresh Soviet division, soon identified through radio traffic as the Forty-fourth, had crossed the border and was advancing slowly westward along the Raate road. Further radio intercepts indicated that the Forty-fourth's commander, General Vinogradov, planned to drive through and link up with the 163d as early as December 22. Finnish intelligence noted with some apprehension that the Forty-fourth was an altogether better division than the 163d, well trained and powerfully armed, with strong armored support.

About the only Finnish troops in a position to stop the Forty-fourth were the two roadblock companies of Captain Mäkinen, still dug in on their little ridge between Lakes Kuivasjärvi and Kuomasjärvi. Siilasvuo knew it was unreasonable to expect two companies, however brave and well led, to halt an entire division. To keep pressure from building against the roadblock, the destruction of the 163d was accelerated, while Siilasvuo also ordered a series of short, sharp attacks launched against the head of the Forty-fourth.

Captain Mäkinen led part of his force on a sally against the enemy's advance guard on December 23, while three smaller Finnish detachments, hurriedly brought up on skis along the "ice road" network, simultaneously struck the Forty-fourth's left flank farther east. A raiding detachment of 200 Finns attacked the enemy column from the vicinity of Haukila farm, just over a mile east of the roadblock, and wrought havoc among the transport elements of an antitank-gun unit, killing dozens of men and more than 100 horses before withdrawing. A battalion of JR-27 hit the Raate road from the south at Kokkojärvi, killing 100 Russians and knocking out a tank, several trucks, and a field kitchen, at a cost of only two dead to itself. The third raiding detachment, a fifty-man guerrilla company that had worked its way north of the road, became bogged down in bad terrain and was unable to make contact.

These jabs did not deal Forty-fourth a serious wound. Yet their timing and ferocity seem to have yielded results all out of proportion to the effort expended. General Vinogradov suddenly became convinced he had been ambushed by superior Finnish forces. As sniper attacks, sudden five-minute mortar barrages from the deep woods, and nocturnal ski raids continued to deprive his men of sleep and hot meals, Vinogradov lost his nerve entirely.

His advance elements got close enough to the trapped 163d actually to hear its final struggles, yet his division as a whole never advanced another meter to its aid.

Siilasvuo stepped up his timetable for the destruction of the 163d. On December 23, 24, and 25, the trapped division made several attempts to break out, using up the majority of its ammunition in the process. By the day after Christmas Siilasvuo was satisfied that there would be no breakout. The Finns had been forced to give ground in some places because of the enemy's firepower and armor, but they always retook their original positions within twenty-four hours, usually at night.

When Siilasvuo launched his all-out counterattack on December 27, the main Finnish effort was directed against the western side of the Suomussalmi perimeter. Two attacks, each two battalions in strength, went in against Hulkoniemi itself and against the main road about one mile north of those straits. Siilasvuo massed his artillery, all eight guns of it, to support these attacks. The Ninth Division's two antitank guns were parceled out, one to each attacking force. Eight miles farther north battalion PPP-6 launched a two-pronged attack on the Kylänmaki road junction. The Hulkoniemi attack began at 8:00 A.M., the Kylänmaki junction attack thirty minutes earlier.

Diversionary and supporting actions were also mounted. Three infantry companies, "Detachment Paavola," took up positions at Ruottula on the eastern shore of Lake Kiantajärvi. This force was ordered to advance across the lake, cutting off any Soviet movement in that direction, then turn southwest along the shoreline until it linked up with the main attacking forces near Hulkoniemi. Smaller detachments went even farther north on the eastern side of Kiantajärvi to prevent any groups of Russians from slipping out of the encirclement.

All of these attacks got underway more or less on schedule, but the main thrust against Hulkoniemi encountered savage resistance, and Detachment Paavola wasted most of its time skirmishing with small pockets of Russians encountered on the open ice, some of them in armored vehicles. The best results of the day attended the actions of battalion PPP-6. It rolled up a sizable part of the road defenses and destroyed six enemy vehicles before it too was stopped, still some distance from its objective, the Kylänmaki junction.

The second day of Siilasvuo's general counterattack brought improved results, though still at a high cost. On December 28, PPP-6 finally secured the road junction at Kylänmaki and held it, just barely, against vigorous counterattacks. The renewed attacks against Hulkoniemi initially ran into the same furious resistance the Finns had encountered the day before. Siilasvuo was tempted to throw in his reserves, but finally decided to keep one battalion fresh in case the strangely quiescent Forty-fourth Division made any attempt to break through to its besieged sister unit. Fortunately for the Finns it did not.

Equally fortunate for Siilasvuo, at about 9:00 A.M. Russian resistance at Hulkoniemi suddenly collapsed. The pressure from so many directions against men already reduced to half efficiency by cold and hunger had finally become unbearable. Some of the Hulkoniemi defenders fled across the straits into the village, where their comrades were still holding out; others simply threw down their guns and ran out onto the ice of Lake Kiantajärvi, in the general direction of Russia. Dressed in khaki overcoats, silhouetted against the bare gray-white surface, they made excellent targets, and Finnish machine gunners on both sides of the lake cut them down ruthlessly.

The resistance in Suomussalmi village itself was fierce, and Russian machine gunners had to be pried out of cellar fortresses one by one by close and dangerous work with grenades and Suomis. But with the Hulkoniemi section of the town overrun, the eastern part could not hold out long. Soon the survivors were themselves streaming across Kiantajärvi, while the Finns brought every gun they could to bear on the ice, filling the air above it with tracers that seemed supernaturally bright against the winter gloom. Siilasvuo's men had already plotted the probable vectors of any breakout attempt from the village; they had prepared for it by erecting barbed wire entanglements under innocent-looking snowbanks and by cutting tank traps in the ice.

By December 28 resistance in and around the village had ceased. The only sizable enemy pocket still fighting back was along the road north from Hulkoniemi. Siilasvuo now could spare some troops to reinforce the hard-pressed PPP-6. This final regimental-sized Russian pocket turned into a bee swarm, as those trapped inside made dozens of wild, uncoordinated breakout attempts. The last significant one erupted on December 29, at about ten o'clock in the morning. It resulted in negligible Finnish casualties and another 300 dead Russians.

Given the primitive nature of the terrain and the confused nature of the fighting on these last days, it was inevitable that some fairly large bodies of Russian troops would slip out undetected. Scouting parties stationed north and east of the main combat zone were able to take these groups under observation and plot their course. As Siilasvuo had predicted, they were making for the Juntusranta road and from there, presumably, the Russian border. Siilasvuo sent truckloads of machine gunners racing up the Juntusranta road to intercept, and for the first and last time in the whole campaign he experienced the luxury of calling in an air strike. Two Bristol Blenheims, about one-tenth of Finland's entire bomber fleet, swooped down low and plastered the largest body of fleeing Russians with antipersonnel bombs. Two of the machine-gun trucks later ambushed another large party of refugees while they were still out on some open ice. They killed 400 men but suffered only one casualty to themselves.

So went that final bloody day and night of December 29–30. When the last firing on the Juntusranta road had died down, the Soviet 163d Division had ceased to exist. The Finns counted more than 5,000 bodies littered along the road from the eastern edge of Suomussalmi to the northern shore of Lake Piispajärvi. No one could even guess at how many thousands more perished in the wilderness during those disoriented breakout attempts.

Russian prisoners told their interrogators the by-now familiar litany of bad treatment, bad food, and poor leadership. One POW told the Finns that he had been visiting the shops in a little town near the Murmansk Railroad, just before the outbreak of the war, for the purpose of buying his wife a new pair of shoes. One of the local commissars had spotted him and dragooned him into the army on the spot, hoisting him by the coat lapels and demanding to know why such a fine specimen of Soviet manhood was not marching to the aid of the oppressed Finnish proletariat. The prisoner had marched into Finland without so much as one hour's formal training; when he was captured, he still had his wife's shoes in his pack. The Finns took pity on the wretch, gave him fresh socks, some cigarettes, and a turn in the sauna bath, the first time in four weeks any part of the man had seen soap and water. He was retained at headquarters as a kind of mascot for the rest of the campaign.

It seems incredible that while these battles were raging, only six miles away the stalled Forty-fourth Division remained in a kind of stupor. Vinogradov did finally schedule an attack against Captain Mäkinen's roadblock on December 28, when it was almost too late to do the 163d any good even if he had broken through, but two company-sized raids by the Finns threw him into such confusion that he canceled the attack order. It is almost possible to pity poor Vinogradov. His division was highly rated, but it was heavily mechanized and trained for mobile warfare. Thousands of pairs of skis had been dumped into his supply train at the last minute before the division went over the border, but nobody knew how to use them, and the handful of men who had volunteered to go out into the forest on them had never come back. Without skis his infantry wallowed uselessly in waist-deep snow. For all its vehicles and mechanized training, the Forty-fourth Division was now blind, surrounded, and virtually paralyzed. Vinogradov had no idea how many Finns were arrayed against him. They seemed to come and go at will, striking and vanishing, and the air superiority he had counted on turned out to be chimerical. There might be dozens of Red Air Force planes overhead during the six hours of daylight, but their bombing and strafing efforts were purely guesswork, as the Finns were completely invisible beneath their vault of pine and spruce. Finally, at the eleventh hour, Vinogradov did draw up an order for an all-out breakthrough attempt; but he never issued it. No one has ever figured out why. Perhaps it was the toughness of Captain Mäkinen's roadblock defenders. One captured Russian officer, a colonel who had taken part in the first attempts to storm the roadblock, told his Finnish interrogators that it had been like "butting your head against a stone wall. . . . it was unbelievable." *

If ever an enemy formation seemed delivered into the hands of *motti* tactics it was the Forty-fourth Division. It resembled a twenty-mile-long link sausage, with its biggest piece, a two-mile segment that started just east of Captain Mäkinen's roadblock, made up of a regiment of infantry, dozens of armored vehicles, and most of Vinogradov's artillery. It was Siilasvuo's intention to slice up the column into smaller and smaller pieces, turn up the pressure, let cold and hunger do their work, and then wipe out each dwindling pocket in turn.

He deployed his increasingly weary men very carefully, making maximum use of the "ice road" network south of the Raate road. Two task forces were organized, one under a major named Kari, the other under a lieutenant colonel named Fagernas. Kari's units went into bivouac near Mäkälä, and Fagernas's troops made themselves comfortable at Heikkilä. A third raiding detachment, a reinforced company, took up position at Vanka, along a crude wagon track that led toward Raate village.

The first heavy blow fell on the Forty-fourth Division on the night of January 1–2. First Battalion, JR-27, advanced to a point about two miles east of the Finnish roadblock. This move was accomplished without detection. The Finns had time to catch their breath, enjoy a hot meal, and perform a careful reconnaissance. The battalion commander, Captain Lassila, took a methodical ninety minutes to organize his attack, basing his plans on observations made from a ridge 400 yards from the Russian perimeter. He assembled two companies behind the ridge and ordered them to advance abreast of one another. Upon hitting the road, one company would swing east, the other west, and roll up about 500 yards of roadway. At that point combat engineers would move up, blow down some trees, plant some mines, and construct roadblocks in both directions. Lassila's third company would stay in reserve behind the ridge. In accordance with the usual Finnish practice, heavy ma-

*Engle and Paananen, 103.

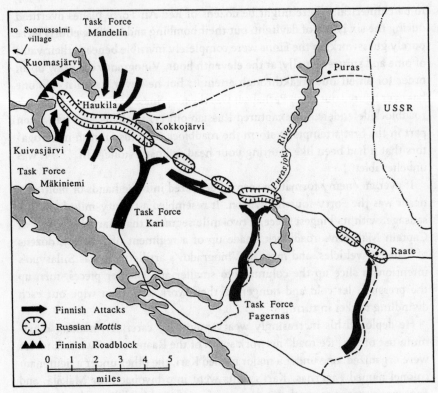

10. Suomussalmi Campaign: Destruction of Soviet Forty-fourth Division

chine guns would be used to augment the limited mortar support available. Fully a dozen Maxim guns were emplaced on the ridge, from which they could fire down into the Russian perimeter, six guns to support each of the two assault companies.

Just after midnight the attack went in. Russian sentries, stationed a mere sixty yards from the road, were taken out first, with little fuss. Then Lassila's men swept on and hit the road hard. Although Lassila thought he was hitting an infantry unit entrenched near Haukila farm, he had actually penetrated an artillery battalion; the Finns' nocturnal navigation had been off by about 500 yards. This mistake, as it turned out, was actually a stroke of good luck. All the enemy's guns were trained to the west, and the Finns were among their positions before they could be reaimed, cutting down the gun crews with Suomi bursts and lobbing hand grenades into dugouts. Several of the Russian trucks mounted four-barrel flak machine guns, and these opened a tremendously noisy and colorful fire, splattering the night with multiple streams of tracer. By the time these weapons could begin firing, however, the attacking Finns were already too close. Most of the fire went over their heads, and the Russian gunners were killed at close range in a matter of minutes. In less than two hours, Lassila had taken his objective and opened 500 yards of road, with only light casualties to his men. By first light, January 2, the roadblocks, both east and west, were up, manned, and covered by mine fields.

Siilasvuo expected his adversary to react strongly to this road-cutting operation; accordingly he took the calculated risk of sending Lassila both of the Ninth Division's Bofors guns. These weapons were manhandled forward from the "ice roads" and were emplaced by dawn, pointing east. They were not a minute too soon, as it turned out, because the enemy launched a heavy attack against the eastern roadblock shortly after 7:00 A.M. In the first fifteen minutes of combat, the two Bofors guns picked off seven tanks, leaving the road clogged with burning vehicles and in effect actually strengthening the new roadblock.

When the fighting died down, hot meals were sent forward on supply sleds to Lassila's men. Stove-heated tents were erected on the ridge from which he had made his battle plans, and the Finns manning the road-cut were rotated periodically to that position so they could thaw out, enjoy a hot cup of coffee, and catch a few hours' sleep. The availability of these Spartan comforts paid tremendous dividends in keeping up Finnish morale.

Conditions inside the surrounded *mottis*, on the other hand, grew worse by the hour as the vise of attrition and exposure closed on them. Elsewhere along the Raate road Finnish snipers, dubbed "cuckoos" by the Russians, shrouded themselves in snow camouflage, tied themselves in trees, and waited patiently, sometimes hours, for an officer to come into their cross hairs. These men fired but seldom, and when they did shoot, rarely failed to kill. With each new casualty the Russians took from their invisible tormentors, the trapped enemy seemed to grow more wildly trigger-happy. Two or three well-aimed shots from the forest would provoke a fifteen-minute counterbarrage from tanks, artillery, machine guns, and mortars, most of whose projectiles did nothing but churn snow and chew up tree branches. So many tens of thousands of rounds of ammunition were burned up on January 2 and 3 that even the more powerful *mottis* were thereafter forced to ration their fire.

The Finns kept up patrols and small-scale raids around the clock. They rapidly established a ring of command posts, supply depots, and camouflaged dugouts around each *motti*, at a distance of 500 to 1,000 yards, depending on the terrain. The ski troopers' schedule called for two hours' patrolling, two hours' rest in a warm dugout, then two more hours of aggressive activity, followed by a four-hour rest period for sleeping and eating. Every two or three days, if the level of fighting permitted, each man would get a turn in one of the frontline saunas, a luxury the Finns could not do without even on a battlefield.

Targets for the skiers' raids were carefully selected: radio sets, command posts, isolated gun pits, ammo storage, and of course field kitchens, which were listed in battle reports alongside the number of enemy tanks and guns destroyed. Anything that offered the surrounded enemy warmth, shelter, or nutrition was mercilessly eliminated. Most of the *mottis* ran out of food only two or three days into the new year. Horses were butchered and roasted over open fires, which in turn drew more sniper fire. The wounded and the weak began dropping in steadily increasing numbers. In such extreme cold the mortally wounded often froze with such abruptness that their corpses stiffened into grotesquely lifelike poses of activity and exertion. Death in the subarctic forests wore a Gorgon's head rather than a skull.

Vinogradov frantically called for more air support, and the skies above his position were thick with Red aircraft during the daylight hours. But all the pilots could see were the *motti* formations. They bombed and strafed the surrounding forest at will, but only rarely, and then only as a matter of luck, did they tag any Finnish targets. Curiously, almost sadistically, only one of the Red Air Force's halfhearted resupply missions seems to have been successful: three small scout planes dropped six bags of hardtack into the middle of an area where 17,000 men were going mad with hunger. By the time those pathetic parcels thudded into the westernmost *motti*, its inhabitants had endured five days of thirty-below-zero weather with nothing to eat but a little barely cooked horse meat.

Late in the afternoon of January 2, the Russians tried to storm Lassila's western roadblock, but flanking fire from the woods to the south of the road turned them back easily. Strange as it seems, Vinogradov never tried a simultaneous counterattack from both east and west, the only tactic that had a chance of succeeding. By hitting first one side and then the other but never both sides at once, he allowed the Finns to deal with each threat systematically and without straining their resources.

Also on January 2 the Third Battalion of JR-27 assaulted the road farther west, near Haukila farm. Here the Russian defenses proved very strong, and the most the battalion could do was tighten its grip on the south side of the road and bring the Russian positions under increased harassing fire. Finnish mortar teams knocked out several field kitchens from their new close positions.

January 2 was a busy day. Siilasvuo also launched attacks from Sangin-lampi farm against Russian positions near Eskola. It took three days of hard fighting to eject the Russians from this important flank position, but by the end of January 4 Task Force Kari had cleared the enemy from that sector and had consolidated its hold on good terrain about two miles from the road junction at Lake Kokkojärvi.

January 3 was given over to improving communications. New ice roads were laid down, poor wagon tracks were widened and their surfaces improved. The besiegers multiplied their advantage of mobility. By January 4 Siilasvuo was ready for another series of attacks. A task force under Colonel Mäkiniemi, comprised of JR-27, a battalion from JR-65, and the highly effective ski-guerrilla unit P-1, would assault the strongest remaining enemy positions in the Haukila farm sector. Siilasvuo allocated three-fourths of his artillery—six guns—to this force. Another task force, under Colonel Mandelin, consisting of two battalions from JR-65 and three attached companies from here and there, would strike the Haukila section of the road from the north at the same time that Mäkiniemi's men hit from the south.

On Mäkiniemi's right (eastern) flank, Task Force Kari would launch sharp flanking attacks on the stoutly defended enemy positions from Tyynelä to Kokkojärvi. Total Finnish forces allocated to Task Force Kari were three infantry battalions and the last two artillery pieces. Task Force Fagernas was to backstop these actions by cutting the road at the Purasjoki River and again near Raate village, about a mile from the Russian border.

Siilasvuo's offensive opened on January 5 against furious, desperate resistance. Task Force Mäkiniemi's assaults gained some ground, but all of his units were halted short of the road by heavy fire from the *mottis*. Captain Lassila's men tried to widen their hold on the road by means of a flanking move on the north side of the road, but the terrain was more open and boggy there, and Lassila's men took heavy casualties from Russian artillery being fired over open sights from within the *mottis*.

After these attacks had failed, Captain Lassila encountered a sergeant who had taken command of an infantry company after all three officers had been killed or wounded. The sergeant himself had been shot through a lung. Lassila stopped by the man's stretcher and inquired as to his condition. The sergeant grinned and said that he found it much easier to breathe with two holes in his chest.

In these aborted supporting attacks, and in repelling several violent Russian probes of its roadblock defenses, Lassila's battalion suffered ninety-six casualties in six hours. His men had been taking this kind of punishment for four days, losing about 10 percent of their remaining strength per day, and Lassila believed they had reached their limit. He requested permission to abandon the roadblocks, deploy his men under cover of the nearby woods, and try to keep the road closed by fire alone. When he finally got through to his superior officer, Colonel Mäkiniemi, he found no sympathy. Mäkiniemi's other battalions were in no better shape and were still pressing their attacks into the teeth of savage Russian fire. Mäkiniemi himself was irate. If Lassila abandoned those roadblocks, he would be court-martialed and shot. Lassila's men hung on.

Task Force Kari moved against the Kokkojärvi road junction at about 6:00 A.M. Despite repeated attacks his men got no closer than a quarter mile from their objective. Kari's troops also tried to capture a section of road near Tyynelä but encountered tanks. Lacking any means to deal with armor at a distance and prevented by the sheer volume of Russian fire from getting at them with hand-thrown weapons, the Finns withdrew to the forest and urgently requested the loan of a Bofors gun.

The day's best progress was made by Fagernas's men. A company-sized raid caused some annoyance and loss to the Russian garrison at Raate, and Fagernas's engineers were able to blow a small bridge about two-and-a-half miles east of Likoharju. Fagernas's main objective, the bridge at Purasjoki, proved to be too well defended. Siilasvuo finally dispatched a company of reserves because Fagernas was making more progress than anyone else, and doing it against much stronger resistance than anticipated. One of his platoons, in fact, ambushed a truck convoy near Mäntylä, which was found to consist of fresh NKVD troops sent over from Russia only two days earlier. Eventually, thanks in large part to the arrival of the reserve company, Fagernas's men succeeded in blowing up the Purasjoki bridge at about 10:00 P.M. Since the river's ice was not strong enough to support vehicle traffic, this demolition effectively sealed off the Raate road west of that point from mechanized or truck-borne reinforcements.

Meanwhile the more lightweight forces of Task Force Mandelin, north of the road, wiped out a number of Russian patrols, brought several sections of the road under fire, and established a strong blocking position on the secondary Puras road, intended to stop any Russian breakout attempts by that route.

If the general attack of January 5 had not wiped out the enemy, it had put the Russians under severe strain, and blowing the Purasjoki bridge had made it almost impossible for Vinogradov to mount a coherent breakout attempt. January 6 was another day of furious combat. In a desperate attempt to break Lassila's hold on the road, the Russians drove herds of horses into the Finnish mine fields. The resulting slaughter sickened and angered the animal-loving Finns but did nothing to shake their grip on the road-blocks. Task Force Mäkiniemi's units finally fought through to the road in several places, knocking out Russian emplacements one by one. By the end of January 6 fighting had generally ebbed as the Russians began to run out of ammunition and stamina.

After taking time to reorganize, Mäkiniemi's forces renewed their efforts at about 2:00 A.M., January 7. This time sizable numbers of Russian troops seemed to break. Abandoning their heavy equipment they fled into the forest, firing wildly in all directions.

Major Kari's forces also renewed their efforts on the night of January 5–6. Since the Russian position at Kokkojärvi was too strong for a direct assault, Kari sent a company, reinforced with extra Maxim guns and one of the priceless Bofors weapons, to establish a roadblock east of that junction. This was done by 3:00 A.M., January 6, and the position held fast despite attacks of such ferocity that Kari was compelled to shift additional machine guns and another sixty infantry to the spot by midmorning.

Another of Kari's units, ErP-15, after three hours of bitter fighting succeeded in reaching the road at a point east of Tyynelä. The Forty-fourth Division, as Siilasvuo had planned, was being hacked into smaller and smaller pieces.

By late afternoon of January 6 it was clear that some of the Raate road pockets were collapsing—substantial numbers of Russians were spotted fleeing toward the Puras track. Siilasvuo accordingly reinforced the new road-block on that all-but-impassable rural cowpath. Other Finnish attacks at Raate village, Likoharju, and the tiny hamlet of Saukko chipped away at the shrinking Russian pockets.

Late on the afternoon of the sixth, General Vinogradov issued what amounted to an every-man-for-himself order for a general retreat. He was about twelve hours behind the situation; since midmorning his division had been melting like April snow. The last organized Russian resistance was snuffed out at dawn, January 8.

Daylight revealed a scene that staggered the senses of even the most battle-wise correspondents who were brought in to see and photograph it. From the high-water mark of the 163d Division, up at Piispajärvi, to the last burned out truck between Raate village and the Soviet border, were scattered the stone-stiff bodies of 27,500 Russian soldiers. Forty-three tanks and 270 other vehicles, trucks, tractors, and prime movers clotted the narrow road or lay, windscreens spiderwebbed with bullet holes and turrets blackened by fire, in the snowy morass of roadside ditches. The victors acquired substantial booty: four dozen pieces of artillery, 600 working rifles, 300 functional

machine guns, a few mortars and salvageable tanks, and a motley but welcomed assortment of trucks and armored cars. Finnish losses amounted to
900 dead and 1,770 wounded.

As for the two Soviet commanders, they met very different fates. Zelentsov's body was never identified. The best theory is that he destroyed his
identity papers, changed into an enlisted man's uniform, and was among
the anonymous dead who failed in their last-minute attempt to break free
through the woods. The Finns searched hard among their 1,300 prisoners
for General Vinogradov. They were curious as to why he had not done more
to relieve the trapped 163d, whose fate he must have been aware of. Some
weeks later the Finns learned, from a Russian staff officer who was captured
at Kuhmo, what had happened to the hapless Vinogradov. He had fled the
battlefield inside a tank, somehow managed to get back across the border,
and was immediately arrested by the NKVD. After a summary court-martial
Vinogradov and three other surviving officers from the doomed Forty-fourth
Division were marched into the woods and shot. The official reason that went
on record for his execution was "the loss of 55 field kitchens to the enemy."

▲ CHAPTER 14 ▲ ▲

Mr. Mydans Visits the Kemi River

Suomussalmi was the cleanest, most decisive, and most spectacular Finnish victory in the northern half of the country—a paradigm of the qualities that made the Finnish ski soldier a legend. The other battles in the north and central parts of the country were generically similar to Suomussalmi, and a detailed analysis of each campaign would be repetitious, eventually tedious. In most cases a summary is sufficient to give the gist of each engagement, although there are of course certain highlights that deserve closer scrutiny.

By all accounts the Finnish high command was initially stunned that the Russians should choose to deploy half of their available infantry and about one-quarter of their available armor in the far-flung wilderness north of Lake Ladoga. The Russian Eighth Army's thrusts toward Kitelä made strategic sense, as did the complementary attacks on Tolvajärvi and Kollaa, which served to draw off so many Finnish reserves. What really struck Mannerheim and his staff as illogical were the four offensives mounted farther to the north, at Petsamo, Kuhmo, Lieksa, and Kemijärvi.

Responsible for the defense of the 400-mile region between Kuhmo and Petsamo was Major General E. V. Tuompo, a farmer's son who had risen by way of the Twenty-seventh Jaegers to become a renowned expert on matters of national defense policy. Tall, slender, an obsessive worker by nature, he was a steady and imaginative officer, an expert linguist, and a respected amateur historian. He would need all of his ability to cope with the unexpectedly massive enemy effort in the northern half of Finland.

As his deputy in command of the Arctic front, from Kemijärvi up to the foggy and storm-lashed coast of the Arctic Ocean, Tuompo had none other than crusty old Kurt Wallenius, the right-wing demagogue who had botched the kidnapping of President Svinhufvud back in the heyday of the Lapuan movement. Wallenius had by now attained the rank of major general. There was, however, no longer any warmth between him and Mannerheim; the

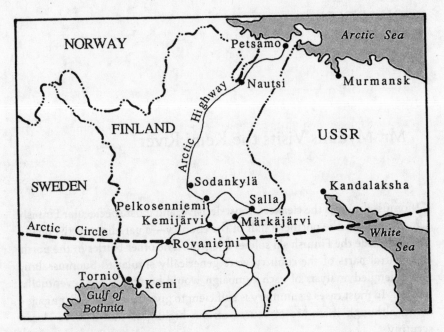

11. Petsamo/Kemijärvi Theater

Marshal even snubbed Wallenius in his *Memoirs*, not mentioning him once by name in the chapters dealing with the Winter War. He had fought the Reds in Lapland in 1918, he knew the terrain intimately, and he was a great tactical improviser; opposing more than three fully equipped Soviet divisions with a few battalions of lightly armed ski guerrillas would certainly require improvisation.

The Arctic front was, paradoxically, easier for foreign journalists to gain access to, thanks to its proximity to Sweden and Norway, than either the Isthmus or the Ladoga front, from which news reporters were barred by Mannerheim's direct order. For correspondents who had cut their teeth on Ernest Hemingway, Wallenius made great copy; he was profane, feisty, and swaggering. His "trademark" for visiting journalists was bare-chested virility, though more than one reporter privately wondered at the sanity of someone who would walk around with his shirt unbuttoned in temperatures of twenty below zero.

When the war started, the Soviet 104th Division came storming ashore on the Rybachi Peninsula, supported by the guns of the White Sea Fleet and by some powerful shore batteries on the approaches to Murmansk. Opposing them was an outfit called the 104th Independent Covering Company, supported, if that is the word, by a four-gun battery of field pieces cast in 1887, half of whose antique shells refused to go off at all.

Petsamo was Finland's only arctic port. In terms of climate, amenities, and general unattractiveness to human beings, it was a poor cousin to Murmansk. It was the northern terminus of Finland's Arctic Highway, one of the young nation's proudest accomplishments, and it had two economic resources that justified habitation: high-grade nickel ore and fish. Nobody minded giving up the fish, but it was annoying to lose the mineral deposits. Still, the Finnish high command was resigned to it. Given Petsamo's remoteness from any centers of Finnish strength and its proximity to a major Soviet base, there was no hope of defending the place.

The Russians took Petsamo after a short firefight and immediately landed some engineer and coast artillery units to garrison the port. Most of the shore batteries and fortifications were aimed toward the ocean, however, not toward the Finns. It was from the sea that any Allied expeditionary force would come, and that was a contingency that Stalin dreaded.

There was little that Wallenius's men could do but retreat and fight delaying actions where they could, and the Lapland fells—treeless, wind scoured, and relatively low—offered poor defensive terrain. It was hoped that winter weather would come to the defenders' aid. As they withdrew, the Finns scourged the region of every man-made or natural thing that might afford the invaders shelter, warmth, or sustinence. Finland had invested heavily in its arctic region, striving to convert this barren land into a habitable and economically viable part of the nation. Every home, every meter of highway, power line, and culvert had been put in place at a great cost of labor, money, and faith. It was not without anguish that the same men who had built these things now blew them up, from the smallest farmhouse to the brand new hydroelectric plant at Salmijärvi, along with several hundred workers' homes recently built around the site.

As a result, there was no shelter anywhere for the slowly advancing Russians. By mid-December this part of Finland was shrouded beneath a pall of perpetual darkness and almost unimaginable cold, often in the form of gale-force blizzards that roared and screamed for days without letup. Glazed with ice, the Lapland fells turned into a savage lunar landscape.

Only rarely did the Soviet invaders see an opponent; if they did, it was an instant's hallucination, a flickering blur of motion as a snow-suited guerrilla flashed across the grayed-out horizon. But there were sniping parties that contested every kilometer of their advance, composed of Lapland natives who had tracked bear and wolves over this same ground and who could drill a man through the head at 1,000 meters with their first shot.

The farther the Russians moved down the Arctic Highway the more vulnerable their lengthening supply line became. More and bolder raids were
launched by Wallenius's men. By January the only way the road to Murmansk could be kept open was by constant armored patrols between block-
house strong points the Russians had erected at five-mile intervals. By the
end of January, with temperatures averaging thirty-five below zero, almost
all military activity had come to a standstill. The front literally froze solid,
with the Russians never able to go one step beyond the tiny village of Nautsi,
close to the Norwegian border. Ten thousand Soviet troops were immobilized between there and Petsamo, paralyzed by the efforts of one-fifth as
many Finns and by their greatest ally, the arctic winter.

Seventy-five miles south of Suomussalmi the Soviet Ninth Army had
mounted a secondary operation intended to siphon off Finnish reserves from
the larger offensive of the Forty-fourth and 163d divisions. Ironically, the
single division the Russians committed to their Kuhmo attack, the Fifty-
fourth, managed to acquit itself far better than the two divisions that were
thrown away at Suomussalmi. Its commander, General Gusevski, was no
fool. He had trained and equipped his men well, and he would fight the victor
of Suomussalmi, soon-to-be-general Siilasvuo, to a standstill.

The Fifty-fourth drove west on two parallel roads, easily knocking aside
a succession of weak roadblocks in its path. Hastily assembled Finnish reinforcements mounted a series of sharp and costly counterattacks and succeeded in slowing the Fifty-fourth's advance by mid-December. By year's
end, however, the forward elements of the Fifty-fourth were less than fifteen
kilometers from Kuhmo village.

No sooner had the dead been counted at Suomussalmi than Mannerheim
ordered Siilasvuo and his entire Ninth Division to move south and do to
Gusevski's division what it had done to the divisions of Zelentsov and Vinogradov. Siilasvuo got his orders on January 18 and dispatched a two-battalion
task force immediately, several days ahead of the rest of his division. The
task force hurried by truck to the town of Nurmes, the only settlement of
any size close to the front. The telephone exchange at Nurmes, in fact, was
the closest communications link that Tuompo and Mannerheim had to the
Finns deploying at Rasti, thirty kilometers away.

The three reinforced Finnish battalions now defending Kuhmo were sufficient to check the Fifty-fourth and compel Gusevski to dig in, but they
were not strong enough to tear up his formations. By the time Siilasvuo was
ready to develop his deadly system of *motti* tactics against the Fifty-fourth,
it had had almost two weeks to fortify its positions. Many of its field pieces
and mortars were lodged in bunkers too strong for Siilasvuo's weapons to

destroy. Gusevski also converted a frozen lake within his perimeter into a landing strip usable by light aircraft. Thus right from the start he was better prepared to cope with Siilasvuo's tactics than either of the divisional commanders had been at Suomussalmi.

To isolate the Fifty-fourth from any relief columns sent from its base at Ryboly, Siilasvuo sent a strong detachment around the *mottis* to occupy a commanding ridge called Löytävaara. No sooner had the Finns entrenched on that position than intelligence reports reached them that another Soviet division, the Twenty-third, was forming up to try and batter its way through to the relief of the Fifty-fourth. The Löytävaara position was the key to Siilasvuo's whole effort. As long as it remained in Finnish hands, the Fifty-fourth was trapped. It would so remain, but just barely, and the battle to hold it would absorb hundreds of men and weapons that were urgently needed to wipe out the *mottis*.

Gusevski's men did not panic. Under heavy covering fire, he sent strong patrols beyond his perimeter to cut down the trees, creating a 100-meter-wide "dead zone" around the *mottis* and making it hard for the Finns to get close. The timber from these cutting operations was hauled back into the *mottis* and used to reinforce the Russians' bunkers. Siilasvuo kept up the pressure as best he could, even hurrying forward a number of Soviet cannon that had been salvaged at Suomussalmi. But Gusevski's blockhouses were strong. The captured 76.2 mm. field guns were too light to destroy them without a long and wasteful battering. And shells for the captured antitank guns, of course, were quite unsuited for such targets, although Siilasvuo's men did use them in the absence of anything more potent.

As Finnish pressure increased, so did Russian pressure on the Löytävaara roadblock. An armored attack was launched against that position in early February, but several vehicles were disabled by mines, and two others received direct hits from a concealed captured antitank gun. Those two vehicles blew up violently, crashing into the rear of the mine-damaged vehicles and creating a flaming knot of twisted metal. Within minutes, the attack evaporated.

Siilasvuo had counted heavily on being able to starve the Russians into surrender, but the Red Air Force flew heavily escorted missions several times daily, and the Fifty-fourth, though hardly comfortable, never experienced the same extremes of hunger that other besieged Soviet units had to endure. For a time, thanks to their superior radio intelligence and the enemy's poor communications' discipline, the Finns were able to imitate Russian signals and have the supplies dropped into their own positions. It did not take the Russians too long to figure out what was happening, however, and one day, instead of supply planes the Finns lured a wedge of SB-2 bombers, which dropped their "cargo" right on target and killed a number of Finnish soldiers. Siilasvuo urgently requested antiaircraft weapons, and Tuompo was able to send him a few of the precious 40 mm. Bofors guns. Siilasvuo also massed everything from captured four-barrel Russian flak-mount machine guns to volleyed rifle fire along the Russians' flight path. This gauntlet of fire brought down five or six Soviet transports and forced the cancellation of daytime resupply missions, but there was nothing Siilasvuo could do about the night flights, and enough supplies got through by means of those to keep the Fifty-fourth Division from starving.

Not only was the Fifty-fourth honored by one of the most successful Red Air Force supply shuttles, it was also the object of a major relief attempt that saw the first massed deployment of Soviet ski troops in the Winter War. Hastily formed from three independent ski battalions, the new unit was dubbed the Siberian Ski Brigade, even though only a portion of its men actually came from that part of the USSR. Totaling 2,000 men, the brigade was comprised of skilled troops, well equipped and blessed at the start with high morale.

The Siberian brigade went across the border on the northern road to the defensive enclave at Kiekenkoski; from there it was to move south, through the heavily forested, lake-spattered wilderness between the two roads, and strike the besieging Finns from behind.

It was a sound plan, and the troops were confident. They were undone, however, by a problem that has been the bane of commanders since the days of Sparta: bad maps. The highly detailed maps of the Kuhmo sector that had been issued to the Siberians bore little resemblance to the real terrain and were filled with misshapen, out of place, or simply nonexistent lakes and ridges. It did not take long for the Siberians to become confused.

Matters were made worse when their commander was killed in their very first encounter with a Finnish patrol. At the same time, the Siberians discovered that their automatic weapons refused to fire. No one had told them that it was necessary to clean the conventional lubricants from their weapons before subjecting them to such intense cold; virtually all of their machine guns and automatic rifles were jammed by gobbets of frozen oil. The skiers fought with a courage and tenacity that elicited grudging admiration from the Finns. Many of them threw down their submachine guns and Degtyarevs in disgust and waded into the Finns with pistols, grenades, and bayonets. Darkness ended the first engagement before either side could claim a victory, but the sudden death of their commander and the sudden loss of confidence in both maps and weapons seem to have generated considerable panic among the Soviet skiers. The unit lost cohesion and split into several fragments, all of them hopelessly lost.

Although the ski brigade never achieved any major successes, its mere presence forced the diversion of large numbers of Siilasvuo's men away from the besieged *mottis*. After the unit fragmented, there were several days of confused skirmishes, as isolated Russian detachments attacked Finnish outposts and support units. After two days of scattered fighting, Siilasvuo's men cornered about seventy-five of the Siberians inside a cluster of wooden farm buildings. After the trapped Russians had rejected several demands for surrender, the Finns set fire to the buildings with Molotov Cocktails and shot down the occupants as they ran screaming into the snow. Not one of the trapped skiers survived.

Eventually about a fourth of the Siberian Ski Brigade managed to find its way back to Soviet lines on the northern road. The others, lost and increasingly desperate, wandered around the area for days, causing various kinds of mischief. One formation of about 100 skiers attacked a Finnish command post near the Rasti *motti* and lost half their number fighting it out with a hastily mustered force of headquarters' clerks, staff officer, medics, and some veterinary specialists who were manning a stable of supply horses.

One intrepid Soviet loner managed to abscond with a sled containing a month's back pay for an entire Finnish battalion. Most of the money was later recovered from the woods. By the time all the alarms and skirmishes died down, 1,400 of the Siberians had been killed, and the rest had either been taken prisoner or had managed to regain friendly lines.

As February gave way to March, the Russians put tremendous pressure on the roadblock at Löytävaara, where a single Finnish battalion had dug into the low, narrow ridge. Theirs was not a very strong position, about two kilometers long and half a kilometer wide. Against this unprepossessing bulwark, the Russians hurled a reinforced division, supported by forty pieces of artillery, which hurled up to 200 shells per minute on the defenders. The Finns could not make any reply to this shelling; they could only endure it and repel the infantry attacks that always followed. By the end of the war, all tree cover had been blasted from Löytävaara, and the front slopes of the ridge had been turned into a barren expanse of overlapping craters. No snow remained visible, only a churned black muck dotted here and there with the remains of what had once been Finnish bunkers.

When the cease-fire went into effect on March 13, Siilasvuo and his men felt cheated of a victory. On one hand, they had neutralized the Fifty-fourth Division, but on the other hand, the Fifty-fourth had also neutralized them, at a time when Mannerheim desperately needed the Ninth Division on the

Isthmus. When the firing stopped and the emaciated but unbeaten survivors of the Fifty-fourth marched back to Russia, Siilasvuo's men finally occupied the vacant *mottis*. They found grim evidence of how desperate the situation really had been inside the pockets: vast piles of clothing, parcels, crates, carts, bicycles, musical instruments, letters, maps, amputated limbs, frozen heaps of human and animal waste, piles of horses' heads near the field kitchen, and of course the dead in their frozen hundreds.

Two rather minor Russian attacks were launched in the area of Lieksa, about forty miles southeast of Kuhmo. Neither attack was pressed very urgently and both were thrown back, without undue difficulty, by relatively modest Finnish forces. By the end of December that sector was quiet, and the Finns transferred their men to more active fronts, except for one ski-guerrilla battalion whose exploits are often spoken about in Finland but whose operations remain "classified" to this day. It remained encamped in the Lieksa area and from that location undertook a number of deep penetration raids into Soviet territory. These included strikes against supply depots, at least one air field, and, according to persistent "unofficial" stories, a number of raids against the Murmansk Railroad itself.

It was on the banks of the Kemi River, close to the little industrial city of Kemijärvi, that the Russians were checked in their most serious incursion into Lapland. They had sent an entire division, the 122d, stabbing westward from its base at Kandalaksha at the tip of the White Sea. The ultimate objective of this attack was Rovaniemi, the capital of Lapland, where the 122d was expected to link up with elements of the 104th, driving down from Petsamo on the Arctic Highway. As already recounted, however, the 104th never covered half that distance, but for a time the 122d looked as though it would do the job all by itself.

A fairly strong packet of armor had been attached to this division, and the Russians used it rather more aggressively on this front than they did at either Kuhmo or Suomussalmi. The forests in this sector thinned out considerably just beyond the frontier zone and offered considerably more room for tank deployment. The Finnish high command had expected nothing more than raiding parties and reconnaissance patrols in this region and so were again forced to scramble for odds and ends of reinforcements to counter this unexpected threat.

Salla was the Russians' initial objective, a tiny picturesque rural village. The road forked at Salla. The northern branch went through Pelkosenniemi and then to Sodankylä, where it connected with the Arctic Highway. If the Russians could reach Sodankylä, Wallenius's troops on the Petsamo front would be cut off from their supplies. Alternatively, from Pelkosenniemi the Russians could turn south and take Kemijärvi, cutting off all Finnish forces fighting between the Kemi River and the border. At Salla, the Russians divided their forces, sending an infantry regiment, a reconnaissance battalion, and a company of medium tanks toward Pelkosenniemi while the rest of the division pushed on toward Kemijärvi.

General Wallenius arrived to take personal command of the defensive battle on December 17; by that date, the enemy was less than twenty miles from Kemijärvi. Mannerheim had augmented the forces at Wallenius's disposal to the extent that he had seven battalions to work with, four of them equipped with little more than their rifles.

Wallenius struck back first against the northern enemy thrust. On the night of December 17, he outflanked them with a battalion that was able to get within 100 meters of Russian lines without being detected. The entire battalion came surging out of the darkness under the arctic pines, firing as they charged, and routed their opponents with surprising ease. Leaving much of its heavy equipment and several vehicles behind, the northern wing of the 122d hastily retreated and did not stop until it had pulled back a total of fifty-five miles, effectively removing it from the action.

This success enabled Wallenius to shuttle reinforcements down to the Finnish defensive line in front of Kemijärvi. The defenders there had already taken out one Russian battalion, killing 600 men in a fierce twelve-hour battle. For the next week, the Russians hammered at Wallenius's line, sending in battalion-sized attacks at the rate of two or three a day. The defenders' positions were superbly camouflaged, and each time they held fire until the attacking infantry was within 150 meters. One Soviet company participated in two such attacks in a single day and was reduced to thirty-eight men by the end of the second assault. Elements of a fresh Russian division, the Eighty-eighth, arrived on the scene, and its battalions were thrown in as they came on line, with no better results.

By the end of December both enemy divisions had shot their bolt. It was all they could do to hold on to the ground they had already won; they were unable to advance a single meter farther to the west. Wallenius was now ready to go over to counterattacks. Beginning on January 2, he struck the Russians with a series of short, hard assaults, keeping them off balance and withdrawing when resistance stiffened, then striking again elsewhere within hours. Gradually the Russians were pushed back. When they reached a series of high ridges, about two miles west of Märkäjärvi, they created a strong defensive line and went to ground behind it. There they stayed for the re-

mainder of the war. Except for routine patrol activity, this sector remained
fairly quiet until the end of hostilities in March.

The Kemi/Salla front, as the Finns designated it in their official bulletins, was
comparatively easy to reach from neutral Sweden, via the railhead at Rovaniemi. Scandinavian, British, European, and American journalists made the
trek, all hoping to get a firsthand look at this strange arctic war.

Among them was Carl Mydans, Time-Life Incorporated's crack photo-
journalist, a pioneering camera artist whose war pictures had the same kind
of force and poetry as those of his close friend, Robert Capra. Fortunately
Mydans was as good a writer as he was a cameraman, and he left some of the
most vivid and haunting descriptions of the forest battles ever to come from
a Western journalist.

The first thing Mydans noticed as he approached the Kemi battlefield was
the surreal quality of the light. In these latitudes, in winter, daylight lasted
about two hours—the sun did not get above the horizon until 11:00 A.M.,
and then it hung low and smoldering in a haze-filmed sky, drenching the
primal landscape with ruddy light.

Even in Lapland, the words "*Life* magazine" carried considerable weight.
Mydans was given a ride to the front by no less a personage than General Wallenius himself. Mydans found him fascinating: an old-fashioned,
strong-man type with a flare for the theatrical, and tough as reindeer hide.
A few kilometers from the battlefield the general's whitewashed staff car
was halted by a couple of zealous sentries who suddenly appeared in the
road, Suomis on their hips, and flagged the car down. The guards loudly
demanded that no one in the car move until all papers had been examined;
there were still Russian stragglers roaming in this area. With grandiloquent
vigor, Wallenius threw open the car door, fairly leaped out into the sentry's
flashlight beam, then flung open his overcoat to reveal a bare, hirsute chest
that bulged with muscle. Both sentries instantly snapped to attention and
began babbling apologies. Wallenius gruffly congratulated them on their
zeal, cracked a parade-ground salute, hopped back in the car, and sped away,
obviously very pleased with himself.

Mydans arrived only a short time after the Russians had begun their withdrawal. He could plainly hear the rumble and crack of the ebbing battle in
the distance. Free to roam the battlefield by himself, he began by wandering
through the recently vacated Finnish positions. He found little that reminded
him of the formal "battle lines" he had seen in Spain and China. Deep
trenches and elaborate earthworks were few; the soil, he quickly discovered,
was as hard as marble. Mostly he found log-roofed huts and bunkers, or

snow-colored tents staked out over shallow foxholes. The larger structures were floored and lined with moss, furs, or some similar form of insulation. The more elaborate bunkers where Finnish ski patrols had rested between actions were filled with handmade blankets, straw, animal hides, lanterns, and small, smokeless stoves. The interiors were a bit funky from occupancy, but they were warm and, given the environment, remarkably cozy.

Mydans had learned, in the course of covering several wars, to "read" the dead. One could tell a lot about an army, he averred, from the condition of its fallen. A helpful Finnish officer answered his first question. No, neither side bothered with steel helmets in the forest fighting; all that inert, frozen metal on top of one's head was more of an annoyance than a protection. Otherwise, he observed that the Russian dead wore heelless, soleless, hard felt boots that looked to be of little value in such a climate. Their padded-cotton uniforms reminded Mydans of the ones he had seen worn by the Japanese in China. While he was poking around, a formation of Soviet aircraft flew overhead. Several nearby Finns, inspecting the enemy dead for documents that might be of value to the intelligence experts, paused long enough to glare up at the sky, make some universally obscene gestures with their fists, and growl something in Finnish that Mydans later figured out was "Fuck you, Molotov!"

It was almost impossible to take pictures of the battlefield. Mydans's cameras froze if he exposed them to the open air for longer than a half minute. He had to carry them inside his clothing, next to his skin. Every time he whipped one out, quickly estimating his focal and light data, he had first to remove his thick gloves, get a secure grip on the camera before tugging it free of his clothing, then set up and grab his shot in a split second. If he left the gloves off of his hands for as long as a minute, his fingers began to throb wickedly from the cold.

He visited a field hospital just behind Finnish lines. There he saw four seriously wounded Russians being given treatment ahead of a group of less-injured Finns. This appeared to be standard practice. The badly wounded were given attention first, regardless of their nationality. A tour of the hospital left Mydans with a feeling that the Finnish medical service was unusually efficient and as well equipped as that of any army he had ever covered. An examination of both the hospital's records and the wounded men still being held revealed what Mydans considered a remarkably high percentage of facial injuries, perhaps accounted for by the close-range nature of the recent fighting.

Mydans then ran into another foreign correspondent, a colleague of long standing. This man had been shown the scene of the bitterest fighting, and he thought Mydans might like to see it too. Mydans returned to the battlefield and later recorded what he saw there:

> The fighting was almost over as we walked up the snow-banked path that led from the road to the river. In the sickly half-light we followed its stained track on to the ice. Here the Russian dead spotted the ice crust. They lay lonely and twisted in their heavy trench coats and formless felt boots, their faces yellowed, eyelashes white with a fringe of frost. Across the ice, the forest was strewn with weapons and pictures and letters, with sausage and bread and shoes. Here were the bodies of dead tanks with blown treads, dead carts, dead horses and dead men, blocking the road and defiling the snow under the tall black pines. Here in the winter of nights with no days, on an obscure river north of the Arctic Circle, in snow that engulfed a man on foot up to his bayonet belt and made him stagger like a dying insect, in temperatures that solidified the lost and wounded into frigid death, here the Finns met the Russians, and stopped them.*

On the road itself the scene was even more horrific:

> Russian Ford trucks with windshields, radiators and bodies bullet shattered. Bloodstained seats told what had happened to the drivers. But back on the narrow icy road and in the woods [alongside it] was a sight that even the most hardened war reporters have called the most horrible they have ever seen. Trucks and supply sleds stood jamming the road. All faced Finland. Here and there they had gone into the ditch on either side, thrown or driven there by necessity. Dead Russians lay about like fallen leaves. With them were their horses, and a shattered truck filled with black bread, a big pile of old leather shoes, heaps of bologna tied with string and hauled like ropes, helmets, gas masks, packages of rice, of red powder for making soup, cases of canned fish, cotton sacks of tobacco, machine gun clips, shells, ammunition, sleighs, harnesses, arms and legs, pink blood in the snow.†

As Mydans was leaving the battlefield, he passed some Finnish officers making a body count of the enemy dead. One of them remarked, in a flat weary voice, "The wolves will eat well this year."

---

*Mydans, Carl, *More than Meets the Eye* (New York: Harper and Brothers, 1959), 19.
†Mydans, dispatch in *Life*, January 29, 1940.

After he returned to the rear, Mydans came upon a group of Finnish soldiers having some sport with a captured Russian. Circling around the man, snarling menacingly, they jeered at him and threatened him with their big knives. They feinted kicks at him with their boots, and clicked the mechanisms of their weapons at him. The prisoner was on the edge of hysteria. Only moments after Mydans arrived, a Finnish officer came for the prisoner and led him from his tormentors into the local command post, an abandoned schoolhouse, for interrogation. Mydans followed, his reporter's instincts in overdrive.

Once the prisoner was seated, he told the Finnish interrogators that he was a dairy worker from Leningrad and that he had left behind a wife and four children. His officers had told the men in his company that they were attacking toward Helsinki. At that point, the "audience" of Finnish soldiers who had crowded into the room began hooting and jeering at the Russian once more. One of the Finns slipped up behind the man and suddenly yanked the blanket from his shoulders. The prisoner gave a tiny yelp of fright and began to shake. Frowning, the major who was conducting the interrogation barked an order, and the onlookers moved back.

Then, his face once more impassive, he paused before starting his questions again. When he did, his voice was very gentle, almost soothing, and the interrogation was soon ended.

Reaching forward, he offered the prisoner a cigarette. The Russian stared at him and his outstretched hand. His tongue, large and white, licked his cracked lips and he slowly raised two blackened and blood-stained hands toward the cigarette. He hesitated, then looked full into the eyes of the Finn. Suddenly tears welled down his dirt-caked face and rolled off his encrusted padded uniform. The room went silent. Gently, the major placed the cigarette on the corner of the table and turned away as if to study the papers before him. For a long moment he sat withdrawn in silence while the Russian continued to tremble, his face now smeared where he had rubbed the tears with his padded cuff.

Mydans thought he had a powerful photograph just waiting to be taken. He reached into his musette bag for his camera and flash gun. "You want to take his picture?" the Finnish major asked. He beckoned for Mydans to come closer. Mydans stepped forward and turned the prisoner around so that he would be facing the camera.

He was rigid and shied from my touch like a mare. . . . I waved several soldiers out of the background and the prisoner watched me frantically.

As he looked and saw himself standing alone, his knees sagged further
and knocked audibly in the silent room.

"It's all right," I said reassuringly, "I'm only going to take your picture." But the major did not offer to translate. I held my camera aloft
to show him, but he only cringed away from me. Through the finder I
saw his hands move up slightly in front of him and then drop. I flashed.

The Russian wheeled around screaming. He sagged to his knees and
grasped the table leg. There he remained, pounding his head on the
table, weeping, stuttering in Russian.

For a moment no one moved. Then, in shame, some of the officers
and men slipped out of the room. The major jumped up and gently
raised the sobbing prisoner. "You're not hurt," he repeated soothingly,
"You're not hurt—we're only taking your picture, we're not shooting
you." He reached for my camera and held it to the Russian's wet face.
"Look through the window," he spoke as one would speak to a child. . . .

The [Russian's] furtive eyes flickered about the room. One eye caught
the finder and two black hands reached up slowly and took hold of my
camera. For a minute he peered through it at me and into the little
group of Finns who waited, quiet and embarrassed. Suddenly there was
a flicker of a smile, then a laugh, then as the major held him he shook
with screams of laughter.

Now the whole room was laughing, and half a dozen hands were
poking cigarettes at him. Someone put the blankets back over his head
and we followed him out through the blackout curtains. The major
turned him over to some guards. . . .

. . . As the major passed me on the way back to the schoolhouse, he
stopped, hesitated before me, started on again. Over his shoulder, he
said harshly in English: "The Russians are pigs!"*

*Mydans, *More than Meets the Eye*, 223.

PART IV

The January Lull

*The Finnins have continual warres with the
Muschovites in the bosome of the sea Finnoni-
cus; using in Sommer the ayde of Shyppes, and
in Wynter they combat upon the ice.*

— George North, sixteenth-century
traveler

▲ CHAPTER 15 ▲ ▲

The Air War

Simultaneously with the epic ground battles, a less publicized but equally one-sided struggle was going on in the air. The first Soviet air attacks had generated considerable shock to the civilian population, but as the raids continued, terror yielded to rage. As would be proven in London and Berlin, the spirits of the bombed do not break as easily as the bombers might wish. Indeed, in terms of overall contribution to the war effort, and considering the fact that by January the Russians were supporting their invasion with about 2,500 aircraft, the Red Air Force had to be judged something of a flop.

The material damage caused by the "strategic" raids of its bombers was relatively slight, with a few notable exceptions, such as Viipuri. Finland, after all, was a most unconcentrated nation; in 1939 nine-tenths of its land consisted of rural wilderness. There were very few modern highways in the interior that offered valuable targets. Much more important was the railway system, and this received a major share of the bombers' attention. Very often the targets would be small village depots. Battered by day-long saturation raids, these would be reduced to splinters, but in terms of results versus effort expended, it was a classic case of using a shotgun to kill a gnat. The rail tracks themselves were cut thousands of times, all over the nation, but there are few transportation targets as easy to repair as a severed rail line, and the Finns usually had trains running again in a matter of hours. A favorite target for roving flights of Red aircraft was the Helsinki-Viipuri rail line, crowded with civilians fleeing west and military traffic moving east.

In the larger urban centers, strict civil defense measures were enforced from the first hour of the war. These precautions had been well rehearsed during the diplomatic skirmishing and false alarms that led up to November 30, and for that reason civilian casualties in the larger towns were surprisingly low.

Helsinki received its worst plastering on the first day of the war and was the target of significant raids only a few times thereafter. With the harbor

187

locked in ice, Helsinki offered few strategic targets and only minor industrial ones; it is possible that the Russians did not think hitting them was worth the consequences if in the process their bombs killed some foreign journalists or wiped out the embassy of a neutral country. Nationwide, only 5 percent of total man-hour production time was lost due to Soviet bombing, and this loss was more than compensated for by volunteers working overtime.

Even so, although the material effect of the Russian bombings was marginal, the aerial invasion did wreak havoc in the private lives of thousands of civilians. Few of the smaller towns and villages could be given any decent antiaircraft defenses. Every gun was desperately needed on the Isthmus, where Soviet tactical strikes, though unbelievably wasteful in terms of expended ordnance, were massive and increasingly bothersome. In some places the local Civic Guard unit might mount an antique Maxim gun on top of the town hall, but most rural localities were defended by nothing more lethal than a forlorn rifle shot or two. The Russians used incendiaries against the villages, many of which were made entirely of wood and insulated with sawdust in the walls, and which went up like torches. For the working-class neighborhoods and peasant farmers subjected to these vicious raids, the appeal of communism suddenly and literally went up in smoke. Incidents of Red aircraft strafing hospitals and hospital trains were so common that the Finns finally painted over any Red Cross insignia that were visible from the air.

All told, there were 2,075 recorded bombing attacks against civilian targets in 516 localities. About 650 Finnish civilians were killed and 2,000 or so wounded. Approximately 2,000 buildings were destroyed and another 5,000 damaged. The ice-plowed harbor at Turku, where most foreign aid was unloaded, was hit very hard, with 48 out of 63 docking facilities destroyed. The industrial city of Tampere received more than 1,500 bombs, most of them aimed, with indifferent accuracy, in the general direction of the state aircraft factory. Viipuri was almost leveled. Nearly 12,000 bombs rained down on that lovely, late-medieval city, along with perhaps 150,000 rounds of artillery, some of it in the form of colossal freight-train shells fired from the outskirts of Leningrad by ten- and twelve-inch railroad guns.

One interesting ordnance experiment tested by the Red Air Force was a device called the "Molotov Breadbasket": a six-foot hollow cylinder packed with 100 small magnesium incendiary bomblets. When the parent bomb was released, metal vanes popped out on the sides, imparting a wild wobbling spin to the cylinder as it fell. This motion flung open the sides of the iron casing and caused the minibombs to spray out in a wide arc. Had these overcomplicated weapons been dropped during a summer dry spell, they might have caused the Finns considerable worry, and those that were dropped on the tinderbox villages certainly worked well enough. It is hard to see why thousands of specimens were lugged aloft and dropped into the forests, however, since everything they landed on was covered with deep snow.

Compared to the wholesale aerial pounding of cities that would become common in World War II, the damage sustained by Finland's civilian population may seem relatively modest. But at the time it was sustained, the world had only seen a handful of comparable aerial blitzes—Nanking, Guernica, Madrid, and Warsaw being the best known—and the world was not yet hardened to these bloody spectacles. The Russians' wanton though often ineffectual attacks on civilians generated a wave of moral outrage all over the world. Typical was the reaction of former U.S. president Herbert Hoover, who denounced the Russian air attacks as a throwback to "the morals and butchery of Genghis Khan."

Sir Walter Citrine, a prominent British Labour politician who was invited to Finland in January 1940, as a gesture of solidarity by the Finnish left, was impressed by the high standards of civil defense discipline. Driving east from Turku one night, he recorded, "nowhere could I see the faintest glimmer of light from the hundreds of houses we passed on the road. The blackout was perfect." * Citrine was able to see some areas that were off-limits to foreign journalists. The seacoast town of Hanko, for example, where Stalin had demanded to be given a strategic base during the prewar negotiations, had few targets of military value but had been singled out for what must have been vengeance raids. Citrine found this once picturesque town in a depressing state: "A little further down the same street a whole series of wooden shops had been destroyed. Sticking forlornly on an upright post, about six feet from the ground, was the stuffed head of an ox, life-size, gazing out seemingly in sorrow across the sea. How odd and strangely pathetic it seemed. The stillness was uncanny. It was worse than going through a churchyard where all the tombstones had been blown down by the wind. We were told that of the 8,000 population, only 2,000 remained. We saw very few of them." †

At the start of the war, the small but highly motivated Finnish Air Force possessed 48 fighter planes, most of them obsolete, along with 34 reconnaissance planes and dive-bombers and a mere 18 modern multiengine bombers. By the war's end shipments of British, French, Italian, Swedish, and American aircraft had raised the total strength of Finland's air arm to more than 200 planes.

Finnish pilots were a superb, elite group. To dive into huge formations

---

*Citrine, Sir Walter, *My Finnish Diary* (London: Penguin Books, 1940), 47.
†Ibid., 56.

of modern warplanes at the controls of a twenty-year-old biplane capable of half the enemy's speed required much controlled courage. At the start of the war the Finns' only modern interceptor was the Dutch Fokker D.XXI—a sturdy, serviceable craft but hampered by an old-fashioned fixed undercarriage and an air-cooled engine that tended to stall at low temperatures and needed constant babying from overworked mechanics. The Fokker mounted four 7.9 mm. machine guns, with 300 rounds per gun, and it could achieve a top dogfighting speed of 286 miles per hour. That made it only 23 miles per hour faster than the SB-2 bombers it was usually sent to intercept and only 36 miles per hour faster than the Ilyushin DB-3.

In late December the Finns received a welcome addition in the form of thirty Morane-Saulnier 406s—sleek French interceptors with superb handling characteristics and a top speed of 302 miles per hour. These were the swiftest planes Finland could send aloft, and they packed the additional punch of a 20 mm. Hispano-Suisa cannon, with sixty rounds, that fired through the propeller hub, in addition to a pair of 7.5 mm. machine guns in the wings. The M.S. 406s did bloody work in March, when they flew sortie after sortie against Russian columns marching over the frozen Gulf of Viipuri. Finnish pilots found them nimble, in particular the men who flew low-level strafing runs, and appreciated the seat armor that had recently been installed in the plane's latest modification. But the French craft was otherwise quite vulnerable to ground fire and could be taken out of the fight by a single rifle bullet.

Britain dispatched some thirty old Gloster Gladiators, those noble bi-winged anachronisms that later flew to their doom, and glory, in the skies over Malta. Once its engine had been adapted to the winter climate, the Gladiator proved to have superior handling characteristics, but its weak quartet of .303 machine guns was useless at long range, and if any were jumped by Russian fighters, they were sitting ducks. In the first ten days they were in action, eighteen of the thirty Gladiators were shot down. The plane was thereafter taken out of action over the Isthmus and Ladoga-Karelia and was relegated to the quieter sectors in the far north. Most of the Gladiators, along with four ancient Hawker Harts, were eventually turned over to some daredevil Swedish volunteer pilots, who tempted suicide by going up in them after Russian formations that outnumbered them five to one. The Swedes acknowledged the situation by painting out the regular Finnish swastikas and covering them with the skull and crossbones. (Finland's use of the twisted cross as an aircraft insignia had nothing to do with Nazi Germany; the swastika was an old Baltic symbol for good luck and had been painted on the very first Finnish warplanes, back in 1918.) Despite the odds, the Swedes brought down six Russian medium bombers and, amazingly, five or six fighters, losing five more Gladiators in the exchange.

The most common Red aircraft in the skies over Finland was probably the Tupolev SB-2, a fairly advanced design that was roughly comparable to the Heinkel He-111. The SB-2 carried 1,100 pounds of bombs, had a range of 435 miles, and protected itself with four 7.62 mm. machine guns. The SB-2's Achilles' heel was its unarmored fuel tanks, located in the wings just behind the nine-cylinder engines. Hit there, the planes usually burst into flames and spiraled out of the sky. Also encountered was the Ilyushin DB-3, which carried 2,200 pounds of bombs at maximum range and more than 5,000 pounds for shorter flights. Missions to Finland permitted the craft to carry even more than that, since the round-trip distance between its forward bases and the Isthmus was so trifling.

Of the many types of Soviet fighters that escorted the bombers, none really gave the Finnish Fokkers as hard a time as the thick, stubby Polikarpov I-16/model 18, an advanced version of the plane Andre Malraux had flown for the Republicans over Madrid, which carried two 7.62 mm. machine guns behind the propeller and two 20 mm. cannon in its stubby wings. An unforgiving plane for novice pilots, the I-16 could attain a top speed of 326 miles per hour above 14,000 feet; its lines had been suggested by several trophy-winning sports aircraft from the early 1930s. At the lower altitudes where most of its dogfighting took place, however, it was only marginally faster than the Fokker D.XXI and somewhat slower than the M.S. 406.

Finnish fighter pilots performed prodigies of valor with their motley collection of planes, diving time and time again into Red formations that outnumbered them ten, fifteen, even twenty to one. Some kind of record was set on January 6, when the leading Finnish ace, a lieutenant named Sarvanto, single-handedly took on a formation of SB-2s and shot down six of them in four minutes. All told, Finnish fighter pilots shot down 240 confirmed Red aircraft, against the loss of 26 of their own planes. It was standard practice to send at least one interceptor up to meet every Russian bomber sortie within range. Not infrequently the appearance of a single Fokker caused an entire squadron of SB-2s to jettison its bombs into the snow and turn tail.

Equal in their dedication were the ground crews who kept the interceptors in the air, even when the planes had been shot to sieves. Most of their work was performed out of doors under camouflaged hangar tents, in temperatures colder than those of a deep freeze. A forward "air base" might consist of a frozen lake, a wind sock, a telephone set, some tents, and perhaps, if they were extremely lucky, an abandoned farmhouse. Hot food was a luxury, as were real beds, sleep, and warmth.

Honor was due, as well, to the women's auxiliary, the Lotta Svard organization. Lotta herself was a folk hero from the days of the Napoleonic Wars, a kind of Nordic Molly Pitcher. Approximately 100,000 women and girls served in the Lottas, and they did much to compensate for Finland's chronic shortage of manpower. They manned air-raid warning posts in high spotting towers, exposed to Russian strafing attacks, bitter cold, and falling shrapnel from Finnish flak bursts. Less glamorous but equally important was their work as nurses, communications specialists, clerks, cooks, laundresses, etc. The "Little Lottas," girls from eight to seventeen, wrote letters to the boys at the front, forwarded gift parcels, and helped out in a hundred other capacities.

Written into the Lottas' creed was the following admonition: "Be not ostentatious in either habit or dress; humility is a priceless virtue." As historian Allen Chew commented: "Their uniform, apparently designed to insure chastity, reflected those Puritan virtues: heavy black stockings, very long, shapeless, somber-gray dresses and floppy garrison hats. By contrast, the modest uniform of the WAACs was daringly provocative." *

Finnish antiaircraft was quite deadly. Estimates of Red planes brought down by ground fire range from 314 to 444, and these include only the confirmed kills, planes whose wreckage fell behind or within sight of Finnish lines. Taking the lowest number as a benchmark, that works out to one kill for every 54 rounds of cannon fire and one low-altitude kill for every 300 rounds of automatic fire, which was remarkable shooting. If the unconfirmed kills are added—planes that were last seen trailing fire and losing altitude—the total number of Russian aircraft lost in the whole 105-day conflict approaches 800.

Finnish bombers, mostly Bristol Blenheims but with a few Italian Fiats added late in the war, carried the war to the enemy as best they could. The Blenheims, nicknamed "Tin Henrys" by their Finnish pilots, had an unpleasant tendency to burst into flame from what should have been minor damage. They could haul a half ton bomb load for a distance of 1,200 miles at 220 miles per hour. Finland started the war with sixteen Blenheims, then obtained ten more in January and a final dozen in February. There were a handful of daring raids against the Soviets' strategic bases in Estonia, but with so many urgent tactical targets closer to home it seems unlikely that such risky, long-range operations were mounted more than a few times, perhaps as morale boosters or just to show the enemy that it could be done. Most Finnish bomber missions had perforce to be tactical in nature—strikes

*Chew, 27.

against gun emplacements and enemy columns—and due to the swarms of Red fighters that protected such targets, all but emergency missions had to be flown at dawn and dusk. This increased the Finnish pilots' chances of getting back alive, but given the primitive state of bombsight technology at that time, it also considerably lessened their chances of hitting anything.

All told, the Red Air Force flew approximately 44,000 sorties during the war, according to Soviet statistics. In the air as on the ground, the Russians learned from their early mistakes, and by late February they were even showing some imagination in their tactics. On February 28, for example, thirty-six Red fighters bushwhacked a squadron of fifteen Finnish planes just as they were taxiing for takeoff, and blew six of them out of the sky with one massive pass.

▲ CHAPTER 16 ▲ ▲

The Outside World Responds

Finland's early victories fired the imagination of the outside world. The so-called "Phony War" on the western front was beginning to bore people. The first month of the Winter War, however, raised the spirits of all those who were opposed to tyranny, especially since so few shots had yet been fired in tyranny's general direction. As historian Max Jakobsen eloquently put it: "So many small nations had been bullied into humiliating surrender, the dictators had won so many cheap victories, that idealism had been left starving. . . . The Maginot Line might have reflected a feeling of security for those living behind it, but it could not inspire them as did the image of a Finnish soldier hurling a bottle at a tank." *

Everybody wanted to get involved, now that it looked like Finland might have a fighting chance. Unfortunately there was a rather extensive global conflict going on, and that made it hard for well-intentioned volunteers to reach Finland. Nevertheless, spontaneous gestures of help were made from every direction. Eight thousand Swedes volunteered, and they at least were both close and acclimated. No other foreign volunteers saw as much action as the Swedes. Eight hundred Norwegians and Danes volunteered. A battalion embarked from Hungary. Italian pilots flew north at the controls of Fiat bombers. Three hundred and fifty Finnish-American volunteers sailed from New York on the *Gripsholm*. Among the stranger volunteers on record were a Jamaican Negro and a handful of Japanese.

From London, the incurably romantic Kermit Roosevelt, son of the Rough Rider president, announced the formation of an "international brigade" optimistically entitled the "Finnish Legion." His recruiting bulletins were worded to imply that anyone who had ever donned a pair of skis was qualified to join, without further training or conditioning. Roosevelt rounded up a total of 230 men for his "Legion" and managed to get them to Finland by

*Jakobsen, 175.

the end of March, too late to fight but not too late for them to become a
major nuisance. The Finns who processed these warriors found them to be
a motley crew indeed: 30 percent were declared unfit for active duty, due to
age, outstanding criminal records, or gross physical infirmities. Several had
only one eye, and one over-the-hill idealist showed up sporting a wooden
leg, just the thing for ski combat.

Their fates were as diverse as their personal stories: sixty of them tried to
return to England via Norway but managed to land in Oslo, in April, at the
same time the German Army did. Some were detained as prisoners, others
managed to scurry back across the border to Sweden. About 100 of them just
settled in Finland, doing whatever came to hand: farming, logging, teaching
English. One man ended up as the resident pro at the Helsinki golf club.
Another, a journalist named Evans, obtained a post at the British Embassy
and eventually became Harold Macmillan's press secretary. The rest simply
vanished from the historical record, blending in with their surroundings
either in Finland or Sweden. It is even possible that a few of them eventually
realized their desire to fight the Russians by serving in the Finnish Army
during the Continuation War of 1941–44.

The Finnish public was certainly flattered by all this attention, and the
rumor mills worked overtime, cranking out increasingly fabulous yarns
about imminent and massive foreign intervention. To the average Finnish
civilian, it must have looked as though the entire Western world was flexing
its muscles to help "brave little Finland."

The muscle flexing, of course, was mostly rhetorical. The sad truth was
that few Western countries, no matter how sympathetic to Finland, were
in any position to help out, due to overriding concerns of foreign policy.
Nowhere was this more true than in neighboring Sweden, where the gulf between cold-blooded political reality and public emotion assumed the dimensions of national schizophrenia. Popular sentiment was accurately reflected
in the recruiting posters of the Swedish volunteer movement:

WITH FINLAND FOR SWEDEN!
NOW THE WORLD KNOWS WHAT IT MEANS TO BE A FINN—
IT IS YOUR DUTY TO SHOW WHAT IT MEANS TO BE A SWEDE!
JOIN THE SWEDISH VOLUNTEERS!!

Apart from the extreme step of actually volunteering, hundreds of "Help
Finland" projects were underway by mid-December; everyone wanted to
help. Everyone, that is, except the Swedish government, who found the Finnish situation acutely embarrassing. Sweden's ruling politicians did not dare

offer enough help to make a real difference in the odds. To do so would have compromised Sweden's neutrality at a very precarious time. Direct intervention on behalf of Finland might have meant war with Russia or, it was feared, some sort of hostile move, eventually, from the Germans. Regarding the Germans, the Swedes were being overly sensitive. It was not, after all, in Hitler's best interests to allow a Soviet republic to be established only five minutes' flying time away from the strategically priceless ore fields in northern Sweden. At the very least, effective Swedish aid would have prolonged the conflict, and that, too, would have been in Hitler's interest, since the Finnish war kept Stalin tied down in the northland and turned away from the Balkans. Hitler would not have moved a finger to stop ten Swedish divisions from marching to the aid of Finland.

Matters were not helped by the hypocritical vacillations of Sweden's leaders. The Swedish people were passionately proud of their volunteer effort, and if a plebiscite had been taken about the matter, they would probably have voted overwhelmingly to go to war for their neighbor and former province. Large segments of the Swedish population viewed their own leaders as spineless and craven. Some public officials resigned in protest and shame. When Foreign Minister Sandler spoke in the Riksdag and labeled his government's policy "neutrality carried to the point of pure idiocy," he was rewarded with a standing ovation.

The Germans allowed some arms to pass through the Reich, until a Swedish newspaper broke the story and Hitler initiated a policy of stony silence toward Finland, in response to frantic diplomatic pressure from his new "ally," the USSR. Oddly enough, however, some of the strongest sympathy for Finland was manifested in Fascist Italy. Huge crowds, including hundreds of Black Shirts in uniform, demonstrated emotionally in front of the Finnish Embassy in Rome, then, carrying the Finnish ambassador on their shoulders, marched to the Russian compound and vigorously stoned it. Italy dispatched substantial shipments of military equipment, including seventeen Fiat bombers and 150 volunteers, one of whom was killed in combat. Väinö Tanner even made attempts to enlist Mussolini's diplomatic influence to help bring about peace negotiations with Moscow. Il Duce, however, brushed aside those appeals. Like Hitler, he too was happy to have Stalin's attention turned from the Balkans, where he had dreams of aggrandizement equal to, if less realistic than, those of the führer.

In America, popular sentiment was almost totally pro-Finland. To the American people, Finland was almost a "pet" nation: a tough, brave little country that always "paid its debts on time," spawned great late-romantic music, and enthralled sports fans with the exploits of its champion athletes.

In New York, Mayor La Guardia sponsored a "Help Finland" rally in Madison Square Garden. The American Red Cross sent substantial humanitarian aid. Stokowski and Toscanini conducted benefit concerts—all Sibelius, naturally.

Franklin Roosevelt was caught in an awkward position by the conflict. He wanted to help Finland, but he was hemmed in by strong isolationist feeling in Congress and by the restrictive neutrality laws that were still on the books from the Spanish civil war. When the first reports of mass bombing of civilians blazed across the front pages of American newspapers, FDR actually contemplated severing relations with the Soviet Union. He was bombarded with so many political arguments against doing that, however, that he finally went too far in the other direction. The American ambassador in Moscow was instructed to deliver a gutless and generalized appeal for "both sides" to refrain from bombing civilian targets, stating that the U.S. government did not approve of bombing nonmilitary targets. The upshot of this policy statement, one historian acidly observed, was that "America was on record as being against evil." * Nevertheless, Roosevelt permitted high-level American diplomats to confer with their Finnish counterparts for the purpose of finding ways to get around the letter of the law. The outcome of these discussions was a scheme by which, under certain conditions, certain types of arms could be purchased by nations friendly to the United States, provided that the deal was made on a cash-only basis, and that any items thus contracted for were shipped from America only in vessels flying the flag of the purchaser.

Finland, of course, had precious little hard currency to spend across the ocean. Nor did it have a merchant fleet capable of convoying arms cargos across the U-boat-haunted North Atlantic. In response to enormous public pressure Congress finally offered Finland a loan of $4 million. On his own authority, Roosevelt upped the total to $10 million, on the condition that Finland would not directly purchase arms with it. This "was like offering a clean shirt to a man asking for a square meal. . . ." † Or, as one congressional critic expressed it for the *Record*: "Because of these limitations, brave Finland cannot have anything but powderpuffs and panties. Finland asks for ammunition, we send them beans. . . . they ask for explosives, we send them tea. . . . they ask for artillery, we send them broomsticks." ‡

But while Roosevelt looked the other way, Finland spent the ten million on surplus foodstuffs, which it then quickly sold for hard cash to block-

---

*Engle and Paananen, 49.
†Jakobsen, 178.
‡Engle and Paananen, 51.

aded Great Britain. Using the pounds-sterling from that deal, Finland then bought weapons from America. As a final gesture, Roosevelt did obtain one-time congressional approval to sell Finland forty obsolescent "Brewster Buffalo" fighters, but only five of them arrived in time to see action in the Winter War.

Other material aid from abroad was substantial in its aggregate total, with Sweden rather shamefacedly leading the list with 100 machine guns, 89 artillery pieces, 85 antiaircraft guns, 77,000 rifles, 18 antitank cannon, and, of course, 8,000 volunteers, many of whom saw considerable action. Other sizable shipments were dispatched by Italy, Hungary, Denmark, Norway, Belgium, France, and the Union of South Africa (twenty-five Gladiators, which did not arrive in time). The aggregate total of this aid was significant and would have marginally strengthened the Finns if it had arrived in time, but because of the political turmoil in Europe, the distances involved, and the logistical problems of merchant shipping during a war, very little came through the narrow end of the funnel in time to be of any use. Finland did, however, equip parts of several divisions with these supplies, in preparation for its second go-round with the Russians in the Continuation War.

Foreign-aid shipments could not go directly to Finland; that was the crux of the problem. Most cargos went first to French or British ports, where they were loaded onto vessels belonging to Finland's small merchant fleet. But these ships had to wait until they could fall in with a north-bound convoy. After sailing as far north under escort as possible, the Finnish ships would break off and dash for the closest ice-free Swedish or Norwegian port. From there the arms and equipment would have to be unloaded and reloaded onto railroad cars for shipment to the Finnish border. Once there, they would again have to be unloaded and reloaded, owing to the fact that Finland had a narrower gauge of railroad track than Sweden. Finally, when the stuff did get to Finland, it had to be uncrated, assembled, and mechanically conditioned for arctic service, and the men who would use it had to translate the instructions and learn how everything worked and how to fix something when it went wrong.

This logistical nightmare was compounded by the fact that the polyglot flow of weaponry arrived in a hundred different models and two dozen different calibers, multiplying the problems of training and maintenance almost beyond the Finns' capacity to deal with them. To cite but one example, by March 1940, there were no fewer than seven different types of hand grenade being issued to Finnish troops in the front lines, each missile with its own fuse length, quirks, and maintenance requirements. Just throwing them safely took an excessive amount of concentration and effort under combat conditions; "our lives were at stake every time we used them," one veteran later said.*

Foreign volunteers included 725 Norwegians and a battalion of Danes that was on its way to the front the day the war ended. A conglomerate band of adventurers calling themselves the "Sisu Legion" embarked from Central Europe but never got beyond German customs. Admiral Horthy's Hungary wanted to contribute an entire corps of volunteers originally numbering 25,000, but only 5,000 men were actually permitted to leave, and only 450 had arrived in time to see a few hours' worth of action just before the cease-fire. The "Finnish-American Legion," 350 midwesterners of Scandinavian descent, saw some hot action on the last day as well, in the collapsing lines around Viipuri. All in all, there were 11,500 foreign volunteers on Finnish soil, and their very presence at least had a tonic effect on morale, even if most of them were too late to have any significant military role.

The Soviet propaganda apparatus continued to crank out shrill, contorted documents attempting to convince whoever was listening that Finland was the real aggressor, that the Kuusinen government was legitimate, and the Mannerheim/Tanner/Ryti regime was enslaving the workers, etc. But the basic arithmetic of the situation defeated them; how could any rational person be convinced that Finland, with a total population of under 4 million, had ever posed a serious threat to the largest land power in Europe? Most American Reds, including those who had recently been so active on behalf of Republican Spain, chose, to their credit, to sit this one out.

One item that was issued for American consumption was a poster featuring a grotesque and unsavory caricature of Gustav Mannerheim, beneath which was printed the following copy:

BUTCHER MANNERHEIM!!

Nuts and bolts clunk into the "Help Finland" collection boxes posted in Detroit auto plants. "Not a dime for Mannerheim!" say the boys on the assembly lines. What guy would be dumb enough to lay his hard-earned dimes on the Mannerheim Line, when that Line is backed by the Hoovers and Fords and Cryslers and all the rest of the fanciest punks?

And their stooge, Butch Mannerheim, the last of the Czar's White Guard majordomos—the Kolchaks, Denikens and Yudenitches who made a bloody shambles of the first workers' republic's early years. In 1918 Mannerheim massacred 30,000 Finnish workers and their wives

*Ibid., 65.

and kids, arming his murderers with money loaned by Britain, France, and the U.S.A. in "the war to make the world safe from Socialism." Today, the Finnish Big Bankers are paying that "war debt" in full—the debt for the slaughtered Finnish workers!!!

Most of these posters, and others like them, were torn down in disgust by the workers who read them.

Propaganda efforts by both sides were amateurish and negligible in effect. During the so-called January lull in the Isthmus fighting, the Russians began using loudspeaker trucks to broadcast propaganda programs toward Finnish lines. The Finns started looking forward to them, since the music was refreshing and the Red artillery had orders to cease firing during the playing of Kuusinen's speeches so the Finns would not miss a word. The Finns used these interludes to "make a break for the head."

Leaflets by the million were airdropped all over Finland, promising an improved standard of living. They were printed on such grossly inferior paper stock that the Finns, many of whom knew a thing or two about the paper industry, disdained to use them in their latrines. In the leaflets Finnish workers were promised an eight-hour day, something they had already enjoyed, by law, for the past twenty years.

Finnish leaflets were not much better, but at least they get credit for originating what would become one of the classic counterintelligence scams of all time: the mansion/swimming pool/starlet offer in exchange for an intact Soviet bomber flown in by a deserter. The "prize" was represented by a still from the 1938 film *Test Pilot*, depicting Clark Gable and Spencer Tracy strolling down the tarmac with Myrna Loy sandwiched between them, airplanes in the background. All the defecting pilot had to do, the leaflet intimated, was to fly his aircraft, undamaged, into the nearest Finnish base, and the good life would be his. The CIA was still dropping specimens of this same leaflet in Angola in the 1970s, only this time using photos of Miami-style mansions designed to entice Cuban pilots. There were no takers at all during the Winter War.

As the most visible symbol of Finnish grit, Field Marshal Mannerheim, despite his general hostility toward journalists, became a magnet for foreign press attention. He forbade any foreign reporters to travel anywhere on the Karelian Isthmus, saying as he signed the edict, "This is a war, not Hollywood." Press headquarters was in the Hotel Kemp in Helsinki—according to some sources, in the *bar* of the Hotel Kemp. From there reporters could file stories based on the basically honest but on the whole quite terse official bulletins issued by supreme headquarters. Using these as their inspiration, the journalists added color from their own imaginations or from the general pool of rumor material. One prominent American newsman got a cable from his home office which read, "Abandon general news. Proceed at once to staff HQ. Attach yourself Mannerheim. Send stories and feature articles." He promptly wired back: "Mannerheim impossible. Shall I try Jesus Christ?"

One foreigner who did obtain a private audience with Mannerheim during the January lull was the well-connected Sir Walter Citrine. Citrine found that the Baron spoke good English, in a "metallic, high-pitched" voice. With unusual candor, at one point in their conversation, Mannerheim told Citrine that he himself had been incredulous about early Russian casualty reports. Battles simply were not that one-sided, in his experience. When one division commander reported that his men had killed 1,000 Russian infantry in a single night, at Taipale, Mannerheim let it be known that he did not believe the figure. Two days later, a terse message came back from the division commander, stating that more than 1,000 Moisin rifles had been collected from the dead and inventoried, if the Marshal would care to come count them for himself. Mannerheim allowed himself a wintry smile as he told the story, adding that he seldom questioned the casualty reports thereafter. "I did not think that my men were so good, or that the Russians could be so bad." *

Gustav Mannerheim was an old man, and unflattering rumors picked and nibbled at the iron stereotype. Stories circulated that he dyed his hair, maintained his manly posture with the help of a corset, donned makeup before each public appearance, etc. But flawed or not, the leadership of Gustav Mannerheim had acquired the same symbolic patina that would soon gather about the head of Winston Churchill. He was, on this and several later occasions in Finland's history, truly "the indispensable man."

Depending on their backgrounds, Finns in the ranks regarded the Marshal in differing lights. To the officer caste, the intellectuals, the urban middle class, and the old Swedish-Finnish aristocracy, he was a figure of almost idolatrous reverence. The working-class Finnish soldiers, on the other hand, were hardheaded individualists, incapable of idolizing anybody. Moreover, many of them harbored a well-founded suspicion that Mannerheim was still not exactly a friend of the proletariat. Even so, the strength of his leadership eventually won their loyalty if not their love. One prominent Finnish historian, Wolf Halsti, recalled overhearing a conversation, during the first week of hostilities, between two burly workmen from Turku. Mannerheim's name came up and was greeted with a few cursory obscenities, after which one of the privates twisted his lips in a wry grin and growled, "Well, I hate to

*Citrine, 105.

admit it, but it's a damned good thing the old butcher-in-chief is still around for this show!"

The Baron's headquarters was in the village of Mikkeli, about eighty-five miles northwest of Viipuri. Each day he was awakened at precisely 7:00 A.M. and arrived for breakfast, immaculately dressed, precisely one hour later. After breakfast he walked from his sleeping quarters in the Seurahunoe Hotel to the operational headquarters, in an abandoned schoolhouse a third of a mile away. At noon, he took lunch in the somewhat formal company of some trusted staff officers. The food is reported to have been good, which means it was probably Continental in nature rather than Finnish, and the conversation was invariably masculine and generalized. Private matters were not discussed, nor was the war itself. One large glass of schnapps was consumed between courses, and smoking was permitted with the postprandial coffee. Etiquette, however, forbade anyone from lighting a smoke until the Marshal had ignited his own custom-made cigar.

After lunch came more operational work. If there were no crises to deal with, and during most of January there were not, Mannerheim would permit himself an afternoon nap, usually sitting in his chair. The evening meal was as prompt as the midday repast and usually finished about 8:30. Afterward, Mannerheim went back to his office and received the final situation reports for the day. He paid particularly close attention to casualty figures, sometimes asking to hear the names of the dead one by one. He seldom got to bed before midnight and often stayed awake until two or three in the morning, in order to savor a drink of scotch—never more than two, but stiff ones—and browse through the foreign newspapers he had always enjoyed reading.

On the fifth of January, Mannerheim's headquarters at Mikkeli was subjected to a saturation bombing that turned most of the village to ashes. Mannerheim calmly ate a final meal at his hotel, which would itself be destroyed later that afternoon, then evacuated his staff and headquarters apparatus to the little town of Otava (The Bear), eight miles to the southeast. From there, he would run the rest of the war, mostly without naps.

Soviet tanks in a "wagon train" circle on the perimeter of *mottis* at Lemetti after a Finnish counteroffensive—*Photographic Center of the General Headquarters, Helsinki*

Remains of an ambushed Soviet column north of Suomussalmi village—*Photographic Center of the General Headquarters, Helsinki*

Russian 163d Division convoy after a Finnish attack in central forests—*Photographic Center of the General Headquarters, Helsinki*

Soviet armor ambushed at the easternmost end of Forty-fourth Division's *motti*, near Raate village—*Military History Museum, Helsinki*

Downed Soviet SB-2 bomber in a forest—*Photographic Center of the General Head-quarters, Helsinki*

One of the Finnish Air Force's thirty French Morane-Saulnier 406 interceptors land-ing in the snow—*Photographic Center of the General Headquarters, Helsinki*

Bristol Blenheim taxiing on a forest air strip. The swastika was an ancient Finnish symbol of good luck—*Military History Museum, Helsinki*

Finnish soldiers sheltered from bombardment preceding the Russian attack on the Mannerheim Line in early February 1940—*Photographic Center of the General Headquarters, Helsinki*

Russian T-28 tank, with a 76 mm. gun in its main turret—*Photographic Center of the General Headquarters, Helsinki*

Finnish artillery during the defense of the Karelian Isthmus—*Photographic Center of the General Headquarters, Helsinki*

Armored shield welded to ski runners, issued to Russian units—*Military History Museum, Helsinki*

Landscape of the once-wooded Summa sector, showing effects of the Russian bombardment—*Photographic Center of the General Headquarters, Helsinki*

Ancient citadel of Viipuri, under fire and burning on March 13, 1940, the last day it flew the Finnish flag—*Photographic Center of the General Headquarters, Helsinki*

Author at the ruins of a Mannerheim Line bunker south of the Helsinki-Leningrad railroad, in 1964—*Author's photo*

CHAPTER 17

The Russians Get Serious

Four days before Christmas, Joseph Stalin celebrated his sixtieth birthday. Fabulous gifts poured into the Kremlin from all parts of the USSR, including jeweled-encrusted portraits of Byzantine splendor that had taken years to create. The Soviet dictator received all the adulation his party could bestow, all the lavish gifts his people's fertile imaginations could devise. Yet Stalin was not happy on this birthday; there was one present missing.

Some weeks before, his old crony Zhdanov, boss of the Leningrad District, had promised that *his* gift to Stalin would be the signed documents of Finland's surrender. But instead of a triumphant parade to celebrate the humbling of Finland, Leningrad was threaded, several times a day, by long, slow trains, their windows covered with curtains, filled to suffocation with maimed, starving, frostbitten Red Army troops. Ten days into December, Leningrad's regular hospitals were swamped; by mid-December so were the emergency wards that had been set up in schools and factories. By Stalin's birthday, the long grim trains no longer even stopped in Leningrad but rolled on eastward all the way to Moscow.

Stalin was not pleased on this birthday. When a thing did not please Stalin, that thing was eliminated or changed. So it was with this infuriating, disastrous abortion of a Finnish campaign. There would have to be payment exacted for the humiliation of the Red Army, and that payment would be heavy.

Stalin was especially furious with the "Leningrad Clique" of Zhdanov, who had assured him that the Finnish war would amount to little more than a police action, a nuisance that could be concluded in two weeks. Beyond that regional sphere, his anger was focused on the People's Commissar of Defense, Voroshilov. Nikita Khrushchev was present at one dinner inside the Kremlin, in late December, when matters came to a head between Stalin and his factotum. "Stalin jumped up in a rage and started to berate Voroshilov. Voroshilov was also boiling mad. He leaped up, turned red, and hurled

Stalin's accusations back into his face: 'You have yourself to blame for all this! You're the one who had our best generals killed!' Voroshilov then picked up a platter of roast suckling pig and hurled it against the table." * †

By the third week of the war, the Kremlin's official tone had changed from bellicose euphoria to cautious apologies and began to include the first of a long parade of excuses. The terrain was terrible, the climate was vile, the Mannerheim Line was stronger than the Maginot Line, the American capitalists had sent 1,000 of their best pilots to Finland (this last fable was reprinted, with a straight face, even in more recent, objective Soviet accounts of the war).

As has already been told, Chief of Staff Shaposhnikov had originally seen the Finnish campaign in a clear, professional, and decidedly pessimistic light; his suggestions were disdainfully filed away by Stalin. Now they were dusted off, and Shaposhnikov was brought in for high-level consultations and given the full authority of the Kremlin to back up any suggestions he might make. It was on his order that the brutal frontal assaults on the Isthmus were suspended in late December and no further adventurous plunges into the northern wilderness were launched, although he did approve vigorous action to extricate some of the units already trapped in the various *mottis*. Instead, the Red Army on the Karelian Isthmus would be built up to such a level of power that it could steamroll its way to Viipuri, if not all the way to Helsinki.

During the first week of January, the disgraced Leningrad Military District was reformed and renamed with the more businesslike appellation "Northwestern Front." To exercise operational command, Stalin chose Army Commander, First Rank, Semyon Konstantinovich Timoshenko, a former barrel maker who had risen in the Red Army through sheer ability and rigorous ideological orthodoxy. His recent handling of the attack on eastern Poland, though undertaken against trifling and disorganized resistance, had con-

---

*Crankshaw, ed., 154.

†Voroshilov was lucky to escape the firing squad; he was, quite properly, sacked as a result of the Winter War blunders, but Stalin kept him around, in Khrushchev's words, "as a whipping boy." Doggedly loyal and subservient, he was clearly too incompetent to pose a threat; Stalin seems to have been fond of him, even as he heaped abuse on him. Voroshilov led a charmed life altogether, surviving purges, upheavals, and a serious post-Stalin denunciation in which his sins were paraded in public. He managed to cling to the skirts of power for an amazingly long time, enjoying reelection to the Supreme Soviet as late as 1962. He died in 1970, at the age of eighty-nine. A mildly pathetic figure at best, the key to his survival seems to have been that nobody, after 1939, ever took him seriously again.

firmed his ability to handle massive formations of troops and equipment. A commanding authority figure with a shaven head, flinty gray eyes, and a powerful drill-field voice, Timoshenko was perhaps the best man in the Red Army to break the Finns. Yes, he assured Stalin when the job was first offered to him, he could crack the Mannerheim Line, but it would not be a cheap victory. He sought, and received, Stalin's promise that he would not be held personally responsible for the butcher's bill that would be presented after the successful campaign.

Timoshenko's chief of staff for the coming operation would be the chief architect of the Red Army's crushing victory over the Japanese in Mongolia, Georgi Zhukov. Zhdanov lost all authority over military matters, something he was no good at anyway, but was given a chance to redeem himself by taking over the political aspects of the new campaign. This he did with redoubled energy, anxious to regain his master's good will, sending thousands of zealous political workers into the ranks of the Northwestern Front's units. Only this time there was a subtle change in emphasis. The usual hackneyed drum-beating party slogans were soft-pedaled in favor of direct appeals to Russian patriotism and pride. Our country has been shamed in the eyes of the world, was the essential message, and it was up to the reorganized divisions of the Northwestern Front to redeem Russia's honor. When the Red Army went back against the Mannerheim Line in February, the battle cries would not be "For Stalin!" but "For the glory of the Fatherland!" It made a difference. The apathy and dim-wittedness so often observed during the December battles was largely replaced by energy and determination. Unit for unit, it made the refurbished Red Army a much more dangerous foe.

In line with this new propaganda strategy, a great show was made of honoring those who had fought well in the December campaigns. In mid-January, the Supreme Soviet, with much pomp and a three-page list in *Isvestia*, awarded medals to more than 2,600 veterans of the early battles.

As might be expected, however, the greatest care was taken in the realm of tactics, for that had always been where the Finns' greatest advantages lay. *Sisu* alone had not accounted for the Finns' defensive victories on the Isthmus in December. The entire Soviet effort had been a tactical botch. Mannerheim likened the enemy's performance to "a badly conducted orchestra." The various component arms had lacked even the crudest coordination. The artillery, though massive in strength and applied against the Finns with Mongol excess, had been poorly directed; its fires merely plowed into a given general area on the map. Field commanders had not been able to call upon direct supporting fire. Barrages had not advanced in step with the infantry, so that some Soviet formations had been forced to advance through curtains of "friendly" shell fire in order to close with Finnish positions. The much-vaunted Soviet armored force had seldom acted in concert with the infantry. Tanks would charge full tilt at the Finns, break through, then simply mill about like herds of oxen, waiting for someone to tell them what to do next. The quality of Soviet leadership, from divisional staff down to platoon leaders, had been almost universally wretched, a fact that may largely be attributed to Stalin's purge of the professional officer caste, a bloodbath that liquidated perhaps three-quarters of the Red Army's experienced professional leadership.

Timoshenko and Zhdanov began working at the top, reorganizing and tightening control. Once that was done, they worked toward the bottom, changing tactical doctrine to meet reality, not theory, and making sure the divisions that would bear the brunt of the assault were well trained and thoroughly supported.

The first step was a total reorganization of the Northwestern Front. All Red Army forces on the Karelian Isthmus were divided into two corps: Thirteenth Army, under General V. A. Grendal, for the right wing on the northern Isthmus, comprised of the three divisions that had been fighting in the Taipale sector, plus new support and reserve units; and Seventh Army, under Army Commander, Second Rank, Meretskov, comprising the much-stronger right wing on the southern Isthmus.

It was Meretskov's men who were expected to break the Mannerheim Line, and his command was strengthened accordingly. Three-fourths of his strength would be massed against the sixteen-kilometer stretch that ran Summa–Lähde road–Munasuo Swamp. Against that already battered sector, Meretskov assembled an overwhelming concentration of force: nine infantry divisions, five tank brigades, one machine-gun division, and enough artillery to achieve a front-wide ratio of eighty guns per mile.

The basic tactical approach was not subtle. It was even dubbed "gnawing through," and it consisted first of piercing the Mannerheim Line with an armored wedge, then systematically expanding the initial puncture, and after that simply continuing to send fresh waves of troops and vehicles against the entire sector until the defenders caved in. It was clear that the Finns were already stretched thin, and it was anticipated that a massive rupture of the line at any point on the sensitive Viipuri Gateway sector would force the Finns to abandon the entire position.

Assigned to be the tip of the wedge was the Soviet 123d Division, and it was given rigorous training. After intense reconnaissance efforts, about three-fourths of the Finns' frontline fortifications were pinpointed. Patrols even brought back samples of concrete for engineering analysis. With this

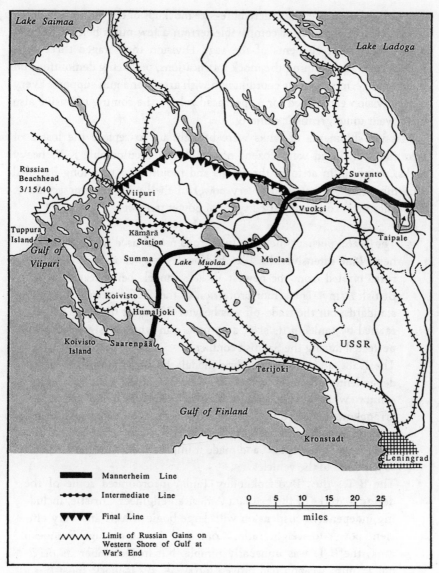

12. Final Russian Offensive on Karelian Isthmus

data in hand, Timoshenko ordered life-size mockups of the Summa defenses constructed in a region of comparable terrain a few miles behind Russian lines. The assault elements of the 123d Division then staged three full-scale rehearsals, storming the mock fortifications, practicing demolitions on them, and perfecting their coordination with armor and gun support. Every other division earmarked for a spearhead role in the coming offensive also underwent tough, realistic training.

Massive shipments of tanks were brought up to replace the losses of December. Included were dozens of the almost invulnerable K.V. heavy tanks, weighing in at forty-three tons and mounting a new long-barreled 76.2 mm. cannon that fired a very powerful shell with extreme accuracy. The other most commonly used types of Soviet tank were:

- The T-26: perhaps the most numerous model used in the Mannerheim Line offensive, the T-26 had been designed using many features pirated from the newest Vickers models being tested by the British Army. The armor protection of the T-26 was weak by 1940 standards, but the trade-off was heavier firepower than was usually carried by tanks of its size: a 45 mm. gun whose design had been perfected during the Spanish conflict.
- The T-28: an interesting hybrid model, the T-28 mounted three independently rotating turrets; the largest housed a short 76 mm. cannon, while the two smaller housings carried machine guns. This arrangement enabled the T-28 to do grim execution when it prowled among Finnish entrenchments, since the triple-turret system did away with "blind spots" and made it impossible for antitank squads to get close to the vehicles.
- The B.T.: the "Byostrokhodny Tank" incorporated some of the design features of the brilliant American engineer Christie, including independent suspension with large bogie wheels and very efficient power-to-weight ratio. Compared to the average European tank, the B.T. was unusually nimble, but in December its original 37 mm. weapon had proven too weak. By January, most B.T.s deployed on the Isthmus had been up-gunned to carry a 45 mm. cannon.

Tank tactics had also been refined. No longer did the operational plan call for Poland-style breakthroughs followed by vaguely defined but wildly optimistic thrusts deep into Finnish territory. The tank units assigned to the new offensive were given realistic, limited objectives and were under strict orders not to outrun their infantry or artillery support.

But by far the most elaborate preparation made by Timoshenko concerned his artillery. The Russian Army had always believed in the power of artillery. If the panzer commander was an elite figure in the Wehrmacht, the artillerist was his counterpart in the Soviet Union. To hammer the Finns until they broke, Timoshenko assembled 2,800 cannon, ranging in caliber from 76.2 mm. to 280 mm. Behind the front, mammoth railroad weapons, nicknamed "ghost guns" by the Finns, heaved gigantic twelve-inch projectiles into Viipuri and other important areas deep in the Finnish rear. Forward observers, equipped with the latest available radio technology, would accompany every attacking formation so that massive volumes of fire could be shifted as required. Area spotting would be done by observers in captive balloons, floating 2,000 feet above the battlefield and protected by fighter aircraft. So contemptuous were the Russians of the Finns' inability to disrupt their preparations that they did not even bother to camouflage any except their most forward batteries. The guns were just lined up wheel to wheel in the open.

On the average, each mile of front was supported by eighty cannon. At the tip of the Soviet wedge, where the 123d Division would smite the Viipuri Gateway, 108 guns were allocated. The most devastating tactical employment of artillery involved the massing of guns to fire directly against the face of concrete pillboxes. In the Lähde road sector, the most hated Finnish strong point had been the so-called Poppius bunker, an immensely strong, multichambered fortress that had been overrun, then retaken, several times in December, and that had been pummeled by hundreds of artillery strikes, but whose guns had never stopped firing. A thousand men had been cut down near that one strong point. Now, under cover of noisy diversionary barrages, the Russians emplaced a six-inch cannon only 500 yards from its embrasures, camouflaged it heavily, and waited for the signal. Other strong points, such as the "Million Dollar Bunker" that had galled the Reds as much as Poppius, were the targets of similar artillery sledgehammers, some of them as large as 280 mm. (approximately eleven inches in caliber).

When Timoshenko opened his offensive, 300,000 shells would crash into the Viipuri Gateway in the first twenty-four hours of the bombardment. Aside from direct flat-trajectory fire against individual strong points, the concentration of cannon was so great that the gunners fired "rolling barrages," simply cranking the gun tubes up and down by increments and not needing to traverse them at all. The sound of that opening salvo, the heaviest since Verdun, would be audible in Helsinki nearly 100 miles away.

▲ PART V ▲ ▲

The Storm

Finland alone, in danger of death—superb,
sublime Finland—shows what free men can do.

—Winston Churchill, January 1940

▲ CHAPTER 18 ▲ ▲

Tidal Wave

By December 27, the Karelian Isthmus had grown relatively quiet. Finnish reconnaissance flights revealed that the Russians were erecting bunkers, a sure sign that, for the moment at least, their thinking was defensive in nature.

Mannerheim did some reorganizing of his own during the January lull: between January 2 and January 5 the burned-out Fifth Division went into reserve, replaced by the Sixth Division, which Mannerheim renamed the Third Division in order to confuse enemy intelligence. As much as the Fifth, the Tenth Division at Taipale also needed relief, but there was no other reserve division to plug in. All Mannerheim could do was rename it, as well, calling it the Seventh Division, so that the Russians might think they were confronting rested troops. It is impossible to say how well or how long these ruses worked; probably not for long. As commander-in-chief's reserve, Mannerheim placed the newly created and wretchedly equipped Twenty-first Division behind the Seventh, in the Pyhäjärvi area.

As round two of the Isthmus fighting began, Finnish dispositions were as follows (southwest to northeast):

Second Corps (General Öhquist)
- Fourth Division: the right flank of the Mannerheim Line, to the gulf coast
- Third Division: on its left, covering the Viipuri Gateway (Summa and Lähde sectors)
- First Division: on the Third's left, as far as Lake Muolaa
- Second Division (formerly the Eleventh): from Lake Muolaa to the Vuoksi Waterway

Third Corps (General Heinrichs)
- Seventh and Eighth divisions, manning the rest of the Isthmus,

from the Vuoksi's northern end, along the Suvanto Waterway, and
Taipale—the extreme left flank of the Mannerheim Line

Reserves

- Fifth, Twenty-first, and Twenty-third divisions, employed strengthening the "Intermediate" and "Rear" lines—the last named, the
  Finns' final line of prepared defenses on the Karelian Isthmus, was
  anchored on the city of Viipuri

Timoshenko's plan called for gradually increasing the bombardment,
wearing down the defenders, and softening up their fortifications, then suddenly escalating the artillery and air punishment on February 1, following it
with strong local ground attacks. After ten days of round-the-clock pounding, the Red Army would go all out on February 11 and try to score the big
breakthrough that had eluded its generals so far.

Factored into Timoshenko's equation was a savage but simple truth. Russian units could be rotated when casualties, exhaustion, or depleted supplies
lessened their performance. Finnish units could not. The cumulative strain
on the defenders was designed to grind them down not only physically but
psychologically, by depriving them of sleep, warmth, hope itself. Eventually, as they shuffled the same increasingly burned-out units to meet threat
after threat, even Finns would reach their breaking point.

When in late January the Finns began to have some conception of what
was in store for them, there was frustratingly little they could do to disrupt
the enemy's concentrations. The air force bombed and strafed troop columns
and gigantic supply depots, but the clouds of Soviet flak and swarms of Polikarpov interceptors made these raids hazardous and restricted them to the
hours of dawn and dusk. Finnish artillery found its maps literally covered
with potential targets, against which it could do nothing. Every Finnish battery was under the strictest orders to fire only against directly threatening
ground attacks, so desperate was the shortage of ammunition. And so contemptuous were the Russians of the Finns' ability to hinder them that they
drove miles-long convoys of supply trucks toward the front with headlights
blazing.

On the morning of February 1 a Finnish reconnaissance plane threaded
its way through some forty Russian fighters and made a hasty photo run
over Russian lines in front of the Summa positions. The film brought back
was quickly processed and enlarged. When the Finnish intelligence team
gathered to examine the still-damp enlargements, there was a spontaneous
gasp from each man's lips. Overnight, the number of enemy cannon em-

placed before Summa had multiplied astoundingly. Counting only the visible guns, brazenly mounted in open, uncamouflaged emplacements, there were no less than 200 pieces of artillery massed to fire against the Summa sector alone. It was nearly as bad everywhere else.

The sound of that first big salvo, on February 1, produced a terrifying convulsion of the earth. An iron wall of sound and vibration crashed into the defenders' nervous systems like the last thunderclap of Armageddon. Overhead appeared the first waves of a correspondingly vast aerial offensive; 500 planes over Summa alone. To the fury of the cannonade was added the impact of concentrated carpet bombing, the heaviest and most sustained aerial attacks in the history of warfare to date.

Day by day the weight and fury of this fire would increase. Finnish dugouts caved in and their occupants were buried alive. The deepest-buried telephone cables were eventually unearthed and ripped to pieces. It became impossible even to heat the Finnish blockhouses; the slightest trace of smoke was enough to summon a punishing bombardment. All resupply had to be done at night. Even the field kitchens could only function after dark. Deprived now of warmth and warm food, the Finns began to show increasing signs of fatigue.

Despite their improved tactics and morale, one aspect of the new Russian attacks remained the same as it had been in December: they were still willing to accept staggering losses in order to reach their objectives. Some attacks, it is true, were screened by smoke, and almost all were heavily supported by artillery and armor, but the infantry assembled, approached, and charged in the open. Whole battalions advanced in dense, cheering columns into which Finnish machine gunners poured streams of bullets, with sickening effect.

These attacks followed a methodical pattern: strong artillery and air bombardment, followed by strong tank/infantry assaults. No matter how many men and vehicles were lost, the attacks would be repeated, in each division's assigned sector, three, four, five times each day, with fresh Soviet units committed each time. Finnish shell fire smashed formations time and time again, but it seemed to make no difference. Armored spearheads of 100 or more tanks were commonly employed. With Bofors guns rationed out at an average of two per regiment, there was no way the defenders could handle such odds; and the Russians' new emphasis on close cooperation between infantry and armor made it suicidal to send out antitank squads armed with hand-thrown missiles.

From the moment of the opening salvos to the fall of total darkness, February 1 was a day of nonstop combat. Yet as heavy as these attacks were, they were still essentially just big probing actions, designed to take out a bunker here and there, feel for the weak spots, and wear down the defenders, setting them up for the all-out blow that would fall on the eleventh.

Each time a Finnish bunker was taken, the men who had defended it were forced to dig holes in the open, or compelled to crowd into the sagging, battered trenches that connected each concrete strong point. Gradually more and more Finns began to feel the effects of prolonged exposure, the mental and physical toll of sleeplessness, and the general deterioration of faculties that comes with prolonged exposure to concussion.

Even at dusk, when the attacks were broken off, the defenders were unable to snatch more than odd moments of sleep. Every man was needed to retake lost positions, repair damaged fortifications, haul forward new supplies of food and ammo, and help bear the shivering wounded to the rear. As the "softening up" entered its third and fourth days and the troops' condition worsened, the frontline troops and the local reserves, stationed a few thousand meters to the rear in the "support line," had to be rotated at shorter and shorter intervals. Even in reserve there was little rest: men in the support line were working frantically to reinforce and repair its defenses and had to be prepared at any time to rush forward and contain Soviet breakthroughs. By the end of the first week of this routine, the units on the line were reaching a state of exhaustion.

In their attacks on February 2 and 3 the Russians repeated the pattern established on the first day, only now the assaults came in greater strength, against a wider frontage of the line. Again fighting was fiercest at Summa, where several concrete blockhouses changed hands five and six times in a single day. One regiment lost its commander three times on February 5. By the end of February 3, it was possible to count more than 1,000 dead Russians on the ground in front of Summa village. By February 7, despite the shortage of antitank weapons, the Finns in General Öhquist's Second Corps had destroyed about ninety Soviet tanks.

And still the bombardment increased. In the Summa sector alone, 400 shells per minute rained on the line. The frozen, granite-veined Karelian soil acquired the consistency of warm paste. Somehow the defenders hung on in their disintegrating positions: deafened, sleepless, half crazy from shock and noise, still they fought back, responding time and time again while the enemy pressed home its relentless assaults, sometimes over mounds of corpses. The layers of snow and soil and sheeting that had hidden the Finnish field emplacements were blown away. Layers of logs and sandbags five feet thick were blown to dust. The outer faces of concrete pillboxes were raked to powder by thousands of near misses, and the steel-reinforced walls of the most massive blockhouses were beginning to crack. So enormous and unrelenting was the concussion from the bombardment that a number of multiton concrete emplacements were finally lifted up and tilted to bizarre angles, ruining their fields of fire.

The inherent weaknesses of the Mannerheim Line forts was becoming grimly apparent: weaknesses that should never have been built into them, regardless of the fact that no one ever expected them to withstand so titanic a battering. The concrete foundations anchoring the newer positions had not been sunk into the ground deeply enough. The concrete walls were not thick enough, nor laced with sufficient steel. Far too many bunkers had been built to command isolated bits of ground, and too few of them could offer support to neighboring strong points when waves of Red infantry swarmed on the tops and sides. Most of the strong points housed no armament larger than the reliable but slow-firing Maxim guns. These wrought mass destruction on attacking infantry but too often could be neutralized by a single determined enemy tank simply parking itself in front of the embrasures, a situation that would never have arisen if the Finns had obtained adequate numbers of antitank guns.

One by one, the Finnish strong points went under, submerged beneath waves of fanatically brave Soviet infantrymen who pressed forward ruthlessly. Time after time Finnish fire would mow down hundreds of men in the first waves of these attacks so that those pressing forward from behind were forced to climb over windrows of dead and dying comrades. As each successive attack dashed itself to pieces, the rows of dead were closer and closer to Finnish lines, until ultimately the assault swept into the trenches and the horror of hand-to-hand combat would erupt. Eventually, no matter how many Russians died in such costly assaults, every Finnish strong point subjected to these attacks was overwhelmed.

In some sectors the Russians captured pillboxes that appeared to have sustained only moderate structural damage, only to find the entire Finnish garrison stone dead inside, without visible wounds of any kind except for rivulets of frozen blood from their nostrils, ears, and eye sockets. These men had died from the cumulative effects of sheer concussion.

Yet somehow, as the offensive moved into its second week, the Mannerheim Line continued to hold. There is no rational explanation for the defenders' endurance. They drew their strength from sources not normally tapped, from the deepest human reservoirs of determination and primitive courage. By the start of the second week, they responded to each new Soviet attack almost as though they were automatons. As soon as the bombardments let up and the attacking formations were visible beyond the shattered wire entanglements, officers would stagger through the trenches, blowing whistles, cursing and yelling, kicking and slapping and threatening each soldier in turn until all of them somehow were on their feet and stumbling to their assigned firing posts. They continued to fight back, and for ten unspeakable days, they held out. The battle for the Mannerheim Line had become, in the word's of contemporary journalist John Langdon-Davies, "the sort of nightmare that might trouble the sleep of an athlete, who finds himself entangled in an unending series of last-laps toward a [goalpost] constantly retreating before him." *

On February 6 the defenses along the Johannes Highway southwest of Summa were assailed by an entire fresh Soviet division. Met by a blistering Finnish barrage, the attack collapsed, and the decimated Russian battalions fled in panic, not even slowing down when their political officers fired into the mob with their pistols.

On February 8 General Öhquist noted in his personal diary: "the men of the Third Division are deadly tired and absolutely must be relieved." That was the opinion as well of the division's commander, who begged Mannerheim to replace his men with the now-rested Fifth Division. The men of the Third were collapsing in their tracks, he insisted, and he was down to a single worn-out battalion of reserves with which he was attempting to counter penetrations made by entire regiments. Mannerheim refused.

Meanwhile, in their rear-area headquarters on the Intermediate Line, the staff of Fifth Division was getting nervous. They knew they were needed in the line, and they were afraid that Mannerheim might eventually order their men up in battalion-sized packets, at the height of some crisis, and thus fritter away the effectiveness of the division as a whole. But that was exactly what Mannerheim was trying to avoid. The Fifth was the only veteran division within easy reach of the "Viipuri Gateway," and it required icy nerve on the old man's part to maintain a firm grip on it when hysterical reports of imminent disaster were flooding the telephone lines to his headquarters. Mannerheim was convinced that these were the pleas of panic-stricken and exhausted men and that there was not yet a breach so dangerous as to require the commitment of the Fifth Division.

Mannerheim's logic was solid, but unfortunately it created a state of mind at supreme headquarters that led to each report of a Russian breakthrough being examined and double-checked with such thoroughness that when a truly lethal penetration did occur, it went unnoticed and uncountered until it was too late. Thus the entire Summa sector was shattered by a breakthrough whose initial penetration was not of itself inherently critical.

*Langdon-Davies, 108.

By February 8 ammunition for all types of Finnish artillery was so low that Öhquist was forced to order new restrictions imposed on all of Second Corps's guns: not a shell was to be fired unless it was to directly repel an attack that could not, in the opinion of the senior officer on the scene, be handled with small-arms fire alone. Öhquist later wrote that this was the bitterest of the many unpalatable orders he had to issue during those grim days. The enemy was forming up for mass attacks out in the open, presenting targets that were the stuff of an artillerist's dream: "the fattest, most impudent kinds of targets one could imagine."*

On the tenth and eleventh the Soviet offensive widened, as attacks thundered against every sector of the line from Taipale to the Gulf of Finland. During the fighting in that area, the Russians tried for the first time to outflank the line by sending powerful infantry columns on a long, curving march across the thick ice. Before these forces could come ashore behind Finnish lines, however, they were spotted and taken under fire by the coastal batteries in the Koivisto sector, particularly the six-, eight-, and ten-inch weapons emplaced near Saarenpää, on Koivisto Island, and at Humaljoki on the mainland. On this occasion at least, the attackers were given a dose of the same kind of punishment the Finns were enduring at the mercy of the Russian artillery. The six- and eight-inch weapons were supplied with shrapnel shells that were fused to detonate in airbursts over the heads of the Russian columns like gigantic shotgun blasts. The heavy coastal battery, armed only with shells designed to pierce a battleship's armored deck, could not cause that kind of damage with their elephantine projectiles, but the enormous weight and velocity with which they struck tore great holes in the surface ice, so that each successive strike enlarged the fractures until they turned into chasms. Hundreds of men drowned in the cold black waters, sucked down by the weight of their gear, or froze to death in a matter of seconds as they tried to swim to solid ice.

On the twelfth, the enemy launched a major attack whose goal was to silence those shore batteries. The biggest push came against Saarenpää, one of the most heavily fortified points in the whole Koivisto region. Screened by a thick ground fog, two companies of Red infantry managed to sneak across the ice and get to within fifty meters of the coastline before being spotted by a small security patrol. These opened fire with small arms and pinned down the attackers until an observer with a field telephone could arrive on the scene and direct the gun laying of a six-inch battery of naval rifles, the only weapons that could depress low enough to hit such a close target. By

*Halsti, Wolf, *Talvisota* (Helsinki: Werner Soderstrom Oy, 1955), 318.

the time the ground fog had burned off, the coastal battery was trained down the Russians' throats at point-blank range. The attacking force was torn to pieces by its bombardment; not a man set foot on the Finnish shore.

Later that same day the Russians sent 76.2 mm. field guns out onto the ice to lay down a barrage, along with twenty-five medium tanks to overrun the defenders while they were still pinned down. Disregarding the shells bursting all around their emplacements, the Saarenpää gunners coolly waited for the armored formation to fill their sights, then opened up a blistering barrage, keeping at least three shells in the air simultaneously until there were simply no more targets to engage. All twenty-five tanks were ablaze or had sunk through holes the explosions had torn in the ice.

Up on the line's extreme left flank at Taipale the Russians charged across the same wide-open, bloody approaches they had used in December, and large formations moved out to turn the Taipale flank by marching across the ice of Lake Ladoga. There, just like the men who tried to storm Saarenpää, they were slaughtered by the shore batteries. The fighting rose in intensity and reached a grim climax on February 14, when in the space of less than four hours, 2,500 Russian infantry were cut down on the ice around Taipale. Thereafter, the scope, if not the intensity, of Russian attacks on Taipale seemed to diminish, as their gains enlarged elsewhere. But there was never a day of real rest for the defenders of Taipale. At no time between early February and the end of the war in mid-March could they count less than 100 Soviet aircraft bombing their positions during any hour of the day.

▲ CHAPTER 19 ▲ ▲

Breakthrough!

What was it like for the Finnish GIs in the trenches to fight in these apocalyptic struggles for the Mannerheim Line? It is not possible to reconstruct every battle in the Summa sector in detail. They raged under conditions of total chaos, and few coherent narratives of them exist that were written from the soldiers' point of view. Finns who survived and wrote accounts of these battles after the war usually admit to breaks in their memories, vortices in which events lose focus and become a blur of violence and exhaustion.

Nowhere on the Mannerheim Line was there any place, after February 11, that could accurately be described as a "quiet sector." Enemy pressure was severe along the entire front. Soviet artillery fire was vicious and heavy against all the defenders' positions. In the Summa sector the scale and intensity of the onslaught passed beyond the power of words to describe adequately, even as it finally passed beyond the Finns' capacity to endure. To gain a clearer understanding of what the February fighting was like, it might be more profitable to "zoom in" on a sector where events were recorded in some detail, where the ebb and flow of battle can be brought into sharp focus.*

In the sector that fronted the Muolaa church—a rural landmark about halfway between Lake Muolaa and the Vuoksi Waterway—the Soviet bombardment was not quite as cataclysmic as the 400-gun flail that pulverized Summa, but it was bad enough. What happened there was a paradigm of what took place all along the line, north and south of the main point of contact at Summa.

The most advanced Finnish position was a country churchyard on the swampy banks of Lake Kirkkojärvi, where troops entering or leaving the

---

*The Muolaa church battles are chronicled in great detail in *Kansa Taisteli* magazine, January–March 1962.

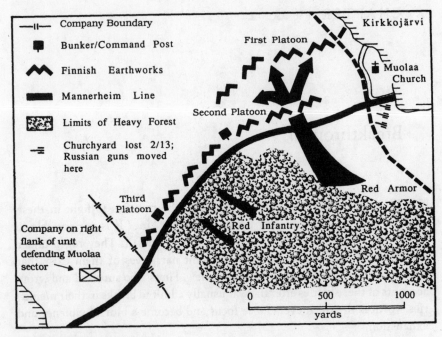

13. Muolaa Church Battle

command bunker, located near the protective stone walls of the church cemetery, had the macabre experience of crawling over a partly exposed coffin.

Russian pressure against the Muolaa church sector grew severe on the morning of February 11, when sappers detonated an enormous chain explosion and blew gaps in the belt of antitank rocks fronting Finnish lines. This overture was followed by a four-hour bombardment that blasted the churchyard into a smoldering ruin and left its cratered surface littered with old bones.

Moments after the shelling stopped, the Russians attacked with twenty-eight tanks. There was not a single Finnish antitank gun left in this sector because all available weapons had been pulled out and sent south to the Summa front. The men defending the Muolaa position had nothing but satchel charges, grenade clusters, and Molotov Cocktails. Their orders were firm: stand fast, ignore the tanks if possible, but repel the infantry at all costs; once the Red infantry withdrew, the tanks would pull back as well— at least that was how it had worked in December.

Although the Red tanks got to within twenty meters of the stone wall surrounding the churchyard, they went no further, apparently fearing a Finnish ambush. Moreover, they did not support their following infantry very aggressively, and the Russian soldiers took heavy casualties every time they tried to advance on their own. Finally, the attacking formations went to ground out near the antitank rocks, about 200 meters behind their own armor. At dusk they withdrew, leaving hundreds of dead.

The Red armor formed a wagon-train circle for the night, each tank parking so it could cover its neighbor with machine-gun fire. With the coming of darkness, the Finns struck back. Taking advantage of their knowledge of the ground, they crept close—while snipers shot out the tanks' headlights—and destroyed seven vehicles with hand-thrown missiles.

Strong attacks were again repulsed on February 12, but the churchyard had to be abandoned on the thirteenth; it was too exposed, and Russian shells had battered down all the cover. The churchyard was immediately occupied and fortified, giving the attackers a good position from which to enfilade the Finns' left flank.

New orders came through from Isthmus Command: the Muolaa position—now held by only a single company—must remain in Finnish hands at all costs, until after the crisis at Summa had been dealt with. No reinforcements or artillery support could be expected. By now, the defenses in this sector were in a very dilapidated condition. There was only one concrete bunker; all the rest were earth and timber fortifications, built by prewar volunteer labor and never intended to withstand this kind of punishment. The trenchlines connecting each strong point were starting to collapse—the soil in this part of the Isthmus was loose and gritty, like coarse sand. The defenders had a mortar or two, but no shells left for them, and they had an artillery observer, but since he had no guns to observe for, he fought as an infantryman.

At 6:00 A.M., February 14, the next Russian assault began, prefaced by a devastating bombardment made even worse by a battery of 76.2 mm. field guns that had been emplaced in the old churchyard. This time, twenty-five tanks advanced, led by a quartet of flame-throwing machines that could shoot a fire stream forty feet long from their turrets. The Finns soon learned that it was possible for a man to run through the fire, provided he covered the exposed parts of his face, without suffering more than a scorched snowsuit. They used this hair-raising tactic to work in close, where the tanks' machine guns could not depress sufficiently to hit them, and disabled several vehicles with mines, grenades, and in one case by the crude but effective method of prying the treads off their wheels with a crowbar.

Again, the attacking infantry hung back, many of them inching forward behind individual armored shields mounted on ski runners. The shields seemed to make the attackers timid, and individual Finns took advantage of their passivity to strike back. One sniper, a platoon commander named Kuusala, went out into no-man's-land with a telescopic rifle and shot fifteen Russians through the legs and buttocks while they crouched behind their shields. On the way back to Finnish lines for more ammunition, Kuusala was spotted by several tanks, which attempted to run over him. He took cover in a shell crater while the vehicles drove back and forth over it, and when he reached friendly lines, his entire back was one vast purple welt from the pressure of the treads.

Once again the Russians withdrew, and the enterprising Kuusala led a squad into no-man's-land and collected thirty abandoned armored shields. These proved extremely useful in shoring up the Finns' crumbling earthworks. There was a lull on the fifteenth, while the Russians replenished their artillery ammunition, and the defenders used it to send out ambush patrols. One Finnish sniper obtained thirty verified kills on that day alone.

On February 16, once again lavishly supplied with shells, the Russians moved to obliterate this stubborn pocket of resistance once and for all. Against the single half-strength company hanging on at Muolaa, they sent a great wedge of fifty tanks, preceded by heavy rolling barrages and accompanied by artillery observers in radio-equipped vehicles.

By eleven o'clock that morning, when the Finnish company commander looked out of his bunker, he could see no movement in what was left of his position—only a churned and smoking landscape. Yet when the enemy attacked again, a few minutes later, using squad-sized armored sleds towed behind huge K.V. tanks, the defenders' trenchline blazed defiantly. Two of the K.V. monsters hit mines that had been planted the night before, and the drivers of the other two vehicles panicked. They turned their tanks around and exposed their infantry passengers to a deadly cone of fire from the Finns.

Finnish discipline almost cracked at midafternoon. The last Finnish machine gun went out of order, jammed by the constant rain of grit on its mechanism, and pairs of Soviet tanks teamed up and started driving back and forth on opposite sides of the defenders' trenches, collapsing their walls and burying some men alive. But eventually the Russians stopped shelling the Muolaa position—their observers could report no visible targets left to shoot at. The handful of Finns still alive at the bottom of their crumbling entrenchments rifled the pockets of the dead and stripped bullets from the belts of their now-useless machine guns. Somehow, they managed to throw back one more battalion-sized attack before darkness fell, and the long-awaited order came permitting them to withdraw.

Out of the company that had defended the Muolaa church sector, less than one platoon walked out that night. Behind them, they left approximately

1,000 dead Russian infantry and the blackened shells of at least sixteen tanks. By that time, no one was counting.

By nightfall on February 11, the nightmare of a decisive Russian break-through had become a reality. But instead of the sudden, dramatic hammer blow that everyone had been expecting, consciously or not, the penetration that caused the abandonment of the Mannerheim Line was first reported almost incidentally, and without much urgency, to Isthmus Command. It was nestled within a host of battle reports that sounded far more disaster fraught than the modest whisper with which the real crisis introduced itself. Instead of high drama, there was only confusion. The Lähde road break-through, which accomplished what hundreds of other enemy assaults had failed to do, was not recognized as a significant threat until the Russian forces within the salient had grown too powerful for the Finns to destroy or eject them. Every action they took to counter the emergency was hours too late, and too weak by hundreds of men.

Manning the defenses in the Lähde road sector northeast of Summa on February 11 were the men of the Second Battalion, JR-9. The Russians had timed their offensive better than they knew: only a few hours before dawn, 2/JR-9 had finished relieving the battered battalion that had held this sector since late January. That battalion was no longer capable of effective resistance; its men had endured everything the enemy could throw at them, had repulsed dozens of attacks, had been overrun by tanks more times than anyone could keep track of, yet they had never broken, never fled the field.

The replacement battalion was dreadfully understrength. To man its mile-and-a-half-wide section of the line, it mustered 40 percent of its peacetime complement, or about 400 men. To compound its problems, this was a battalion of Swedish-speaking Finns attached to a Finnish-speaking regiment. Under normal civilized conditions, so many Finns are bilingual that this would not have been a problem; in the tension and chaos of battle it was one more strain on an already overburdened communications system. Its commander, a major named Lindman, was wound too tight before the fighting even started. When he saw the wave of men and steel inundate his positions, he caved in and remained stunned to inactivity during the most crucial moments. The Second Battalion would fight a leaderless battle, a battle of company commanders and noncoms doing what they could with what they had.

As luck would have it, the Lähde road sector was the very place that had made General Öhquist apprehensive during the prewar debates about the Mannerheim Line's final configuration. The sector was very close to

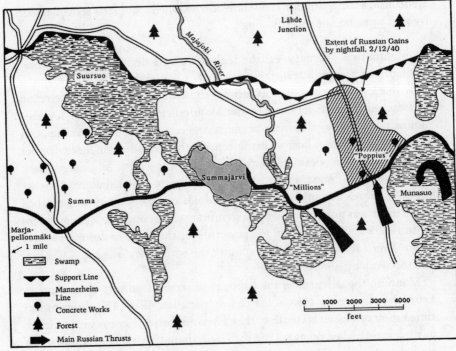

14. Russian Breakthrough of February 12, 1940

that critical "elbow bend" at Summa, and its worthiness as a defensive line
rested solely on the two modern fortresses that dominated its approaches,
the Million-Dollar Bunker and the Poppius bunker. Otherwise the fortifications were not impressive: three more concrete pillboxes designed and
poured almost twenty years earlier and all three badly damaged by shell fire,
plus numerous trenches, log bunkers, and dugouts, all badly mauled by February 11. Moreover, except for the left flank, where the Munasuo Swamp
remained boggy and treacherous beneath its crust of winter ice, the terrain
leading to the defenses was open, lightly wooded, and gentle in slope: good
tank ground. There had been extensive mine fields, antitank rocks, and wire
entanglements, but the ten-day bombardment had reduced the rocks to broken stumps, blown up most of the mines, and cut the barbed wire into useless
little curlicues standing in clumps, with big cleared avenues in between.

It was pitch black when the battalion took over this sector. Its men had no
chance to become familiar with the terrain or to establish any psychological
or visual contact with whomever was on their flanks. While in reserve, the

men had of course heard numerous horror stories about the new kind of war Ivan was waging.

February 11 was a Sunday, cold (−7° F) and foggy. During the night Timoshenko moved up eighteen fresh divisions and five tank brigades across the entire width of the Karelian Isthmus. At Lähde the Russians wheeled up additional artillery batteries by hand, so as not to alert the Finns, and unmasked their hitherto-hidden sharpshooting pieces, the guns that had been sighted to pour flat-trajectory fire against the embrasures of Finnish strong points.

In front of the Lähde sector the Soviet 123d Division made ready for the attack it had rehearsed so carefully. It was an anxious night for the division's soldiers and their officers. Their primary task was to take out both Poppius and Millions, and they were certain the eyes of the Kremlin would be on them.

There was now even more importance attached to this sector than before. The Summa defenses had proven so tough that Meretskov had decided to make the Lähde sector the focus of his main thrust. If he scored a breakthrough here, Summa would have to be abandoned. About 1,000 meters behind the main fortifications was a support line. Once the 123d had punched through that, it was within easy striking distance of road junctions whose very sensitivity would force the Finns either to abandon the whole Summa sector or bleed themselves white in counterattacks.

At first light a vodka ration was issued to the troops. By eight o'clock the 123d Division and its attached armor, the Thirty-fifth Light Tank Brigade, were in position. The curtain went up in the form of a two-and-a-half-hour bombardment of unprecedented weight and fury. The hitherto-masked sharpshooter weapons opened up on the Poppius and Millions bunkers, tearing great chunks out of their concrete and buckling their armored embrasure shields.

All three companies of JR-9 were in line between Lake Summajärvi and the Munasuo Swamp. On the right, covering the Millions bunker, was Lieutenant Ericsson's company; in the center, covering Poppius and the Lähde road itself, was Lieutenant Malm's company; on the left, dug in behind Munasuo Swamp, was Lieutenant Hannu's company.

At noon Leningrad time, two regiments of the 123d Division launched their attacks. One entire regiment came against Ericsson's men and the Million-Dollar Bunker, while a battalion supported by two companies of tanks went for Poppius. Poppius resisted furiously. Lieutenant Malm's men defended the bunker so successfully that the first Russian attack faltered and broke after only twenty minutes. Then a second, fresh battalion was added to the Poppius attack, and this time the Red tanks, despite losing four of their number to shell fire, drove right up and parked in front of the bunker's firing ports, ignoring the machine-gun fire that sparkled and whanged off their turrets.

This was not a new tactic; when it had been tried before, the bunker's garrison had called for fire from the Bofors guns or had sneaked out the rear entrance and plastered the vehicles with cocktails and grenade bundles. It was not possible to do that now. The Russians had improved their tank-infantry tactics to the point where each vehicle was adequately covered by men with automatic weapons, and every single Bofors gun in the Lähde sector was out of action, not from direct hits but from concussion.

Now the Poppius garrison had no choice but to spill out of the strong point and take up the fight from what was left of the earthworks around it. As they closed on the position, the Red infantry encountered savage resistance, leaving about 200 dead sprawled within a 100-meter radius of the bunker. Even so, at approximately 12:30 P.M., officers watching from the 123d's start line were delighted to observe a red banner going up on top of Poppius. There were cheers, the first cheers some of these men had heard since the war started.

Over on the Finnish left, Lieutenant Hannu's men at first faced only infantry, since the swamp would not support the weight of armor. Attacking across the shallow weed-fringed expanse of the bog, the Russians lost so many men that the survivors referred to that place as "The Valley of Death." But Hannu eventually had to order a withdrawal when he spotted a score or more of T-28s moving in behind him from the direction of the Lähde road.

Only on the right flank, where the Million-Dollar Bunker stood, were the defenders able to maintain their original line. Ericsson's men fought on all day. Several times the strong point was submerged beneath waves of Red infantry, and each time it was cleared off with grenades and Suomi fire. Individual Russians tried to wriggle in through the firing ports, and there were a number of hand-to-hand encounters. Resistance continued all night at the bunker, even after the fortress was completely surrounded. The Russians twice called out for the platoon inside to surrender and were answered with obscenities. Then at 5:00 A.M. on the morning of February 12, enemy sappers placed a 500-pound block of TNT on top of a shell-fire crack on the roof of the main chamber. The resulting blast killed every man inside and left a thirty-foot hole in the roof of the fortress. Even then, their number reduced to less than fifty, Lieutenant Ericsson's men continued to resist. His ordnance people even got one of the Bofors guns working again and knocked out three or four passing tanks with it before it jammed for good. Finally, at noon on the twelfth, the survivors withdrew, still in good order, to the support line behind Lake Summajärvi.

By nightfall the 123d Division and its tanks had secured a lozenge-shaped salient down the Lähde road as far as the Finnish support line. No attempt was made to rush those defenses, not with the light fading and the possibility of imminent Finnish counterattacks. The Russians secured the ground they had seized, formed a strong defensive perimeter, and broke out some more vodka.

They deserved it; nowhere else along the entire line had the big push of February 11 made much of a dent. Fierce attacks on Summa had been repulsed, and everywhere else on the fronts of the First, Second, Third, and Fourth divisions, all Russian lodgments were eliminated by counterattacks during the night.

A counterattack was in order against the Lähde road penetration, too, and if the Fifth Division had been closer and the danger had been realized earlier, it might have succeeded. As it was, Mannerheim did not release the Fifth Division's three regiments, JR-13, -14, and -15, until the morning of the twelfth. The plan was to throw all three regiments against the Lähde salient in a division-sized blow, but events were outstripping the Finns' ability to cope. General Öhquist was forced to commit one regiment, JR-13, to bolster the support line at the head of the salient, and to parcel out another, JR-15, to a danger spot near the boundary between Third and Fourth divisions. That left only JR-14 immediately available for the counterattack.

Action was also heavy elsewhere on February 12. Summa received five separate attacks on that day. All were thrown back. Second Division's front was penetrated in three places, all retaken by vigorous counterattacks. By the end of the day the Mannerheim Line was still intact except for the Lähde salient, and the Russians had again suffered terrible losses. But Timoshenko's long-range strategy was to grind down the Finns by forcing them to mount continuous counterattacks against localized threats, stretching their dwindling resources to the breaking point. On the twelfth alone, Isthmus Army suffered 1,200 casualties. Timoshenko could lose ten times as many men in one day. Mannerheim was now defending regiment-sized fronts with scarecrow battalions, and there was no way it would get better.

The counterattack against the Lähde bulge went in on the morning of February 13. The plan called for two battalions of JR-14 to hit the salient from the Majajoki River valley while two other battalions launched secondary attacks, one from the support line against the head of the salient and one against its right from the boggy ground at the head of Munasuo Swamp. As it happened, intense bombing, shelling, and armored probes kept the former battalion pinned down, and the latter battalion had to check its advance to meet a new Soviet thrust to the northeast of Munasuo. That left the two battalions of JR-14 to carry out the whole operation. Up until about midday they made a brave show of it, driving the enemy off of a hill north of Summajärvi and getting some companies across the Majajoki, but by that time forward observers in the Russian salient were calling down enormous concentrations of artillery upon the attackers. After suffering heavy casualties, including the regimental commanding officer and four successive battalion commanders, and with their left flank in danger of being turned by tanks, the two battalions withdrew to the support line.

Finnish historian Wolf Halsti, serving in the quartermaster arm of the Fifth Division, was an eyewitness to these events. After the collapse of the counterattack, he noted in his diary:

> The tactical situation in and of itself is *not* hopeless! Only the means to deal with it are lacking! If only we had some heavy weapons! Those poor bastards from Turku! [The battalions attacking that morning were made up of men from the Turku district.] I wonder if they know whose fault this mess really is? What a pleasure it would be to form a battalion out of politicians and bureaucrats and then order *them* to make such an attack, without the tanks and artillery their stupidity has deprived us of today!!*

Up at the head of the salient, in midafternoon, the Russians mounted a ferocious armored attack. There was a desperate close-range melee at the point of heaviest contact, an antitank ditch walled on its western side by a log palisade. One Finnish company lost eighty-six men that afternoon. Massed fire from the tanks' cannon blew down the log wall, and Russian infantry filled the ditch with bundles of brush, logs, and in some places their own bodies. After two-and-a-half hours of bitter combat, a wedge of fifty Soviet tanks crashed through and barreled west, into the Finnish rear. Frenzied efforts were made to counterattack them by tank-killer squads armed with explosives and bottle bombs, but with the Russian infantry vigorously following the tanks, it was suicidal. The first position the tanks overran was a battery of ammunitionless howitzers that had first seen action in 1905 against the Japanese in Manchuria. More serious was the loss of ten 150 mm.

*Halsti, 318.

guns still farther back, which were overrun so quickly that there was no time to spike them, much less pull them to safety.

Then, only one mile from the Lähde road junction and with a clear run on good tank ground all the way into Viipuri, the armored spearhead halted, regrouped, and waited for additional units to catch up. Historians can only guess why, with total victory in their grasp, the Russians held up their best punch of the war. The most likely explanation is that they could not believe that the road to Viipuri lay open before them, or that the Finns' defenses had been as badly shattered as they really were, and so reverted to old habits and the tactics of caution. By the time they got moving again, the Finns had shored up their sagging defenses, and the Russians' opportunity was gone.

Elsewhere on the thirteenth the situation reports read like paraphrases of those from the previous two days. Taipale was pummeled by 50,000 shells and attacked by five regiments, but the defense did not break. Second Division, including the battered men defending the Muolaa churchyard, bent under severe pressure but did not break either. A further counterattack against the Lähde salient was contemplated early on the night of February 13–14, but the continued lack of artillery support and the relative lack of cover made it look hopeless, and the operation was canceled before it was fully planned.

There was a tense meeting at Second Corps headquarters on the morning of February 14. Present were the exhausted General Öhquist, General Östermann, overall commander of the Isthmus Army, and Marshal Mannerheim. All three generals agreed on one thing: since the Lähde road bulge could not be eliminated, it would be necessary to make a major adjustment in the whole of Second Corps's front. Beyond that point there was disagreement. Predictably all three generals gave differing accounts in their memoirs. Östermann favored pulling all the way back to the Rear Line, anchored on Viipuri, and using the half-finished Intermediate Line only as a delaying position. Öhquist, prodded by Mannerheim, came out in favor of making a determined stand along the Intermediate Line. In the latter stages of the conference, Mannerheim pointedly snubbed Östermann and talked tactics directly with Öhquist, who was, after all, Östermann's subordinate. This violation of the chain of command was only the latest symptom of the friction that had been growing between Mannerheim and his Isthmus commander for some weeks.

Although Mannerheim had made his basic feelings clear, he left to return to Otava without having issued any firm orders. As usual the Baron offered no explanation for his actions, but it is likely that he wanted to check on diplomatic developments before passing such a crucial order. Alone of the three men in the room that day, Mannerheim knew that peace talks were at a delicate stage and that Finland retained some power to influence diplomatic events only as long as its army appeared to the outside world to be unbeaten. It was this political consideration, and not bloody-minded stubbornness, that made Mannerheim insist on holding every inch of Finnish soil until the last possible moment.

February 14: repeated attacks were launched over the ice against the gulf flank of the line. All were thrown back with heavy loss. In the Lähde sector the Russians widened their salient and rolled up portions of the support line, losing a battalion's worth of men but exerting such pressure on the rear of the Summa sector that it became necessary to start withdrawing the defenders. It was a bitter moment for them: Summa had held out for seventy days against the heaviest blows the Red Army could throw. The withdrawal was accomplished without the Russians finding out, and the next day, February 15, they launched a tremendous attack with two divisions and more than 100 tanks, only to find their opponents had vanished. When the Kremlin received word that Summa had "fallen," Stalin at first did not believe it and had to be reassured by a high-ranking eyewitness who had actually seen the red flag hoisted over the gutted pillboxes.

In the interior of Finland, the "bottom of the barrel" was being scraped for replacements. Sixteen-year-old boys, reservists in their mid-fifties, and convicts with light sentences were being issued rifles and uniforms and rushed through basic training or refresher courses. Odds and ends from less-threatened areas in the north and central wilderness, a company here, and a company there, were being shuttled south as rapidly as possible, while the Red Air Force redoubled its efforts to chop the rail net into pieces, causing constant delays.

To block the Russians' next move from the Lähde salient, the worn-out remnants of JR-14 and some teenaged Civic Guard recruits from the Viipuri area were hurriedly deployed in a thin defense line anchored on the open, barren terrain of Kämärä Ridge. There was little tree cover and no time to dig foxholes. The Finns just burrowed into the snow and pointed their rifles east.

Historian Wolf Halsti was present with the supply echelon of the withdrawing Fifth Division when the boy soldiers went into battle:

2/15/40: In the early afternoon, there appeared in front of our tent a reserve ensign, really nothing more than a child, asking if we could spare some food for himself and his men. . . . he was in charge of a platoon of "men" scarcely old enough to shave. They had come straight from training school with two new antitank guns. They were cold and scared and hungry and were on their way to join the troops at the roadblock in front of Lähde. . . .

2/16/40 (afternoon): Same reserve ensign back again, blood on his clothes, asking for more food. . . . he lost both guns and half of his men when the Russians broke through. . . . his men were scattered, the tanks drove right over his guns and crushed them. . . . I asked why he had not nailed the tanks before they got that close. The wretched fellow explained that his men had received the guns, still covered with canvas, straight from their freight cars, in pitch darkness; since they had to move forward right away, they left the covers on the weapons as they went to the front. It was not until the guns were emplaced in the forward positions that they had a chance to remove the wrappings and then they were sickened to learn that these were not the same type of weapon they had trained with. They did everything they could to figure out how to load and fire the guns, but there was not enough time to get ready before the Red tanks attacked and drove straight over them. . . ." *

At four o'clock on the afternoon of February 15, Mannerheim authorized a general retirement of Second Corps to the Intermediate Line.

*Ibid., 301.

▲ CHAPTER 20 ▲ ▲

Dance of the Diplomats: Round One

Since the day he had assumed power, Finnish Foreign Minister Väinö Tanner had attempted to reopen talks with Moscow by every means he could think of. He had made personal appeals, he had sent secret emissaries to the Baltic states, and he had tried to make contact through the offices of a number of sympathetic neutral nations. Moscow's only response had been a chilly silence.

Then in early January, Tanner received a letter from a lady named Hella Wuolijoki, a feminist leftist playwright and prominent Finnish Communist who was known to have been a confidante of Boris Yartsev, the Russian agent who had first approached the Finns about leasing some territory to Stalin. Wuolijoki had connections, and among them was the Soviet Union's ambassador to Sweden, Alexandra Kollontay. In her letter to Tanner, Wuolijoki offered to contact her friend and have a woman-to-woman conversation about the prospects of getting peace negotiations started. Tanner had never heard of a more unusual method of initiating diplomacy, but he was at a dead end in his own efforts, and even something so weird as this was worth following to its outcome. He consulted hurriedly with other top members of the Finnish government, and they agreed. It all sounded cockeyed, and there was one chance in a thousand of anything coming from it, but why not give it a try? Excited by the go-ahead, Wuolijoki soon departed for Stockholm.

She arrived on January 10. For the next three weeks she and Kollontay met secretly every day in a room at the Grand Hotel. Their method of conducting international diplomacy, in Max Jakobsen's description, was "horribly unconventional and haphazard: they kept no records, they drew freely upon their own vivid imaginations to embellish and improve upon their official instructions, they freely spiced their reports with personal comments; in short, they acted like two matchmakers determined to lead, or if need be, *mislead* a reluctant and suspicious couple into matrimony. But, in the end, they succeeded where orthodox diplomacy had failed: they got Finnish-Soviet peace negotiations started." *

Moscow's initial response was cautious. Then on the last day of January Molotov finally sent a note through Swedish diplomatic channels that tacitly recognized both the existence and the legitimacy of the Ryti-Tanner government. With this brief letter the Kuusinen regime in Terijoki officially ceased to exist. With one stroke of Molotov's pen, both the man and his entire government were consigned to the "limbo of lost Communist causes." One can almost feel pity for Kuusinen, who was mothballed in a bureaucratic post in the Karelian SSR and rarely heard from again. For two long decades he had brooded over the lost civil war and faithfully toed the party line, yet his pathetic hour on the stage had come and gone in less than a hundred days. His reward had been empty, and his fall from grace was both sudden and pathetic.

This de facto abandonment of the Kuusinen apparatus was quite an opening concession. There is no hard evidence for it, but it seems likely that Stalin himself was never wholeheartedly enthusiastic about the Kuusinen charade and had let himself be talked into it while he was feeling angry and frustrated over Helsinki's intransigence. The world had ridiculed the Kuusinen government without mercy, and its existence had become a gross stumbling block in the path of ending the war.

And end it Stalin wanted to do—after, of course, first redeeming the reputation of his armed forces. This whole Finnish affair had mushroomed far beyond Stalin's original intent. Conceived as a quick-and-dirty sideshow involving regional forces, it had turned into a major military debacle whose diplomatic and material damage would prove costly to repair. The campaigning season in Europe was not far away. Who knew what military events might occur? Here Stalin was with a significant percentage of his *total* military resources sucked into a grueling campaign that still had no conclusion in sight, as of the end of January.

There was also a new and worrisome factor in the picture. The shadow of Anglo-French intervention, a remote and utterly theoretical possibility in December, had suddenly become tangible. Soviet intelligence reports whispered of contingency plans to attack the Caucasus oil fields as well as send troops to Finland itself. All in all, then, the Finnish campaign was not only an embarrassment, it had become a dangerous disruption, a wild card in the

*Jakobsen, 209.

whole European equation, whose temporary balance was important to the security of the Soviet Union.

Yet it would not do for Stalin to rush into negotiations. He could not afford to be seen to fold easily; his original demands would have to be met with interest and penalties, and the Finnish Army would have to be humbled in order that the USSR might emerge from this bloody shambles with its credibility still intact.

France had been one of the earliest and most vocal supporters of Finland's cause. Even the French Socialists had come out against the Soviet Union in this episode. Seeing the depth and passion of public feeling, the French government concocted a much-too-subtle scheme for striking obliquely at Germany by weakening Germany's major ally, Russia. The driving logic behind this plan was an overestimation of the importance of Russian exports to the Nazi war economy, and a ludicrously overoptimistic projection of how effective the Allied "blockade," such as it was, might become if those exports were stopped. The neatest thing about the scheme was that the Russians appeared to be such military pushovers. What the whole concoction amounted to was a way to hurt the Germans without actually having to fight them.

Beneath this objective were still deeper motives: the desire to convert some remote part of Europe into a major theater of war, rather than France itself, and the possibility of converting the war's main purpose from that of fighting Hitler, which many Frenchmen were not keen to do, particularly now that France was off the hook with regard to Poland, to that of aiding "brave little Finland."

Two schemes were being plotted. One involved French help in rearming all the Polish exile units, transporting them up to Petsamo, and helping them join forces with the Finns, thus avoiding the nastiness of a direct violent confrontation with the Russians. The other entailed making a massive air strike, with Turkish cooperation, against the Caucasus oil fields. Matters got as far as discussions with Mannerheim's staff about the Petsamo operation, which the Marshal regarded as feasible and potentially useful. The hitch was that it could not be brought off without British cooperation, and that was not in sight until late December.

The British became interested because one of the most crucial loopholes in the Royal Navy's "blockade" of Germany was the flow of ore from the Swedish iron fields, which supplied up to 40 percent of Germany's needs. In summer those ore shipments went through the Gulf of Bothnia and were therefore beyond Britain's reach. But in winter they went to Narvik in Norway and thence to Germany in convoys that hugged the fjord-cut coastline well inside Norwegian territorial waters. Churchill had suggested as far back as mid-September that the Royal Navy plant mine fields along those inland routes and force the Germans out onto the high seas where they could be reached.

On December 16 he revealed a revised plan, fully aware that, on the British side, it involved a blatant violation of international law, and on the German side an almost certain military response somewhere in Scandinavia. Given the Allies' naval superiority in surface ships, however, Churchill felt they would have a significant advantage if a major campaign should break out in the northern reaches. At first there was no mention at all of Finland in this mining scheme, which soon came to be known as "The Small Plan." By the time the British cabinet met to discuss the issue on December 18, they had also been apprised of the French scheme to aid Finland and of the League of Nations' expulsion of Russia. The cabinet's decision was to back away from French proposals of immediate intervention and to refer the whole untidy Scandinavian business to the chiefs of staff.

Thus, when General Gamelin came out against direct military aid to Finland in a December 19 meeting of the Supreme War Council, the British were content to let the matter lie, for the moment anyway. The council did elect to send notes to Norway and Sweden, urging them to help Finland and promising them Allied support if they got into hot water for doing so. If things fell out that way, it would offer a perfect opportunity for cutting off the Germans' ore supply without taking on the opprobrium of violating Norway's territorial integrity. Such a note was duly sent on December 27, and on January 5 the two Scandinavian neutrals sent their reply. Individual volunteers for Finland and war materials donated by foreign states could freely transit Swedish and Norwegian territory. Beyond that, the two neutrals would not go.

While these first dance steps were being executed, the British chiefs of staff had concluded a study of Scandinavia as a potential theater of war. On January 2, they presented a new scheme for the region, an alternative to Churchill's original ideas, which was soon to be dubbed "The Big Plan." It was primarily the brainchild of General Sir Edmund Ironside, who saw in it a chance to redeem the Allies' reputations, now badly tarnished by their failure to act on behalf of Poland, and to upset any German timetable for spring offensives. Obviously the Allies could not spare major forces for a Scandinavian adventure, but Ironside saw in that region a set of transient circumstances that might allow a relatively modest force to achieve a greatly disproportionate effect: "the chance to get a big return for very little expenditure" was how he phrased it in his diary.

The Big Plan called for the Allies to declare openly their intention to send aid to Finland, citing the League of Nations resolution as their justification, and then simply demand that Norway and Sweden give them the right of passage. The expedition would land at Narvik and proceed toward Finland by rail, along rail lines which, coincidentally, just happened to pass through the Swedish ore fields. A base would be established at Lulea, which, also coincidentally, was the port through which the Germans' warm-weather shipments passed. Naturally the Germans would respond violently to this move, but by the time they got around to it, the Allies would be dug in and waiting for them with superior air and sea power.

For all its neatness, the plan did have some drawbacks. First and foremost was the assumption that both Sweden and Norway would permit themselves to be used as convenient battlefields. Second, the original expeditionary force of 30,000 men was clearly not large enough to guarantee success. By the time Ironside got beyond his rough draft, the "big return for a little expenditure" had metamorphosed into a major strategic operation. Finally, there was the bothersome fact that few if any of these forces would actually end up helping Finland. As Ironside admitted privately in his diary, "Any brigade that reaches Finland would have to remain near the railway and the frontier so as to avoid getting too close to the Russians, or being cut off by the Germans." *

At first the cabinet found the Big Plan too big for comfort. The Small Plan was dusted off, and new notes were sent to Norway and Sweden on January 6, informing them that their neutrality was actually working to the Nazis' advantage, a hint that dire consequences might result if they hewed too closely to the neutral posture. Those two countries replied on January 12, rejecting the British interpretation and affirming their intention to resist any infringement on their neutrality no matter whence it came.

But by that time the British cabinet, goaded by Ironside's memoranda and by French pressure that seemed to increase every day, had switched directions again. On January 11 the chiefs of staff were authorized to work out operational details of the Big Plan. It was at this time that the concept of some kind of Scandinavian expeditionary force began to acquire a momentum of its own. The plans were drawn up by January 27 and were approved by the cabinet on January 29. France, whose generals had hitherto favored the Petsamo scheme, now swung in behind the British plan, making that decision formal at a Supreme War Council meeting on the same day.

The main points of the new plan were now these: Finland had to make an

---

*Macleod, Roderick, and Denis Kelly, eds., *The Ironside Diaries* (New York: David McKay Co., 1963), 188 (hereafter referred to as *Ironside*).

open appeal for assistance. The Allies would then ask Norway and Sweden for permission to move the expeditionary force across their territory. Technically the forces would be labeled "volunteers" for Finland, but in order to "secure their supply lines," troops would have to be stationed at Narvik and at points along the rail line to the Finnish border. Finally, in order to protect this line from German action in the south, additional Allied units would have to be put ashore at Namsos, Bergen, and Trondheim. Narvik would get two brigades and the southern ports five battalions. At the narrow end of the funnel, Finland, for whose benefit all this was ostensibly being done, would get a single brigade group. It would be no small operation: 100,000 British troops, 50,000 French, and considerable naval and air resources. The supply convoys would sail on March 12, and the landings themselves would begin on March 20.

The lily-white cause of aiding brave little Finland had now assumed in truth the secondary role that was always implicit in these deliberations. As Ironside noted in his diary, "We are quite cynical about everything, except stopping the iron ore."*

Viewed as a flanking threat against Germany, the plan sidestepped the whole issue of declaring war on the USSR; Hitler, it was hoped, would be provoked into a counterattack that he could not sustain and that could be met on ground of the Allies' own choosing, conveniently remote from the mainland of Europe, where Hitler had already demonstrated what his armies could do. Hitler for his part was not insensitive to the danger on this northern flank and had ordered contingency planning for such a counterstroke as far back as mid-December. By February the German preparations were at least as far advanced as the Allied ones.

The major weakness in the Allied plan remained what it had always been: the fact that the whole thing hinged on Norway and Sweden giving their permission. Astonishingly, no serious thought seems to have been given to what would happen if they did not. General Pownall, chief of staff of the British Expeditionary Force in France, was quick to jump on that point when the plan was first revealed to him: "I cannot for the life of me see why they should agree, for what do they get out of it except the certainty that Germany will declare war on them and part of their countries at least will be used as a battleground. . . ."†

In reply to such arguments, the plan's advocates could only respond that the pressure of public opinion, once Finland had actually made its public cry

*Ibid., 215.
†Upton, 58.

for help, would force the neutral countries to grant passage, whatever noises they might be making at the moment. Thus beneath all the verbiage and rationalizations the entire Allied scheme was really a gamble on the power of moral persuasion, a political force whose stock at that moment in history had seldom been lower.

Nor could anyone guarantee that Finland would play the game. By now the Finnish government had begun to grow suspicious of the various Allied promises that were being floated toward them. If the offer to help were genuine, then the forces that would arrive in Finland did not seem to be large enough or powerfully enough equipped to be of more than marginal value. If the offer were not genuine, then the Finns were being counted on to defraud their own best interests.

Initial contacts between Finland and the Allies were handled through military channels. Only in February did the Finnish political leadership get brought into the picture. Tanner saw the Allied schemes as an obstacle to his efforts to get negotiations going. Others saw them as a source of international leverage against the Russians, a bargaining chip. It does not seem that anyone in the Finnish government was overly impressed by the offer to help in and of itself. The forces actually earmarked for Finland seemed pathetically inadequate even to the civilians, but the *threat* of intervention might be useful as a means to pressure the Soviets, or for that matter to coerce the Swedes into giving more aid, as a better alternative than being used as a battlefield.

Intense discussions were conducted in Helsinki between February 8 and 12. There was general agreement about the nation's diplomatic priorities: first, open direct negotiations with the Soviets; second, get Sweden to join the war; third and definitely last, make an open appeal to the Allies, and let the chips fall where they may. As a basis for negotiations, Finland would offer the Russians a sizable chunk of the Karelian Isthmus and the island of Jussaro, in return for monetary compensation, cash being a much more needed commodity than a big patch of sparsely inhabited Karelian wilderness.

Once the Finnish government's inner circle had these things nailed down, Tanner and Ryti sought to enlist the Foreign Affairs Committee of the government. At an important session on February 12, the new concessions were agreed to, most reluctantly, by President Kallio, which put him on the side of Tanner, Ryti, and the influential banker-statesman J. R. Paasikivi, who had been part of the original negotiating team in Moscow. Three other ministers balked at offering the Russians any new concessions whatsoever. Their preference was for an appeal to the Allies, the sooner the better. The only immediate course of action everyone agreed on was that Tanner should make one final trip to Stockholm, in a last-ditch effort to obtain Swedish intervention. The pro-peace faction did agree among themselves to pass word to the Russians of the new concessions. On the very day Tanner left for Stockholm, however, the negotiation process was utterly transformed by a single fact that emerged from the battlefield.

The enemy had at long last broken through the Mannerheim Line. For the first time in seventy-odd days the Finnish Army was about to make a general retreat.

▲ CHAPTER 21 ▲ ▲

Fighting for Time

The strength of the Intermediate Line varied widely from sector to sector. In the "Gateway" section, from Lake Muolaanjärvi to the Vuoksi Waterway, it was as strong as the Mannerheim Line itself had been. Indeed, in one prewar configuration, it *had been* part of the Mannerheim Line. Elsewhere the secondary line was not impressive; one Finnish general called it nothing more than "a colored line on a map." Made up of scratched-out trenches, a few bunkers, and barbed wire entanglements, the Intermediate Line was thin, brittle, and poorly reinforced with concrete, and the troops who were digging in along its forward edge were already exhausted.

By late afternoon of the sixteenth the Russian Seventh Army had wrested Kämärä Station from its stubborn but undergunned defenders after a three-hour battle that cost both sides heavily. Otherwise it was not until the seventeenth that contact became general along the Intermediate Line, offering a few priceless hours for the Finns to catch their breath, throw up some sandbags, plant a few mines, and sight their Bofors guns up the relatively open roads to the east.

By the afternoon of the eighteenth most of the enemy's armored strength had reached the Intermediate Line, and massive attacks were launched at several points. By now, however, the Finnish gunners had redeployed their batteries and registered the ground, and a taste of victory had made some of the Russian tank commanders reckless. Reverting to the tactics of December, they charged ahead of their infantry support and were hit hard in the open terrain, losing more than fifty vehicles between February 19 and 21.

Over in Third Corps's sector on the left flank of the Isthmus, there had been no retirement. The original Mannerheim Line positions still held. Looking at their maps the Russian commanders could see their own left growing longer and longer, and the Taipale sector looming more and more as a salient deep behind their right. If Finland had been hoarding a division or two, here was the perfect place to use them. To prevent this from happening, and if possible to eliminate the Taipale salient altogether, the Russians redoubled their efforts to smash the stubborn defenders there.

February 18 came to be known as the "Black Day at Taipale." An entire Soviet division, supported by the usual stupendous artillery and aerial bombardment, smashed into a green replacement regiment and drove it from the field in panic. A dangerous dent was hammered into the front lines, and several important strong points fell, but the support line, manned by the battered but battle-wise veterans of the sector, held out. The Taipale line remained unbroken, though only barely so.

The following day there was a dramatic shakeup in command. General Östermann had clearly fallen from Mannerheim's favor, and his own confidence was further shaken by the news that his wife had been seriously wounded in an air raid. On February 19, Östermann resigned his command, citing reasons of health. Mannerheim accepted the resignation, then added to the command-level friction by ignoring the next man in line for the job of Isthmus Commander, General Öhquist, and appointing in his stead General Heinrichs, of Third Corps. To replace Heinrichs, Mannerheim imported the victor of Tolvajärvi, General Talvela.

A general reorganization followed these changes in command. First and Second divisions were grouped into a new corps, the First, between Second and Third corps. The purpose of this regrouping was to allow General Öhquist and his now-streamlined Second Corps to concentrate all their attentions on the defense of Viipuri and the Gulf of Viipuri.

By February 22 it was obvious that Koivisto Island could not be held any longer without its garrison being cut off. The island's shore batteries had all but paralyzed daytime traffic along the coastal roads, destroying tanks, artillery batteries, and supply columns. But a massive enemy buildup across the straits from Koivisto gave promise of an all-out assault on the island, and its garrison was urgently needed for the defense of the gulf. Therefore on February 23 the coast artillerymen began evacuating their positions, blowing up what they had to leave behind only after firing off nearly every shell in their magazines, subjecting the assembled Russians across the straits to one of the most devastating concentrations of Finnish shell fire encountered by any Soviet units in the war.

With the galling obstacle of the offshore batteries removed, the pace of the enemy drive quickened along the gulf coast. Spearheaded by fresh units of elite shock troops, several Soviet divisions drove past Koivisto and battered against the portion of the Intermediate Line held by the Finnish Fourth Division. Pulliniemi, the long, thin peninsula leading from Koivisto city out into the wide neck of the Gulf of Viipuri, was hardest hit, and by the end of

February 23 all but the tip of that promontory had fallen. Crossing the ice from Pulliniemi, the Russians captured a nearby islet. Ominously, this was the first position in the actual gulf to fall into enemy hands.

General Öhquist asked Mannerheim for permission to draw up plans for a general retirement to the Rear Line, should the need for such a withdrawal suddenly arise. But Mannerheim refused to permit any further open discussion of retreats. To Öhquist and other subordinate officers the Marshal's attitude appeared stubborn and unrealistic, but as before, Mannerheim had his reasons. He knew that every foot of Finnish soil remaining under his army's control gave Finland that much more leverage at the peace negotiations. Besides, the last-ditch defense line, running through Viipuri itself, was far from ready for occupancy, and every hour that was bought by the Intermediate Line gave the overworked engineers time to strengthen those defenses. There was, as well, the principle of the thing. In Mannerheim's view an army whose generals started talking about defeat was already halfway there.

By February 24 the Intermediate Line was bending in several places. The situation was especially grim at Honkaniemi Station, where the defending companies had been reduced to forty or fifty men. It was here, at 6:30 A.M. on February 26, that the Finnish Army launched its one and only armored attack of the Winter War. Employed was a single company of Vickers tanks purchased just before the outbreak of hostilities, but only now outfitted with their armament of 37 mm. guns. The very appearance of these vehicles caused a panic among troops who had never laid eyes on a *Finnish* tank before. Initially the attack enjoyed some success, probably due to Russian astonishment at the appearance of Finnish armor, but several of the tanks broke down just inside Russian lines, and the others soon ran into some enemy tanks whose turret armor deflected their 37 mm. shot harmlessly, but whose 76 mm. guns devastated them in return. The whole operation had a ring of desperation to it and shows the negative side of the usually successful Finnish doctrine of aggressive counterattacks. A great deal more service could have been gotten from those tanks by using them as mobile antitank guns instead of wasting them in a charge.

Timoshenko planned an all-out offensive against the whole Intermediate Line on February 28, but by that time Mannerheim had given permission to start the withdrawal to the Rear Line. The signs were not good. The Mannerheim Line had held out in most places for seventy-eight days. The Intermediate Line had held out for twelve. How long could the third line be held? And what would happen when it, too, was shattered? There was no fourth line.

The massive assault launched on February 28 largely fell on empty trenches. Here and there, however, the Finns manned delaying positions that cost Timoshenko dearly. In front of one such position, the massive artillery bombardment was not followed up by the expected infantry attack. Instead, all during the afternoon the Finns heard a single Russian voice, out in no-man's-land, screaming over and over again, "Stalin! Stalin!" It was a lone wounded man, hopelessly caught in barbed wire. The Finns decided that if the enemy sent a patrol out for him, they would not fire. But the hours crawled by and there was an eerie lack of movement in front of the delaying position. At regular intervals the man on the wire continued to throw his head back and scream at the gray heavy sky: "Stalin! . . . Stalin!" Finally, the Finns put him out of his misery with a burst of Maxim fire.

Before withdrawing, the delaying force sent out a patrol to see what the strange lack of enemy movement signified. The patrol soon came upon the assembly area for the ground attack that had never been launched. Inside a two-acre killing ground, they counted 400 corpses, stacked on top of one another. The Russian bombardment had fallen one kilometer short. The heaviest weapons in the Red arsenal had been used, including the twelve-inch railroad pieces firing from just over the border and several of the monstrous sixteen-inch shore batteries in the outer belt of Kronstadt defenses, and it had all landed here. The Finnish patrol eventually came upon the enemy's forward artillery observer—dead, in a sitting position, a map across his knees and the telephone receiver, whose wire ended in midair, still clutched in his fist. He had been trying to report the shortfall of rounds at the moment of his death. The entire battalion, it was learned from documents, had just been graduated from the Leningrad noncommissioned officers' academy; they had died clean shaven, wearing neat new uniforms and brand new flannel underwear.*

*Engle and Paananen, 128–29.

▲ CHAPTER 22 ▲ ▲

Dance of the Diplomats: Round Two

Foreign Minister Väinö Tanner departed Helsinki for Stockholm on February 12, the offer to cede Jussaro Island to the Russians in his pocket. The offer was obsolete before Tanner arrived. The Russians had already informed the Swedish government that, as a consequence of recent military victories, they still required the base at Hanko as well as the whole of the Karelian Isthmus.

On the morning of February 13 Tanner met with the Swedish defense minister, prime minister, and foreign minister and received their unequivocal answer to Finland's plea. No Swedish Army units would be allowed to serve as "volunteers" in Finland, and no Allied units would be granted freedom of passage across Swedish territory. The reason given to Tanner was Swedish fear of German intervention. But the Swedes knew Hitler's true feelings about the Scandinavian situation, so this answer was just one step removed from an outright lie. Sweden's actual motives were cold-blooded in the extreme. Finland would be forced to make peace with Russia in order to preserve its independence, which would leave the nation of Finland in place as an armed buffer between Sweden and the Soviet giant. None of the Swedish diplomats involved in this policy found it easy to stomach, but there it was in a nutshell. The last thing Sweden wanted was to encourage further Finnish resistance.

Three days later a leading Swedish newspaper broke the story that Tanner had come, hat in hand, begging for military aid, and had been rebuffed for the most cynical of reasons. The bluntness of Tanner's plea, and the coldness of his rejection, stirred considerable popular anger in Sweden, not to mention outrage in Finland. The outcry reached such dimensions that the king of Sweden felt compelled to make a tactful restatement of his nation's policy. After voicing his own heartfelt regrets, he spelled it out in no uncertain terms: "I am convinced that if Sweden intervened in the Finnish war, we would be in the greatest danger of being drawn not only into the war with

Russia, but also into the war between the Great Powers." The force of such an unusual public statement from the king effectively ended the possibility that public opinion might force Swedish intervention.

There is no question but that Hitler simply wanted the whole Scandinavian problem to die down quietly. Not until he got wind of what the Allies were planning did he revise his thinking. Planning for a German operation in Scandinavia, code-named *Weserubung,* got under way on January 23.

On February 17 the German Foreign Office approached Tanner and offered its services as a mediator in peace talks with Russia, not aware that such talks were already under way through Stockholm. On that same date Hitler's determination to go ahead with his own Scandinavian operation was fueled by news of the seizure of the prisoner ship *Altmark* by the British Navy. The formal directive to execute *Weserubung* was issued on March 1. Now it no longer was of much concern to Hitler how long the Russo-Finnish conflict lasted, as long as he continued to have peaceful relations with Russia while his westward adventures unfolded. The German offer to mediate was therefore withdrawn. The German ambassador in Helsinki tried to deprecate the offer, saying that it had been merely a private, as opposed to an "official," initiative, after which Tanner angrily showed him to the door. Official German involvement in the Winter War was now terminated.

Even the revelation that Swedish aid was but a chimera had not been enough to force many Finnish politicians to face reality. Many still refused to believe that the situation at the front was as grim as it really was, or that the Russians' new demands could be as harsh as they really were, or that the Allied expeditionary force was little better than a cruel illusion.

On February 25 the new Soviet demands were spelled out in detail: the cession of Hanko as a Russian base for a period of thirty years, the cession of all the Karelian Isthmus back approximately to the frontier line of Peter the Great, and the signing of a mutual assistance pact between Finland and the USSR.

Meanwhile the Allies were dangling sets of numbers in front of the Finns, including the supposed arrival dates of the first troops, but in view of the Swedes' now-public declaration of neutrality, they remained disconcertingly vague about just how the troops were supposed to arrive. When pressed by the Finns, Allied representatives insisted that a public cry for help from Finland would generate such moral and political pressure that the Norwegians and Swedes would be forced to let the Allies through. None of the Finns could bring themselves to ask the logical follow-up question: Or else what?

A mood of paralysis gripped the Finnish government. Russian conditions must be modified, or else the Swedes must be persuaded to let the Allies through. Other alternatives did not bear thinking about. So Väinö Tanner went back to Stockholm and met with Prime Minister Hansson again on February 27, less because Tanner believed there was any chance of the Swedes changing their mind than because another turndown would help him rally his own countrymen to the proposition that peace must be made, at whatever cost, without further delay.

It is interesting to speculate, at this point, just what Sweden and Norway would have done if the Allies had bullied their way ashore. Documents captured later by the Germans in Norway indicate that resistance would have been pro forma rather than violent, but in actuality the entire Allied plan would have come crashing down in ruins if the rail line to Narvik were knocked out of commission. Since much of that railroad was electric, all the Norwegians had to do to negate the entire Allied effort was just to cut off the power. Not a shot would have had to be fired.

Hansson told Tanner just what Tanner expected, by now, to hear. Finland must make peace on whatever terms the Russians would grant, consistent with its continued existence as an independent state. To palliate the message, Hansson did tell Tanner that Sweden was willing to consider a defense alliance once peace was concluded, as well as significant economic aid to Finland. And that was what Tanner had really come to Stockholm to hear: something positive, something positioned in time *beyond* the passions of the war, that would happen as a result of making peace now with the Russians.

By the time Tanner met again with the rest of the Finnish government on February 28, the Soviets had demanded a Finnish response to their terms and set a deadline for it: March 1. The Allies had also revealed the true scope of their intervention effort, and it was hardly inspiring. Several key, wavering politicians now swung over to Tanner's viewpoint. A new and hopelessly pessimistic assessment of the military situation arrived the next day from Mannerheim, and with it the last holdouts for continued resistance reluctantly joined the peacemakers. On February 29, word was sent to the Russians that Finland "accepted the terms in principle" and was willing to enter into immediate negotiations in Moscow.

When word of the Finns' commitment to sue for peace reached the Allies, it provoked responses ranging from the quietly hysterical, in Britain, to the bizarre, in France. French prime minister Daladier had all but mortgaged his government on the scheme to aid Finland, hoping to turn an unpopular war into an anti-Bolshevik crusade that would engage the passions of the French right wing at the same time as it moved the main theater of war about as far from France as it could get. On the night of February 29, without bothering to consult the British, Daladier sent an infamous cable to Helsinki promising 50,000 French troops in Finland by the end of March, and 100 bombers to be dispatched as soon as the Finns openly asked for help. The offer was, naturally, contingent on continued Finnish resistance.

This offer had no basis whatsoever in reality, and Daladier must have known it. Instead of calling his bluff, when they found out about it, the British, too, fell victim to the spell of the north and contemplated launching their amphibious expedition without bothering to obtain permission from Sweden and Norway. Fortunately for Finland, certain British officials insisted that the size and timing of the operation not be inflated as Daladier had done with the French statistics, and it was this little bit of sobering honesty that kept the Finns from grasping at new illusions.

Nevertheless Daladier's cable had quite an impact. When the Finnish government convened on the morning of March 1, everyone was, for a little while, taken in by it. The original acceptance message to Moscow was hurriedly modified to buy some more time, but the Swedish foreign minister refused to transmit it to Moscow unless the Finns added a sentence from their original response, agreeing "in principle" to Moscow's terms. Pumped up by visions of Daladier's imaginary bomber squadrons and divisions of *chasseurs alpins*, the Finns balked, and the entire peace process froze in its tracks.

Disillusionment arrived in the form of a British "clarification" of Allied intentions. Daladier's "50,000" men were explained away as being the total number of soldiers involved in the whole venture, not a separate French expeditionary corps; the British statement further added that only the first echelon of that force, a mere 12,000 men, could possibly arrive on Finnish soil before mid-April.

It was clear now to every politician in Helsinki that the proposed "aid" was neither large enough nor timely enough to materially improve Finland's prospects on the battlefield. The Finns' only hope was that intelligence of the Allies' expedition might have made the Soviets moderate their demands. The "open appeal" to the Allies had to be made by the end of March 5 if the plan were to be put into motion in time for anything at all to reach Finland. But March 5 came and went without any word from Moscow. The only message that did reach the Finnish cabinet was from Mannerheim, informing them that the tactical situation around Viipuri was deteriorating by the hour and saying flatly that he could no longer guarantee being able to hold the city.

Thus the Finns came full circle, and after having their hopes cruelly raised and dashed were forced to send to Moscow the "agreement in principle" statement that had been drafted originally on March 1. Daladier's contemptible little gesture had wasted five days and cost the lives of thousands on both sides.

A Soviet reply to the March 5 note arrived within hours. There would be no armistice before the final agreement was reached. The Red Army steam-roller was in high gear now, and it would continue to exert pressure on the Finns. On March 6 the Finnish peace delegation was chosen: Paasikivi; Ryti; a general named Walden, to represent the Finnish military; and a member of the Foreign Affairs Committee of the Diet, Voionmaa by name, to show the flag of domestic politics. The four men and their staff went to Moscow via Stockholm, arriving on March 7. They were armed with only one bargaining chip: the Allies had agreed to keep their offer open until March 12.

It was to the Finnish delegates' credit that, inexperienced though they were in the arena of international affairs, they were ultimately able to look beyond their nation's immediate and emotionally wrenching situation and perceive the Allied offer for the hypocritical sham that it was. In reach-ing that conclusion they were no doubt prodded by the recent examples of two other small democracies that had trusted in offers of Allied protec-tion: Czechoslovakia and Poland. Although the main reason for spurning the Allies was simply that their offer was too little and came too late, the Finns had come to grips with the fact that Finland's cause was now merely a pretext for the implementation of other, regional strategies.

If nothing else, the rejection of Allied aid showed that basic good sense had not deserted the Finns. When the same, or very nearly the same, Allied strategy went into high gear after the German attack on Norway, it proved an utter disaster, and there is no reason to think it would have worked out any better in March. The Allies couldn't even hold on to one little port city, Nar-vik, against aggressive German countermeasures conducted by moderate-sized forces. It is likely that if the Allies had deployed 50,000 men along the railroads from Narvik to Finland, the net result would have been a debacle on the same order of magnitude as Dunkirk or Crete.

When the Finns arrived, they were ready to dicker over terms. Their first shock was the realization that there would be no dickering. From the open-ing moments of the first session, on March 8, the Finns were presented with two choices: sign or keep fighting. Stalin did not even bother to attend, a sure sign that the Russian position was firm and nonnegotiable.

Ryti's opening statement amounted to a plea for lenient terms as the groundwork for harmonious relations in years to come. Molotov was frigid in his reply. Finland had proven itself to be a tool of the British and French imperialists, just as Stalin had feared back in November. Molotov pointed out that the London *Times* and *Le Temps* in Paris had both openly advo-cated military action against the Soviet Union. Ryti protested that his own government could hardly be held accountable for rabble-rousing statements that appeared in the foreign press. True, interjected Zhdanov, but the Finns had never bothered to repudiate such statements. Molotov then grudgingly conceded that perhaps Finland may not have wished to be a pawn of the Anglo-French strategists, but nevertheless that was how it had worked out and it was from that diplomatic and strategic fact that the current discussions would have to proceed.

He then read out the peace terms. To their horror the Finns now learned for the first time that the terms would be even harsher than they had originally thought. In addition to the border changes on the Karelian Isthmus and the cession of Hanko, Finland would have to cede the entire Rybachi Peninsula in the far north and a band of territory in the Salla district, and would be required to build at its own expense a rail line connecting the Murmansk Railroad with the strategic port of Tornio on the Swedish frontier at the end of the Gulf of Bothnia. The stunned Finnish delegates protested that they could not possibly agree to such terms without further consultations with their government in Helsinki, and the discussions were adjourned so they could do that.

These new demands were heatedly discussed in Helsinki on March 9. Outraged though they were by the new stipulations, the Finns were even more alarmed by the latest situation reports from the Isthmus. Battalions were down to the strength of companies, artillery ammunition was exhausted, and the weapons themselves were worn out to the point that many Finnish guns no longer had much rifling in their barrels.

Molotov had apparently never communicated all of his demands to the Swedes for fear that the cession of territory in central Finland and that curious demand for a railroad might be interpreted as a threat to Sweden and dampen Swedish enthusiasm for a quick peace settlement. But it was too late to try the Swedes again.

A message was therefore sent to the Finnish delegation in Moscow: "Headquarters has furnished situation report; not sanguine about chances of carrying on. . . . As continuation of war on the basis of aid promised is difficult, and as contact with you is slow, we authorize you to decide the matter in all respects, provided you are unanimous."

Mannerheim thought that wording was not urgent enough and insisted that a second message underscoring the desperate military situation be sent as a follow-up. Neither message had reached Moscow, however, by the time the Finns had their next meeting with Molotov, on March 10. They tried to bargain for more concessions, but Molotov was unwilling to discuss substantive changes. If the Finns did not agree, he pointed out cynically, he could always call the Kuusinen government back from the dead, sign a quick agreement with them, and let the military chips fall where they might. When

Paasikivi pointed out that even Peter the Great had paid a large monetary compensation for his Finnish border back in 1721, Molotov snapped, "Then write a letter to Peter the Great—if he orders it, then we'll pay compensation!"

The formal permission to sign, on the basis of the new and most severe set of Soviet demands, reached the Finnish delegation on March 11. Ryti tried once more to move Molotov toward some kind of concessions, however minor, by pointing out that Russia had not militarily conquered most of the territory it was demanding. Molotov, in tones of contempt, replied that if the Finns wished, they could come back and discuss the matter *after* the Red Army had taken those places. Yielding to the inevitable, the Finnish delegation started drafting the text of a peace treaty that incorporated all of the Russian demands.

Meanwhile, in Paris and London the Allied leaders were becoming frantic about the possibility that the Finnish "appeal" would not be made. Their precious Scandinavian front was slipping farther away from them with every passing hour. Daladier, for one, knew that his own government would not survive the collapse of the project, and he exerted frantic pressure on London to do something, anything, to keep the whole shabby business alive. On March 11 matters reached a crisis. At the insistence of Finnish president Kallio, Finland made yet one more appeal to Norway and Sweden about the right of Allied passage. No one expected an eleventh-hour change of heart on the part of those neutral countries, but then, this appeal was being made for the record, to generate something that could be used to cushion the shock of public response when the severity of Russian terms became known. Finland's government had had no choice, the reasoning would be, because there was no way the Allies could get there in time. All the Scandinavian parties involved in this last-minute two-step understood it for what it was, but to the Allies it looked like the Finns were wavering.

On the same day, March 11, the French ambassador demanded that the British launch their expedition without Norwegian and Swedish consent. Ironside, who had maintained a fairly rational attitude until these new developments looked about to generate a serious Allied setback, now came out in favor of just bullying through regardless of any neutral opposition. Admiral Evans, the Royal Navy representative on the Chiefs of Staff Committee, agreed. Only the Royal Air Force delegate, Air Marshal Newall, kept his perspective, saying: "I think the whole thing is hare-brained."

Later that day, both Chamberlain and Daladier announced in Parliament that their governments stood ready to help the Finns "with all the means at their disposal." Chamberlain called in the Finnish ambassador and told him that if the appeal were made, a dozen bombers would fly to Finland immediately. The only question remaining, assuming that the Finns made their public appeal, was whether or not the big convoy would embark without the consent of Norway and Sweden. Ironside, who thought this matter had already been decided, was shocked to find that the cabinet was still arguing the question as late as the morning of March 12. Privately he described them as "a flock of bewildered sheep faced by a problem they have consistently refused to consider. . . . I came away disgusted with them all." *

The final decision was a compromise: to launch the Narvik part of the operation but to hold back the southern wing of it until German response offered a provocation for such action. The orders issued for this action, however, were so vague, so curdled with contradiction, and so open to interpretation that they could be studied as a textbook invitation to military disaster. They surely reflected the confusion and duplicity of motive that characterized this entire effort from the start.

One extract from these orders should suffice to give an idea of their incoherence:

It is the intention of His Majesty's Government that your force should land, provided it can do so without serious fighting. . . . Fire on Norwegian or Swedish troops is only to be opened as a last resort. Subject to this, you are given discretion to use such force as may be required to secure the safety of your command. . . . It is not the intention of the government that this force should fight its way through Norway or Sweden. . . . The decision as to the size of the force to assist the Finns and the terms for its dispatch are left to your discretion. It is important that the force to assist the Finns should be dispatched as soon as possible.†

Some clarification of this prose masterpiece is obtainable from reading the minutes of the meeting held by the ministers and their commanders on March 12. Evidently the expeditionary force was expected to elbow their way past the Norwegians and proceed to the Swedish border, where they would demand passage. Should this be refused, the troops were not expected to fight their way forward but simply to encamp where they were. The possibility of becoming embroiled in a shooting war with Russia, though quite real in the event that Allied soldiers went into Finland, was dismissed as a

*Ironside, 226–27.
†Upton, 144.

mere annoyance. The force would bluster its way ashore, there would be no violent opposition, Hitler would be goaded into a blundering counterattack, and everybody could get on with the real business at hand: fighting the Germans.

As the clear-eyed General Pownall noted on March 13, "Of the four or five divisions that might have been sent . . . not one division was intended for Finland—perhaps a brigade or two, if they were lucky. . . . The rest were simply for occupying and holding the iron-ore mines. . . . they weren't intended to go anywhere near Finland. It is really a most dishonest business." *

Fortunately, the Finns sensed that dishonesty and did not make the appeal that would have set the whole sorry enterprise in motion. On March 12, the Finnish government met to reach its final decision, based on the news from Moscow. Two ministers balked at the last minute, stunned by the severity of the terms, and tendered their resignations rather than their signatures. As President Kallio signed the document that gave the Moscow delegation authority to conclude the war on Moscow's terms, he growled, "May the hand wither that is forced to sign such a document as this." A few months later, the old man suffered a stroke that left him paralyzed in his right arm.

The actual treaty was signed in Moscow in the early hours of March 13. A cease-fire was scheduled to go into effect at noon, Leningrad time.

*Ibid., 145.

▲ CHAPTER 23 ▲ ▲

Time Runs Out

The Gulf of Viipuri had never figured in prewar planning by the Finnish Army. It had been assumed that any threat to the gulf would be naval and could be taken care of by the powerful and well-sited shore batteries that covered the approaches. The islands that screened Viipuri from the sea were fortified, but not against an over-the-ice offensive from the Finnish coast. Nothing had been done at all, not even map exercises, to prepare a defensive plan for the western coast behind Viipuri. Under ordinary wintertime conditions, by late February, the ice over the gulf would have become too unstable and too dotted with thin spots, to support heavy vehicle traffic. But this year, it remained frozen as solid as ever, capable of bearing the weight of trucks, light tanks, and up-to-medium-caliber field artillery. "General Winter" had turned traitor.

But before the Russians could strike at that vulnerable coastline, they had to fight their way across the gulf itself, and this required the subduing of garrisons on several dozen islands that were not technically part of the Rear Line but that were situated so as to form breakwaters, delaying and blunting the edge of the invaders' columns. The defenders of these isolated positions knew that every hour the enemy spent fighting them was another precious hour gained for strengthening the defenses around Viipuri.

It cost the Russians heavily to subdue these positions. Little Tuppura Island, for instance, just west of the Pulliniemi Peninsula, held out for twenty-four hours against a full Russian division, its garrison killing about 1,000 enemy infantry and knocking out a dozen tanks, at a cost of 260 Finnish dead. In addition to the two six-inch coast defense guns on the island itself, the Tuppura defenders were supported by a battery of twelve-inch rifles at Ristiniemi, across the mouth of the gulf. The heavy armor-piercing shells from those huge guns blasted gigantic cracks in the ice, sinking tanks and spilling hundreds of infantry into the fatally cold water. Here is a Russian survivor's description of one of the assaults on Tuppura:

We heard noises behind us—our tanks were arriving. They drew abreast of us and we formed up to advance behind their sheltering steel. The range decreased steadily . . . now the machine guns on the beach opened up . . . now our tanks shuddered as their big guns began shelling the island; then they fired their machine guns, and we could see tracers splintering the rocky parapets on the beach ahead. . . . It is hard to describe my feelings: we were entrusting our very lives to these tanks and the protection they gave us from the rain of Finnish fire. . . . the Finns' main battery began firing shrapnel, and soon there were wounded men writhing on the ice all around. . . . a sound in the air like a rushing freight train: those infernal shore batteries across the Gulf began hitting us again, sending over shells that weighed many tons and that burst through the ice so violently that it shattered like glass. . . . this caused great shock waves of water to surge up and wash out over the surface, making it necessary for us to advance through pools of soupy, ice cold mush. . . . although our bodies were well-clad, our feet soon felt the effects of having to march in boots filled with this slush. Suddenly, there was a great roar as one of those heavy shells struck the ice close by. . . . the tank behind which we were advancing suddenly shuddered to a halt and began to rise into the air at an alarmingly steep angle; then, with a huge gulping sound, the vehicle took a nose-dive and instantly slid out of sight through a jagged rupture in the ice.*

The Red Army was now battering at the very gates of Finland, hurling its inexhaustible power against the Rear Line. Beyond that line lay the cultural, economic, and psychological heart of Finland. Mannerheim was taking a grimly calculated risk by standing and fighting it out at the Rear Line— further westward, where numerous lakes, some of them very large, channel the land into narrow corridors, there was better defensive ground, even without time to fortify it. But those areas were a long way beyond Viipuri, and continued retention of Viipuri was one of the few bargaining chips Finland still held. If the Isthmus Army could just hold out a little bit longer, until the spring thaw melted the gulf and frozen lakes and turned the ground in front of Viipuri into a quagmire, then it might well be possible to halt the Russian drive in place, giving Finland an improved negotiating position. The Red Army command was of course aware of spring thaws, too, and it assaulted this final defense line furiously.

*Lyytinen, A. E., *Koivisto Ja Viipurinlahti: 1919–1944* (Helsinki: Werner Soderstrom Oy, 1958), 98.

The worst danger spot was the western coast of the Gulf of Viipuri. Adding that terrain to the Rear Line lengthened its frontage beyond the Finns' manpower capacity. Troops had to be found, a command had to be organized. Mannerheim prevailed upon the commander of the Swedish Volunteers to take his men from training depots and use them to replace Finnish battalions tied down on the quiescent Salla front. Beginning on February 22, 8,000 Swedes and 725 Norwegians took over that front, releasing five experienced Finnish battalions and a handful of artillery pieces for redeployment on the gulf coast. These units, in addition to the three coastal battalions already in the area, were now designated "Coastgroup." To command the new task force, Mannerheim imported the blustery victor of the arctic battles, General Kurt Wallenius.

The old pirate had done extremely well up in the wide, open spaces of Lapland, where he had proven himself a master of fluid guerrilla tactics and where he had more or less run the whole show. When Wallenius arrived on the Isthmus on February 28, however, he found a different kind of war. He took one long look at the chaos, the terror, the desperation, the sheer, screaming, overwhelming noise of the Isthmus battle, went back into his command post, and began drinking heavily. He stayed reeling drunk for three days, barely able to stand up during important command conferences. On March 3, Mannerheim summarily relieved him of his command and forbade him ever to serve in the Finnish Army again. General Oesch, the hard-working chief of the general staff, dutifully replaced him and achieved a minor miracle of organization in shaking down Coastgroup into a coherent tactical command.

On the same night that Oesch took command of Coastgroup, the Soviet Twenty-eighth Corps pushed across the gulf in force and wrested two small beachheads on the western coast at Vilaniemi and Haranpaaniemi. Simultaneously the Russian Tenth Corps thrust over the gulf on a northward curving axis that lay east of Tervajoki, attacking without letup the clusters of defended islets that guarded the inner harbor of Viipuri. Savage counterattacks threw back the earliest Russian lodgments; when they retreated, they left hundreds of dead and the blackened hulks of fifteen tanks.

Once joined, the struggle for the gulf would mount steadily in intensity until it reached a climactic fury that equaled the Summa battles of February. Sensing that the gulf was the most sensitive and vulnerable point in the Rear Line, and knowing that they had only a limited time before the ice began to break up, the Russians shifted the greatest weight of their entire offensive effort in that direction, sending wave after wave of men and machines out over the ice.

As the surface of both gulfs grew crowded with thousands of moving men, the Finnish Air Force made its last, bravest, and most desperate effort, flying sortie after sortie until its pilots collapsed from exhaustion, strafing the advancing columns from treetop levels, and braving umbrellas of interceptors and rain forests of flak. Finnish ace Eino Luukkanen left a vivid impression of one such mission:

> We did not have to search for our target, for no sooner had we crossed the shoreline than we could see, about six miles away, a column of men and horses trudging across the ice. I judged that the column, which looked like a long black snake, was a reinforced battalion of about five hundred men, and from the air the troops appeared motionless. Suursaari was covered by fog, so we had little to fear from Russian fighters, and as we closed with our target our Fokkers lined up in single file for the strafing run. We could not have been offered a better target. The Russians were not even wearing white parkas as camouflage, and were sharply defined against the snow-covered ice. I gently eased the stick forward to commence my strafing run. I can only assume that the Russians had been promised some form of air cover, for they made no attempt to break column at the noise of our engines. I levelled off at thirty feet, loosing a lethal stream of bullets into the column from all four guns.
>
> Panic immediately overtook the Russians as I roared past their heads. Some dropped in their tracks, some endeavored to hold the frightened horses, while others scattered in all directions, slipping and sliding on the ice. My undercarriage almost scraped their heads. . . . Backwards and forwards we roamed across the remnants of the column, pouring some eight thousand rounds into the Russians from our thirty-two machine guns.*

Observers at a Finnish shore battery, who witnessed the massacre through their immense spotting glasses, later passed the word to Luukkanen's squadron that they had killed at least half of the entire column.

On March 5, the Russians hurled an entire division at Vilaniemi Peninsula, supported by 100 tanks. This gigantic formation was taken under fire by the shore batteries at Ristiniemi. Tight clusters of huge shells designed to smash through battleship armor rained down on the attacking columns, blowing enormous crevices into the ice, shattering the broken surface so

*Luukkanen, Eino, *Fighter over Finland* (London: MacDonald, 1963), 70–71.

violently that entire companies of men were swallowed by the fatally cold waters, in a manner unforgettably similar to the climactic scenes of the film *Alexander Nevsky*.

Elsewhere along the Rear Line contact became general by the end of March 2. Near Tali, northeast of Viipuri, there was good tank country. Here, too, the loamy, sandy soil typical of the eastern Isthmus yielded to bare rocky ground, making it difficult for the Finns to dig trenches and multiplying the effect of Russian artillery, whose exploding shells filled the air with splinters of granite. To block the enemy in this sector, Finnish engineers opened the gates of the Saimaa Canal, flooding the low-lying terrain to a depth of three feet. The Russians towed their tanks right through the flood, and their infantry was preceded by companies of incredibly brave sappers who crawled through frigid water up to their chins in order to close with the defenders. In the opinion of the Finns who fought them, these were the most courageous Red soldiers they had ever seen.

March 4: There were now the equivalent of thirty Russian divisions hammering the gulf and the Rear Line, supported by at least 1,200 armored vehicles and 2,000 aircraft. Positions changed hands a dozen times a day in some places. The Finns recaptured Vilaniemi but could not hold it against tanks. Out in the gulf the island of Uuraas was lost, and heavy attacks continued against all other islands still in Finnish hands. Each of these attacks on the inner ring of Viipuri's fixed defenses was pressed into the teeth of intense shore battery fire. Entire battalions were mauled by these weapons, but they were replaced.

March 5: The strain of circumstances was merciless. Mannerheim was taking the worst gamble of his life, and doing it while confined to a chair with a severe case of the flu. Even those who hated him had to admire the iciness of his nerve at this point, knowing that if the Russians did expand their beachhead on the gulf coast, there was nothing between them and Helsinki except a few companies of teenagers with ten days' training. If Mannerheim gave the order now, it might still be possible to disengage and retire to more defensible lines west of Viipuri. In twenty-four hours it might be too late.

March 6: Coastgroup put through an emergency call to Öhquist, begging for artillery ammunition. Öhquist, in anguish, had to refuse: in the entire Finnish Second Corps, there remained a reserve supply, for all calibers of guns, of 600 shells. Along the gulf coast the defenders sawed or blasted holes in the ice, but within hours it refroze as solidly as ever. In Viipuri itself Finnish commanders estimated they could not possibly hold the city for longer than four or five days. Heavy fighting had reached the outskirts.

March 7-8: The Finnish Twenty-third Division fell apart. One entire battalion broke and ran away, the first time this had happened in the Finnish Army. When ordered to retake the lost ground in counterattacks, another battalion simply pointed its rifles at its officers, climbed out of its trenches, and walked off the battlefield. The Russians expanded their beachhead on the gulf coast, and for the first time artillery rounds began dropping on the Viipuri-Helsinki highway. If the Russians occupied that road, they would cut Coastgroup off from Second Corps and be in a position to surround Viipuri. Radio communications had broken down utterly; only runners got through, sometimes. Each Finnish company, each platoon, was fighting its own bitter and personal battle.

March 9–10: The order went out to evacuate all island positions still in Finnish hands. Portions of the Third and Fifth divisions began setting up for house-to-house resistance inside Viipuri itself. Russian shells battered the ancient citadel near the harbor, but even modern artillery could do little more than chip those stout granite walls. At his headquarters, General Öhquist, still in the dark as to the status of peace talks, wrote in his diary: "This is an awful gamble we are taking! It is possible that we can keep Viipuri in our hands until tomorrow night. If we are ordered to continue resistance beyond that time, it means that either the city or the troops will be doomed." *

The Finnish Army had begun the war with approximately 150,000 men under arms. By March 10 its losses from all causes totaled about half of that figure. It was thus fighting with half its original strength, along a line twice as long as the line it had originally held, against an enemy whose reserves for all practical purposes were inexhaustible.

March 11–13: It was no longer possible to speak of a Finnish "line" on the gulf coast: from the Baltic shore to the farthest Russian advance, now just six kilometers from the western edge of Viipuri, the entire shoreline was a chaotic tangle of savage delaying actions. The Finns' situation was by now truly desperate; yet so too was their will to resist. The Russians were never able to break through and surge forward those last few kilometers that stood between them and total victory.

March 13: The cease-fire was to take effect at 11:00 A.M. Helsinki time. During the final hour, the firing died down slowly, ceased altogether in many places along the 100-mile front. By 10:45, the defenders had begun to relax and stretch in their cramped dugouts and foxholes. Thoughts turned to home, to loved ones, to the sheer ecstasy of having survived 105 days of unbelievable horror and violence.

*Öhquist, Harold, Talvisota—Minun Nakokulmastani (Helsinki: Werner Soderstrom Oy, 1949), 350.

And at precisely 10:45, for the sheer vindictive meanness of it, the Russians unexpectedly opened up a furious last-minute bombardment that even their own historians admit was nothing more than a gesture of revenge. There was not the slightest military reason for this savage act; hundreds of Finns were killed or wounded in a spasm of childish rage.

The defenders of the Karelian Isthmus marched out of their battered positions with their heads high. Following them was virtually the entire civilian population, streaming westward with only as many belongings as they could pack onto sleds or into carts, abandoning homes, farms, land that had been won by their forefathers; yielding as well the beautiful and historic city of Viipuri, once called "The Paris of the North." One Finnish officer wrote to his family:

All belongings were being hastily taken away in order that they might not remain behind for the Russians, who had the right to occupy the village the next day. . . . it was upsetting to see villages left burning behind you in battle; it is even more upsetting to leave these undamaged houses for the Russians. But one thing was clear: we have not fled. We were prepared to fight to the last man. We carry our heads high because we have fought with all our might for three and a half months. More than that, one can scarcely demand.*

British journalist John Langdon-Davies was sitting in a Helsinki restaurant when news of the surrender terms was broadcast to the public for the first time: "Every now and then, as the true tragedy unfolded itself, my eyes caught a quick movement from first one table and then another. It was the movement of a man or woman suddenly brushing away tears. . . . I could not understand anything that was being said, except for the proper names. It was words like 'Viipuri' and 'Hanko' that produced this movement—a stifled, spasmodic cry that seemed to come from almost everybody in the room, as if in response to a physical blow."†

His assignment to cover the war for *Life* concluded, Carl Mydans boarded a train for Sweden. It was crowded, and he had to share a sleeping compartment with three Finnish officers, one of them a colonel. During the night, all four men maintained a polite silence. The following morning Mydans was dressing and, like two of the other men, discreetly trying to maintain as much decorum as he could inside the cramped quarters. The Finnish colonel

*Goodrich, 70.
†Langdon-Davies, 124.

was shaving, balancing his straight razor delicately against the swaying of the train. He caught Mydans's eye in the mirror.

"You are an American?" he asked in clear English. Mydans nodded, noticing that the other two Finnish officers were studiously averting their eyes. The colonel began to scrape at his chin once more.

"At least you will tell them that we fought bravely."

Mydans felt his guts knot. He whispered that he would, indeed.

The colonel carefully wiped his razor, then dabbed at himself with a towel. He had cut his cheek and there was a tiny bubble of blood swelling there. When he had taken care of that, he began to button his tunic. Mydans observed that the officer's hands were trembling.

Suddenly he peered up at Mydans with an expression of anguish twisting his features. He began in a hoarse, quiet voice: "Your country was going to help. . . ." Then, in a louder voice: "You promised, and we believed you. . . ."

Then he grabbed Mydans by the shoulders, his fingers digging in, and screamed: "A half-dozen God-damned Brewster fighters with no spare parts is all we got from you! And the British sent us guns from the last war that wouldn't even work!"

The other Finns turned their backs and self-consciously finished dressing. The train rattled into the station. The Finnish colonel dropped his hands, fell onto a bunk, and wept convulsively.

▲ CHAPTER 24 ▲ ▲

Aftershocks

For its unwillingness to meet Stalin's demands, Finland paid a high price. In addition to all of the islands mentioned in the prewar negotiations, Finland lost the entire Karelian Isthmus, Hanko and some adjacent coastline, the entire Rybachi Peninsula, and a great slice of Karelia north of Lake Ladoga: roughly 25,000 square miles of land, including every strong natural defense line Finland possessed. In human terms, the war cost 24,923 killed and 43,557 wounded; approximately 420,000 Finns lost their homes. If those casualty figures seem disproportionately low, the reader should put them into perspective. The entire population of Finland at that time was less than 4 million; if the same percentage of losses had been inflicted on the United States in 1940, it would have been the equivalent of 2.6 million casualties in 105 days of war.

One Soviet general, looking at a map of the territory Russia had acquired on the Karelian Isthmus, is said to have remarked: "We have won just about enough ground to bury our dead."

How many Russians died in those violent weeks? Molotov's "official" figures, issued just after the war, listed 48,745 dead and 159,000 wounded. No one seriously believed them at the time, and even the Soviets acknowledge much more serious losses in their post-Stalinist accounts of the Winter War. The actual figures will probably never be known with any certainty. Khrushchev, in his memoirs, stated flatly that "we lost a million men," but that is hyperbole. Modern Finnish historians, who keep close tabs on anything about the war that appears in the Russian language, now estimate Soviet dead at 230,000 to 270,000 and another 200,000 to 300,000 wounded.

To those figures must be added the 5,000 Russian POWs who were repatriated from Finland. No "smoking gun" evidence has ever seen print, of course, but several defectors who were in a position to have access to such information have sworn that every single prisoner was packed off to secret NKVD camps in the wilderness near the White Sea, interrogated, then shot.

The immediate military consequences of the war were played out fifteen months later, when the Germans opened Operation Barbarossa—their all-out offensive against the Soviet Union. Before then, the Supreme Military Soviet had met in urgent conclave in April 1940 to sift through the lessons of the Finnish campaign and recommend reforms. The role of frontline political commissars was considerably reduced, and old-fashioned ranks and forms of discipline were reintroduced. Clothing, equipment, and tactics for winter operations were thoroughly revamped; so were tank and aerial tactics. Professionalism, in short, was put back in its proper place. Not all of the reforms had been completed by the time the Germans struck, but enough changes had been wrought so that the Red Army was a far tougher and better equipped opponent than it would have been had the Winter War never happened; there was at least a thin margin of improvement that enabled Russia to survive, just barely, the stupendous onslaught of the world's finest professional army.

As a result of its victory over Finland, Moscow did acquire some depth to its Leningrad defenses, although the mortal danger to the city, ironically, came from the other direction. During the period of cobelligerency with Germany, Finland's army was under strict orders from Mannerheim not to advance beyond the old border, and not to shell Leningrad from its Isthmus lines. In the first, worst winter of the Siege of Leningrad, when the city's defenses were stretched to the breaking point, a determined Finnish assault from the west would probably have caused it to fall.

Once the Baltic Republics succumbed to the Germans, the coast artillery and air facilities at Hanko were not only rendered useless but proved impossible to defend; Stalin was forced to evacuate the garrison for use nearer the city. Only in the far north, where the dismal headlands of the Rybachi Peninsula and the high ridges north of Salla gave the Russians good positions from which to repulse the German drive on Murmansk, did the Finnish concessions materially strengthen the USSR's defenses. The Soviet-built railroad to Tornio was seldom used, and its true purpose remains mysterious to this day.

The so-called Continuation War with Russia saw Finland go to war with a completely revamped army of sixteen divisions, decently if not spectacularly equipped with artillery and armor (a lot of it converted Soviet weaponry taken during the Winter War), and a polyglot air force quite unlike any other in the world. So many nations had aircraft "in the pipeline" to Finland at the Winter War's end that its airmen flew the machines of every belligerent in World War II with the exception of the Japanese.

That Finland should fight the Soviet Union again, only fifteen months after the end of the Winter War—and that in so doing it should compromise its national image if not its honor—seems a cruel twist of history. That Finland fought at the side of Nazi Germany, officially as a "cobelligerent" but in every practical aspect as a close ally, seems tragic. There was a disturbing aspect to the Continuation War in that a nation that only fifteen months before had been held up as a shining example of freedom and democracy should now make aggressive war at the side of one of history's most ruthless totalitarian regimes.

No subject in Finnish history remains more clouded than the Continuation War. Finnish writers have spilled rivers of ink debating the complex chain of events and machinations that brought Finland into the conflict on Germany's side. But even today there remain many unanswered questions, gaps of knowledge, and ambiguities. Was there a concerted plot on the part of certain Finnish generals and politicians to plunge the nation into war? Was the primary motive of these men—if indeed there was such a cabal— simply to regain the lands that Russia had seized in March 1940, or did vaster and more sinister schemes of aggrandizement fuel their machinations? Or was the nation simply a helpless victim of the inexorable pressures of circumstance and geography? No consensus on these matters exists in Finland itself, so it would be folly to presume one in these pages. The merest outline of events will suggest their complexity as well as their ambiguity:

Finland's worst mistake, clearly, was in choosing the losing side. But at the time that choice was made, it seemed quite reasonable. So poorly had the Red Army performed in the early stages of the Winter War, so crude had been the steamroller tactics that finally gave Stalin his victory, and so stunning were the early conquests of the Nazis, that military experts the world over gave the Russians no chance at all of surviving a German onslaught. General Marshall advised Franklin Roosevelt, a few days after the German attack in June 1941, that the Red Army would be utterly defeated in no more than ninety days. British analysts gave the Russians about sixty days, and some predicted that Hitler would be in Moscow by September 1.

Who can blame the Finns for seeing in this situation a perfect chance to regain the land that had been wrested from them? After Norway and Denmark fell to the Germans, Finland was geographically isolated. No military aid could reach it from the Allies except through Petsamo, which could easily be sealed off by the Germans in Norway or the Soviets in Murmansk.

Stalin, moreover, pursued a heavy-handed and antagonistic policy toward Finland, undercutting the political impact of the many sensible Finns who wanted only to mend fences with their eastern neighbor. When Finland sought a rather innocuous defense pact with Sweden, under the by-then somewhat tattered umbrella of Scandinavian neutrality, Soviet pressure, some of it crude in the extreme, ruined the scheme. When Russia annexed the Baltic Republics in August 1940, a shudder of fear went through Finland.

It was during that same month that Hitler, frustrated in his attempt to bring England to the peace table through aerial bombing, began seriously to plan Operation Barbarossa, his invasion of the Soviet Union. Informal talks between Finnish and German diplomats resulted in Finland granting the Germans right-of-passage through the arctic provinces—ostensibly just overflights to and from the remote German bastion at Kirkines, Norway, but once the agreement was in place, it could certainly be used to give legality to more substantial troop deployments, against Murmansk for example. The Finnish public, by this time, had become so uneasy about the nation's isolation that it was ready to welcome all the German troops Hitler wanted to send.

Stalin could still have wooed the Finns back into a mode of neutrality, but he was preoccupied with larger concerns and continued to treat Finland in an offensive and threatening manner, permitting Kremlin agents to interfere in domestic Finnish politics and publicly threatening to retaliate against Finland if men such as Tanner or Mannerheim were elected to high office. When Stalin learned that there had been informal discussions between German and Finnish military teams, he responded by cutting off desperately needed food shipments (shipments supposedly guaranteed by treaty) and by violating Finnish air space. Every maneuver seemed almost designed to increase Finland's sense of dependence on Germany.

Despite exhaustive efforts by Finnish historians, it has so far proven impossible to pinpoint the exact date on which Finland was taken into confidence about Operation Barbarossa. The "paper trail" is tantalizing but leads only to dead ends and side paths, not to any benchmark conference or dates. Probably no formal agreements were necessary. The Finnish generals who were privy to joint planning were mostly German trained and intimately familiar with the German way of waging war. There was also a certain amount of coyness on both sides. Joint operations were discussed, all during the spring of 1941, in purely hypothetical terms, and neither the Finns nor the Germans were ever entirely candid with one another as to their national aims and methods. In any case, the step from contingency planning to actual operations, when it came, was little more than a formality.

Three days after the start of Barbarossa, Stalin handed the Finns a perfect excuse by launching some air raids. War was declared on June 25, 1941. After weeks of intense Soviet pressure, Great Britain felt compelled, on the same day the Japanese attacked Pearl Harbor, to make a formal declaration of war against Finland. No British leader had the slightest intention of waging active war against Finland, however, and the only practical military result of this uncomfortable alignment was a single rather lethargic air raid on Turku, during which most of the Royal Air Force pilots intentionally dropped their bombs into the sea.

Finland strained every national fiber in this crusade of reclamation. Fully 16 percent of its population went to war, including 80,000 women auxiliaries and a field army of 475,000 men. Germany had augmented Mannerheim's forces with heavy artillery, modern fighter aircraft, and 100 or so Czech tanks. An entire corps of German troops prepared to enter Finland from Norway for the purpose of launching a drive against Murmansk.

Even Germany's enemies understood why Finland had gone to war again; they also understood the military necessity of its partnership with Hitler. When Mannerheim's troops reached the old border, one of the first statesmen to offer congratulations to a Finnish minister was American secretary of state Cordell Hull.

In most sectors, Mannerheim permitted no advance beyond the old border, except minor operations for local tactical reasons. The one area where this policy did not prevail was East Karelia. Pressure from Finnish right-wing political groups and nationalist societies forced the government to annex a vast area of Karelia, as far east as the Svir River. To the Finns' discomfiture, they were not everywhere welcomed as liberators. Massive resettlement programs carried out by Stalin in the 1930s had altered the demographic makeup of many Karelian districts to the extent that most of their inhabitants were indifferent if not actually hostile toward Finland.

Militarily, there were two distinct campaigns launched from Finnish soil. The German drive above the Arctic Circle against Murmansk was quite separate from Finnish efforts in Karelia. It was also a failure. Bitter Russian resistance, terrain difficulties, and the generally mediocre quality of the Wehrmacht troops committed in the far north all combined to halt the attack some distance from Murmansk.

By mid-February 1942, however, the Finns had reached all of their objectives. Static trench warfare set in all along the Karelian front, and some 180,000 Finnish troops were demobilized in order to ease the strain on the nation's economy.

By the start of 1944 Finland realized that Germany was losing the war. Peace feelers were sent out, but when Hitler got wind of them, he interrupted shipments of food and weapons, just to remind the Finns of how dependent they were on his favor. Finland's dilemma was agonizing. If it sought peace unilaterally, Hitler threatened military occupation (as he did in

Hungary when that nation tried to leave the Axis). If it did not, sooner or later the Red Army would turn its attention to the north.

After two years of inactivity, the dreaded blow fell on June 1944. Against a demoralized Finnish Army of 268,000 men, the Russians unleashed a stupendous attack by 450,000 infantry, 800 tanks, 10,000 cannon, and 2,000 aircraft. The Finnish Army reeled back everywhere. Viipuri was lost (in one day, after desultory resistance) a mere ten days after the start of the Russian offensive.

Mannerheim had no choice but to beg Hitler for emergency aid. Stukas and assault guns were sent from the Baltic front, and a flotilla of PT boats delivered several thousand of the new "Panzerfaust" bazookas. As a condition for this aid, Finnish president Ryti had to pledge fealty to Hitler. He was cagey enough, however, to do this by means of a signed personal letter to Hitler—a document not legally binding to the rest of the Finnish government.

Miraculously, the Finnish Army rallied and did not break. Thanks to the Stukas and the Panzerfausts, the Finns blasted more than 200 Russian tanks in early July. Late in the month, up near Ilomantsi, they even showed some of their old Winter War spirit by routing two entire Soviet divisions.

The Russian offensive ran out of steam. The planes, tanks, and cannon were urgently needed on a more important front if Stalin were to realize his dream of getting to Berlin ahead of the Americans. Stalin was also deterred by the very practical question of what to do with Finland if he went ahead and conquered the whole nation. The prospect of a festering guerrilla war in the forests, a struggle for which the Finns had made contingency plans, could not have been pleasing. Having humbled Finland and reexerted Russian dominance over its political will, Stalin was content to let Finland become his commercial window to the west, a nation still formally independent but never likely to be a threat to its giant neighbor again.

An armistice was signed on September 19, 1944. As part of its obligations under that treaty, Finland was required to turn upon its former German allies and eject them from the northern quarter of the country. A sideshow war was then fought between an outnumbered portion of the Finnish Army and some 200,000 German troops. Personnel casualties were moderate, but damage was immense, for the retreating German units destroyed everything of value in their withdrawal to Norway. Even today, the hills of Lapland are dotted with the blackened chimneys of humble farms that were put to the torch during the "Lapland War."

When this last and most distasteful conflict was over, Finland was again at peace. And it remained a free state. The finest achievement of Gustav

Mannerheim and his soldiers is just that fact. Of all the Baltic nations that negotiated with Stalin in 1939, only Finland resisted aggression. Only Finland survived as a free nation.

The Winter War also had severe political repercussions beyond the Baltic region. Neither Daladier nor Chamberlain recovered from the failure of their Scandinavian designs; both men were out of power within weeks. The humiliating British defeat in Norway was the direct outgrowth of the "Save Finland" scheme and gives a bleak indication of what would have happened if the expedition actually had sailed in response to the Finns' call for help. The strategic might-have-beens are quite formidable, starting with the disorienting scenario of Britain and France waging war against Germany and Russia simultaneously, and probably laying waste to most of Scandinavia in the process.

The mythology of the Winter War was powerful but short-lived. Too soon after the surrender of brave little Finland, it was the turn of numerous other brave little countries. But for a period the Finns' gallant stand against their huge and bullying neighbor gave the democracies something to feel good about at a time when they needed it. Or, as historian Max Jakobsen put it, in his splendid book, *The Diplomacy of the Winter War*:

> The Finns were defending democracy and freedom and justice, all the things the western democracies stood for, but had had, at the time, little actual chance to fight for. Many a modern Byron on skis volunteered to go to the scene of the action, and, though few got as far as the firing line, in most countries of the west, there are men who think of Finland, a little wistfully perhaps, as the country they almost died for.[*]

From the farewell order of Field Marshal Gustav Mannerheim to the soldiers of the Finnish Army:

> Soldiers! I have fought on many battlefields, but never have I seen your like as warriors! . . . After sixteen weeks of bloody combat, with no rest by day or night, our army stands unconquered before an enemy whose strength has grown in spite of terrible losses.
> . . . Our fate is hard, now that we are compelled to surrender to an alien race land which for centuries we have cultivated with our labor and sweat. . . . Yet we must put our shoulders to the wheel, in order that we may prepare, on the soil left to us, a home for those rendered

[*]Jakobsen, 177.

homeless, and a better life for all; and, as before, we must be ready to defend our diminished homeland with the same resolution and with the same fire with which we defended our undivided homeland.

We are proudly conscious of our historic duty, which we shall continue to fulfill: the defense of western civilization which has been our heritage for centuries. But we also know that we have paid, to the last penny, any debt we may have owed the West.

. . . That an army so inferior in numbers and equipment, should have inflicted such serious defeats on an overwhelmingly powerful enemy, and, while retreating, have over and over again repelled his attacks, is a thing for which it is hard to find a parallel in the history of war. But it is equally admirable that the Finnish people, face to face with an apparently hopeless situation, were able to resist giving in to despair, and instead to grow in devotion and greatness.

Such a nation has earned the right to live.

1917

November 7:   Bolshevik revolution breaks out in Russia.

December 6:   Finland declares independence from Russia.

1918

January–May: Civil war in Finland, following leftist coup d'état. Ends
                 with a crushing victory by the White forces under
                 Mannerheim (with substantial aid from Imperial
                 Germany).

1919

July 17:   Finland adopts a democratic constitution, among whose
                 principles are: a president elected for a six-year term by a
                 300-member electoral college; a prime minister, to be
                 chosen by the president; and a 200-member single-
                 chamber parliament, elected through universal suffrage
                 to a four-year term and to which both the prime minister
                 and the cabinet are held accountable.

1920

October 14:   Russia and Finland sign the Treaty of Tartu, which
                 provides for mutual de jure recognition and a settlement
                 of the Karelian borders, including demolition of all
                 preexisting tsarist-era border fortifications.

1932

January: Russia and Finland negotiate a nonaggression pact.

1939

August 24:   Russo-German nonaggression pact signed; secret
                 protocol places the Baltic region, including Finland,
                 within the USSR's sphere of interest.

September 17:   USSR invades Poland.

September 22:   Estonian foreign minister invited to Moscow.

September 29:   USSR-Estonian "mutual assistance pact" signed.

October 1:   Latvian foreign minister invited to Moscow.

October 3:   Lithuanian foreign minister invited to Moscow.

October 5:   USSR-Latvian "mutual assistance pact" signed; USSR invites Finnish negotiators to Moscow to discuss "territorial adjustments."

October 9:   Helsinki government orders mobilization.

October 10:   USSR-Lithuanian "mutual assistance pact" signed.

October 11–12: Finnish delegation meets with Kremlin leaders in Moscow and receives stunning demands for concessions.

October 14:   Finnish delegation offers counterproposals, which Moscow rejects.

October 31:   In a speech before the Supreme Soviet, Molotov asserts Russia's right to adopt strong measures in the name of security; again, concessions are demanded of Finland.

November 3:   Finns make their final offer to Russians.

November 13:   Negotiations are broken off in Moscow—on a ludicrously jolly note by Molotov—and Stalin orders plans for an immediate offensive against Finland.

November 26:   Russians fabricate a pretext for war by staging the so-called Mainila shots incident and accusing Finland of a "hostile act."

November 27:   Finland denies firing the shots, submits eyewitness accounts that claim the rounds were fired from the Soviet side of the border. Moscow renounces the existing nonaggression treaty.

November 29:   Moscow breaks diplomatic relations with Helsinki.

November 30:   Helsinki bombed; Soviet columns totalling about 600,000 men cross Finnish border; Mannerheim assumes command of Finnish armed forces; a state of war exists.

December 1:   The puppet government of the "Democratic Republic of Finland" is conjured in the village of Terijoki, under old-time Finnish Bolshevik O. W. Kuusinen.

December 3:	Finland makes eloquent, but futile, appeal for intervention by the League of Nations.
December 7:	Russians reach main line of Finnish resistance on the Karelian Isthmus.
December 14:	Russia expelled from League of Nations.
December 22:	Having repelled all Russian attacks against the Mannerheim Line, the Finns launch an ill-considered and badly organized counterattack, with negligible results.

1940

January 8:	Finns win their most spectacular victory of the war, at Suomussalmi, encircling and annihilating two Russian divisions.
February 1:	Start of Russians' all-out offensive on the Karelian Isthmus.
February 5:	Britain and France agree to intervene in Scandinavia, ostensibly to help Finland but mainly to seize control of Norwegian ports and Swedish iron ore.
February 11:	Russians score decisive breakthrough of Mannerheim Line in the Lähde sector.
February 12:	Finnish cabinet authorizes government to seek peace terms.
March 1–5:	Furious, seesaw fighting in and around Viipuri; last Finnish reserves committed.
March 5:	Finnish delegation departs for Moscow to begin peace negotiations.
March 9:	Finns evacuate last toeholds in Gulf of Viipuri.
March 12:	Peace agreement signed in Moscow; Russia receives 16,000 square miles of Finnish territory.
March 13:	Cease-fire goes into effect at 11:00 A.M., after a final savage bombardment by the Russians.

1941

| June 22: | Finland attacks USSR as "cobelligerent" with Germany; "Continuation War" begins. |

December 6:   Great Britain declares war on Finland, to soothe Stalin's
                  feelings, and then, apart from a single token air raid, does
                  absolutely nothing to prosecute it.

1944

September 19:   Soviet-Finnish armistice; Finns lose everything they lost
                  in 1940 all over again and become economically and
                  politically indentured to the USSR. Finns undertake to
                  drive remaining German troops from northern Finland,
                  which they do—almost—after some additional fighting
                  and considerable destruction.

▲ NOTES ON THE SOURCES ▲ ▲

There seems no point in listing, in a formal way, the Finnish-language sources consulted, as the titles are not available outside of Finland and would be unreadable if they were. Suffice it to say that I read everything I could during the year I lived there—very slowly at first, as I struggled with the demonic complexities of written Finnish—and was able to cover a fair-sized shelf of basic titles. Included were several one-volume histories, the memoirs of General Harold Öhquist, and the official history of the Finnish Coast Artillery, which contained far more detailed accounts of the Gulf of Viipuri fighting than could be included in this book. Tactical accounts and first-person combat narratives by the hundred were also available, thanks to the editor of *Kansa Taisteli*, Finland's magazine of popular military history, who donated five years' worth of back issues to the cause. To supplement my Finnish-language reading, I interviewed anyone who would sit still for it, including veterans of all ranks. The names of some of the most helpful interviewees appear in the acknowledgments at the start of this volume.

The best narrative of the war in English is Allen Chew's *The White Death* (East Lansing: Michigan State University Press, 1971). Eloise Engle and Lauri Paananen (an American/Finnish husband-and-wife team), in *The Winter War* (New York: Scribner's, 1973), recount numerous fascinating anecdotes not found elsewhere and include some valuable appendixes—such as the most detailed breakdown of foreign aid I have seen in any book outside of Finland. But their book is too sketchy and lightweight to be of more than supplemental value.

Mannerheim's autobiography *The Memoirs of Marshal Mannerheim* (New York: E. P. Dutton, 1954) is of course essential, because of who and what he was, but it is disappointingly flat and reticent; reading it is a duty, not a pleasure. The diplomatic and political dimensions of the Winter War have fared much better in English than its military aspects. The list of references is short, but every title is distinguished, starting with what is, all things considered, perhaps the best short history of the war ever written, Max Jakobsen's *The Diplomacy of the Winter War* (Cambridge, Mass.: Harvard University Press, 1961), a lively, authoritative, and surprisingly witty account that also contains excellent brief summations of the military events.

Finnish domestic politics—some comprehension of which is necessary for an understanding of the war's origins—are clarified admirably in Marvin Rintala's *Four Finns—Political Profiles* (Berkeley: University of California Press, 1969). The historical background, back to the time of the Mongols, is colorfully treated in Oliver Warner's history of the Baltic, *The Sword and the Sea* (New York: Morrow, 1965). Väinö Tanner's *The Winter War* (Stanford, Calif.: Stanford University Press, 1957) is certainly illuminating, given Tanner's vital role in the Finnish government, but it, too, is a chore to read and is recommended only to those with a special interest in the subject. The tangled but fascinating relations between Finland and the Great Powers are explicated with clarity and style in Anthony Upton's *Finland, 1939–1940* (Newark: University of Delaware Press, 1974).

Because of the war's distance, short duration, and inaccessibility to correspondents, few accounts written during or immediately after the conflict retain much validity today. Exceptions are John Langdon-Davies, *Invasion in the Snow* (Boston: Houghton Mifflin, 1940), which contains valuable data on weapons and tactics drawn from interviews with Finnish officers, and Sir Walter Citrine, *My Finnish Diary* (London: Penguin Books, 1940), which offers a rare first-person glimpse of Finnish society and domestic politics during the war, written by an experienced and eloquent visitor.

Churchill, in *The Gathering Storm* (Boston: Houghton Mifflin, 1948), provides a predictably vigorous but politically sanitized account of the Winter War's impact on Allied foreign policy. General Edmund Ironside, by contrast, in *The Ironside Diaries* (London: McKay, 1963), gives an intimate and robustly cynical view of the actual behind-the-scenes machinations surrounding the abortive "relief expedition." Nikita Khrushchev's memoirs, *Khrushchev Remembers* (Boston: Little, Brown, 1970), contain only a few pages about the Russo-Finnish conflict, but each one is a gem—salty, irreverent vignettes of how things were done in the Kremlin in those days. (The tone of the memoirs has always seemed utterly authentic to me, although some still question their origin.)

Readers who wish to know more about Finland itself are directed to Eino Jutikkala's *A History of Finland* (New York: Praeger, 1962), David G. Kirby's *Finland in the Twentieth Century* (Minneapolis: University of Minnesota Press, 1979), or Wendy Hall's *The Finns and Their Country* (New York: Paul Eriksson, 1968), a warm and affectionate valentine of a book that nonetheless conveys a great deal of solid information.

▲ INDEX ▲ ▲

About the Author

William R. Trotter was raised in Charlotte, North Carolina, and educated at Davidson College, where he earned a B.A. in European History. He has worked as a regional music critic, a book reviewer, and a freelance historian and feature writer.

Trotter has published twelve books as well as many articles—in *The Independent* (North Carolina), *Spectator Magazine*, the *American Record Magazine*, *Film Culture*, *Military History Monthly*, and dozens of other magazines. Since 1987, he has been a senior writer for *PC Gamer Magazine*.

In 1995, Trotter won the Finlandia Foundation's Arts and Letters Prize for *A Frozen Hell*, and the book is required reading for the 2nd Marine Division. In addition, his biography of Mitropoulos, *Priest of Music: The Life and Times of Dimitri Mitropoulos*, was selected as one of the "ten best 'arts' books of the year" by National Public Radio, and one of his novellas has been nominated for a Bram Stoker Award.

William Trotter lives with his wife and their youngest son in Greensboro, North Carolina.